I Glanced Out the Window and Saw the Edge of the World

I Glanced Out the Window and Saw the Edge of the World

Catherine Halsall

RESOURCE *Publications* • Eugene, Oregon

I GLANCED OUT THE WINDOW AND SAW THE EDGE OF THE WORLD

Copyright © 2020 Catherine Halsall. All rights reserved. Except for brief quotations in critical publications or reviews, no part of this book may be reproduced in any manner without prior written permission from the publisher. Write: Permissions, Wipf and Stock Publishers, 199 W. 8th Ave., Suite 3, Eugene, OR 97401.

Resource Publications
An Imprint of Wipf and Stock Publishers
199 W. 8th Ave., Suite 3
Eugene, OR 97401

www.wipfandstock.com

PAPERBACK ISBN: 978-1-7252-5899-0
HARDCOVER ISBN: 978-1-7252-5900-3
EBOOK ISBN: 978-1-7252-5901-0

Manufactured in the U.S.A. 06/22/20

"A Clare Benediction" by John Rutter © Oxford University Press 1998, text reproduced by permission. All rights reserved.

Final verse of "Counter Attack" by Siegfried Sassoon, reproduced by kind permission of the Estate of George Sassoon.

Vera Brittain material is included by permission of Mark Bostridge and T. J. Brittain-Catlin, Literary Executors for the Estate of Vera Brittain 1970.

Text by Adrian Roberts from Robert Grandin's *The Battle of Long Tan: As Told by the Commanders*, published by Allen & Unwin, Crows Nest, 2004, reproduced with permission from Adrian Roberts.

Lines from Dante's *Inferno: The Divine Comedy (Volume 1, Hell)*, translated by Robin Kirkpatrick (Penguin Classics, 2006). Translation copyright Robin Fitzpatrick 2006. Reproduced by permission of Penguin Random House UK.

Translation of "To Death" by Gerrit Engelke, reproduced with permission of the translator, Merryn Williams.

Scripture quotations from New Revised Standard Version Bible, copyright © 1989 National Council of the Churches of Christ in the United States of America. Used by permission. All rights reserved worldwide.

Dedicated to

George Samuel Halsall
13th Light Horse Regiment Royal Australian Army Corps, WWI

Jeffreys Bannister Horne
19th Field Ambulance Royal Australian Army Medical Corps, WWI

John Douglas Henderson
2/4 Dental Unit Royal Australian Army Dental Corps, WW2

Arthur James Stammers
Signals 9th Division 2nd Australian Imperial Force, WW2

Colonel Adrian Roberts (Rtd)
Formerly Troop Commander, 3 Troop APC at Long Tan, Vietnam

. . . as they went on they got the strangest impression that here at last the sky did really come down and join the earth—a blue wall, very bright, but real and solid: more like glass than anything else. And soon they were quite sure of it. It was very near now.

But between them and the foot of the sky there was something so white on the green grass that even with their eagles' eyes they could hardly look at it They came on and saw that it was a Lamb.

"Come and have breakfast," said the Lamb in its sweet milky voice.

Then they noticed for the first time that there was a fire lit on the grass and fish roasting on it. They sat down and ate the fish, hungry now for the first time for many days. And it was the most delicious food they had ever tasted.

"Please, Lamb," said Lucy, "Is this the way to Aslan's country?"

"Not for you," said the Lamb. "For you the door into Aslan's country is from your own world."

"What!" said Edmund. "Is there a way into Aslan's country from our world too?"

"There is a way into my country from all the worlds," said the Lamb; but as he spoke his snowy white flushed into tawny gold and his size changed and he was Aslan himself, towering above them and scattering light from his mane.[1]

C. S. Lewis, *The Voyage of the Dawn Treader*, 1952

---

1. Lewis, *Chronicles of Narnia*, 540

Contents

Acknowledgments | ix

PART ONE: THE GREAT WAR | 1
  1. The Beginning of the War to End All Wars | 3
  2. The Start of the Great Adventure | 15
  3. The Horrors of Reality | 48
  4. The Role of Christianity | 72
  5. Brutality, Survival, and Grief | 87
  6. A Peace for the World? | 102

PART TWO: WORLD WAR II | 109
  7. From Humiliation to a Reich under Hitler | 111
  8. The Scourge of Nazism | 114
  9. The Collaboration of the Christian Church | 139
  10. The Personal Cost | 149
  11. A Forerunner of the War in the East | 158
  12. Japan's Ambitions in the Pacific | 161
  13. War and Racism | 177

PART THREE: THE WARS CONTINUE | 183
  14. Korea: The Forgotten War | 185
  15. Vietnam: The Lonely War | 190
  16. The Raging of Wars Never Ceases | 214
  17. Death and Killing | 217

18. Christianity Must Play an Effective Part | 238
19. The Place of Days of Remembrance and Memorials | 246
20. Can War Ever Be Justified? | 252

Bibliography | 263

Index | 275

Acknowledgments

IN THE WRITING OF this work I extend much gratitude to the following people:

All the members of my family—my children, grandchildren, and my special niece—who, over a period of some years, were always there with support, encouragement, and practical help. Pauline Brockett, my friend and mentor, for all her constructive criticism and suggestions. Annette Cousens and Lorraine Haldon for reading my original manuscript and believing in it. Father John Sanderson who provided me with valuable information on chaplaincy. The Reverend Doctor Roger Chilton for his advice and encouragement. Kevin Forde who gave me the confidence to tackle new computer skills. All those, sometimes unknowingly, who helped in the planning and direction of the work. Many friends who continually reassured me in the task I had set myself. Ariana Klepac, my formatter and copyeditor, who persevered with my amateur approach to publishing. My publisher, Wipf & Stock, for their advice and patience. Lastly, to my lovely man, Ian, my mainstay in life for over fifty years, who has already crossed the Jordan from the Edge of the World.

Part One

The Great War

The Great War is long ago and far away. And in the clay that is soft and springy under your feet at Boesinghe it is still with us, loaded with mysteries and heavy with sadness and thoughts of things that are unspeakable.

LES CARLYON, *THE GREAT WAR*, 2006[1]

---

1. Carlyon, *The Great War*, 777.

1

The Beginning of the War to End All Wars

THE BATTLE OF VERDUN of 1916 was the longest battle of World War I. French casualties during the battle were estimated at 550,000 with German losses set at 434,000, half of the total being fatalities. The only real result of this tenacious battle was the huge number of casualties of both armies—no tactical or strategic advantage was achieved by either side. As a combatant, Second Lieutenant Alfred Joubaire wrote, "Hell could not be worse. Men are mad!"[1] In the 1920s the bones of soldiers were gathered from the battered earth and placed in the crypt of the gigantic ossuary built on the site of the Ferme de Thiaumont. The number of these anonymous dead runs perhaps to 75,000, maybe even 150,000 bodies, which had been pulverized into the mud and snow. The building above them stands in somber magnitude with its tower looking like a huge artillery shell. This tower surveys a seemingly endless military cemetery with a host of smaller graveyards lying near and far beyond—these entombing the bodies of those who could be identified. Everywhere one travels in this small village, the final resting places of a whole generation of youth stretch as far as the eye can see.

Reflections on World War I: Causes and Reasons

In researching a work by Fischer: *Griff nach der Weltmacht: Die Kriegszielpolitik des Kaiserlichen Deutschland 1914–1918*, published in Düsseldorf by Droste Verlag in 1961, Lewis-Stempel notes that: "Dr Fritz

---

1. Ousby, *The Road to Verdun*, 304.

Fischer showed persuasively that a reactionary German elite used the crisis caused by the assassination of Archduke Franz Ferdinand to carry out long-held plans for the creation of a German-dominated Mitteleuropa and Mittelafrika. In other words, Germany caused the First World War... The Germany of the Kaiser was a right wing military dictatorship bent on the subjugation of Europe."[2]

Feeling rejected by his mother because of his withered arm, Willy (later Kaiser Wilhelm II) easily came under the strong influence of his grandfather, Kaiser Wilhelm I who, although he believed himself to be a true servant of his people, also believed in the divine right of kings. The army and the battles in which he had taken part, formed the strongest aspect of his personality. He slept on an iron camp bed in the barest of rooms with few essentials. In such a room with a library of army regulations, drill books, law compendia, and military reports, he ate with his young grandson, recounting stories of battles and victories and thus creating an intimate and lifelong bond with him. As a result, Willy scorned his parents, to the delight of the Prussian court, and labeled his peace-loving father as weak and too strongly influenced by his English wife. Willy's military ambitions were born in that small, cold, airless cell and were fostered by the chancellor, Otto von Bismarck, and his nationalistic policies. Over the latter part of the nineteenth century, Bismarck had built Prussia from one of the weakest German states into a great German empire feared and envied by other European nations. A short successful war with Denmark scored the duchies of Schleswig and Holstein for Prussia and Austria respectively; a war with Austria, after stirring up the hearts of its Hungarian subjects, resulted in the German states, which supported Austria being annexed to Prussia and their rulers deposed; and the manipulation of written communications between Napoleon III and the Kaiser concerning the possibility of a member of the Prussian family accepting the throne of Spain, resulted in victory over the French in the Franco-Prussian War and the annexation of Alsace and Lorraine. All this Bismarck achieved by preliminary diplomatic scheming with other nations, such as Russia and Italy, to ensure he could go ahead with his plans for expansion without the fear of such powers intervening. An author of the times, Theodor Fontane, commented on the nineteenth-century rise

---

2. Lewis-Stempel, *Six Weeks*, 9.

of Prussian militarism: "The mere glorification of the military, without moral content and elevated aim, is nauseating."[3]

Thus, due to the empire building of Bismarck, the Germany of the Kaiser at the beginning of the following century was obsessed with militarism, power, and expansion. It had a large standing army and great numbers of reservists. Its army officers were well trained and efficient compared to the Turkish and Russian armies of the time, where officers were barely competent. Britain also had drawbacks—its army was smaller and spread throughout its empire plus it was the only European nation where there was no conscription. A common saying of the times was, "if anyone wants a disastrous war, then let him pick a quarrel with a German."[4]

When Wilhelm became Kaiser in 1888, he initially sought to challenge the supremacy of the British navy by building a mighty fleet of warships and constructing the Kiel Canal. He also desired to have an overseas German empire equal to that of Britain and, to this end, Germany pursued cruel and punitive measures to secure and maintain its sovereignty both in German South West Africa and German New Guinea. With his physical deformity constantly at the forefront of his mind, the Kaiser strutted the European stage. Amazingly, when Victoria of England died and Wilhelm's uncle Edward took the throne of Britain, he saw himself as the elder statesman because he had been Kaiser of his empire for some thirteen years. Little Willy saw himself as the prototype of a ruler for the whole of Europe.

Wilhelm's arrogance can be viewed even today in the commercial district of Kurfürstendamm Avenue in Berlin. Here the Kaiser Wilhelm Church is a permanent reminder of one man's overwhelming belief in his own glorious position in the world. Under his direction this church was built in the 1890s, in honor of his grandfather, Kaiser Wilhelm I, the man who so strongly and completely molded the young Wilhelm. Although the building was badly damaged in bombing raids in World War II, its narthex and spire remain. As you enter you are confronted, on the surrounding walls, with murals of Kaiser Wilhelm II and his family—it therefore appears as a memorial to these pompous persons and is incongruous to a sanctuary normally dedicated wholly to the glory of God.

---

3. Craig, *Theodor Fontane*, 92.
4. Passingham, *All the Kaiser's Men*, 15.

From the very beginning of his reign, Wilhelm's belligerent attitude to all other nations was obvious. It is well illustrated in his address to the German soldiers who were sent to relieve the garrison in China during the Boxer Rebellion: "When you come upon the enemy, smite him. Pardon will not be given. Prisoners will not be taken. Whoever falls into your hands is forfeit. Once, a thousand years ago, the Huns under their King Attila made a name for themselves, one still potent in legend and tradition. May you in this way make the name German remembered in China for a thousand years so that no Chinaman will ever again dare to *even squint at a German!*"[5]

How vastly different Germany may have been under the reign of his father, the peace-loving democratic Kaiser, who ruled for only ninety-nine days—and then as a dying man. Friedrich recorded the following words in his diary during the Franco-Russian War: "I maintain even today that Germany could have conquered morally, without 'blood and iron' [in Bismarck's phrase] . . . It will be our noble but immensely difficult task in the future to free the dear German Fatherland from the unfounded suspicions with which the World looks upon it today. We must show that our newly acquired power is not a danger, but a boon to humanity."[6]

When the assassination of the heir to the throne of Austria-Hungary, Archduke Franz Ferdinand, took place in Bosnia, Kaiser Wilhelm immediately reacted with a flurry of telegrams—the Serbs must be dealt with and any action Austria took to this end would be wholeheartedly supported by Germany. Even if Russia intervened in support of the Slavic people, Germany would stand by Austria. It seems incredible that such a rash reaction would result in the Great War of 1914 to 1918 for, although the assassins were Serbians wishing to free the Slavs from the yoke of Austrian rule, they belonged to a conspiratorial faction who were actually at odds with the government of Serbia. The Black Hand did comprise a number of army officers but they did not have the backing of the army in which they served—they were a small number of individuals acting solely without any official recognition or support. In fact, a classified report delivered to the Austrian capital some short time later, absolved the Serbian government from any involvement in the assassination.

Any previous wars that had broken out in the Balkan states had been restricted to that area, so most countries did not foresee that the

---

5. Palmer, *The German Wars*, 57.
6. Passingham, *All the Kaiser's Men*, 2.

assassination would develop into anything other than a local crisis. Even the conflicts between Turkey and Italy and between Russia and Japan in earlier years had been contained to just that, without involving any other powers. However, the belligerent attitude of the Kaiser and his political leaders, almost accusing Austria-Hungary of cowardice if it did not take decisive action, pushed the situation to boiling point. Germany saw a future Russia as a threat to its power and influence in Europe and reasoned that the possible involvement of Russia coming to the support of Serbia whilst still not at its zenith, would help to prevent such a scenario.

An Austro-Hungarian ultimatum consisting of fifteen demands was delivered to Serbia. Serbia, realizing that its fighting capacity was limited against such an empire, accepted most of the conditions outlined. Nevertheless, the Serbians were very much against having Austrian officials participating in the judicial process or their having the right to influence any decision on punishment for those found guilty. It was requested that this demand should be submitted to the International Tribunal at The Hague. Only then would Serbia agree to the terms. The Tsar then intervened, proposing that negotiations should commence on this pretext. The British called for a four-power conference but the Kaiser, excited by the possibility of a suppression of Russia, would not accept any such proposal.

Amazingly, after he read the Serbian reply in detail, the Kaiser suddenly had "cold feet." He decided that if the Austrian army temporarily occupied Belgrade and then negotiations followed, there would result a great moral victory and it would cancel the need for full-scale military action. *But it was too late*—within an hour of the Kaiser expressing these thoughts on paper, war had been declared. Willy had been like a spoilt child who was completely devoid of realizing the possible consequences of his rash words and actions. Kaiser Wilhelm had made a blundering and momentous miscalculation. In 1917 he made another. He instigated a policy of unrestricted submarine warfare knowing that in doing so he risked the possible entry of the United States into the war.

With the advent of the war the Kaiser moved to proceed on his grandiose plans. He misunderstood the words contained in a conversation between his brother Prince Henry and the British King George V and, wrongly believing Britain would remain neutral, he decided to invade France through Belgium and then turn to defeat Russia. Germany would become the great European power and he the great emperor of all its domains.

Through the success of artful diplomacy and successful wars over the previous fifty years, Germany was now surrounded by potential enemies. Nevertheless, though hated, there was no nation strong enough to challenge its power. The German population had increased by 50 percent and there had been tremendous growth in the manufacturing industries and in the export trade. The Fatherland was continually expanding and equipping its army and its reserve; developing new weapons such as machine-guns and motorized tanks; and the use of such weapons and improvement in battle tactics and operations were practiced and improved. An entire chain of command was established with officers given much more initiative throughout. In fact, the Prussian army had always been a sophisticated body and as the empire widened the army continued to develop and embrace newer methods of warfare. Even the simple practice of each soldier carrying entrenchment tools, as well as arms, gave them an advantage over the armies of other nations. Railways were extended and wireless technology developed. Other nations such as France followed the example, especially in the building of its railway system. But no other country had the huge, disciplined and experienced military force of the Kaiser.

However, the major drawback for the Germans, when entering the war of 1914, was that their past experience of rapid and decisive victories was not going to be so easily attained in the new age of industrialized fighting. Their past had established their might but had not necessarily secured their future.

Britain and Its Leaders at the Onset of War

As the British approached the beginnings of World War I they were, in some ways, blissfully unaware of the turmoil and change that lay ahead. Certainly, they seemed to have learned little from experiences of the past century. The Great British Empire reached to the four corners of the world; the British navy was master of the seas; and in all things the British regarded themselves as part of a superior race—more virtuous, more intelligent, and most of all, more gentlemanly. Les Carlyon, in his work *Gallipoli*, writes: "The stalwarts of the British empire tended to dismiss soldiers who did not look, act and dress like them, as though a man who lacked the sense to fasten a kilt around his waist and a bearskin on his head must be from a lower caste and quite likely a heathen as well."[7] Even in battle itself the British soldier was first and foremost a gentleman. During the Crimean War: "Captain Morgan of the 95th, who had held aloft the Colours at a moment of crisis, and personally shot a Russian sharpshooter, was summoned before his senior officer, where the following conversation took place: 'Morgan, do you think you were justified in shooting that Russian yesterday?' 'I think I was, sir.' 'I think you were not; it is not the duty of an officer. You should have told one of the men to shoot him.'"[8] Ponder also the reaction of the Duke of Wellington to Lord Uxbridge's dilemma at the Battle of Waterloo when he was hit by a cannon ball: "'By God, Sir, I've lost my leg'– had elicited the brisk Wellingtonian response, 'By God, Sir, so you have.'"[9]

Involvement in wars of the previous two centuries had produced few lessons learned—how long, for example, did it take the army to realize that soldiers garbed in vibrant red jackets were easy targets for Native Americans and the later patriots of the War of Independence. In 1880 the British navy was still using the muzzleloaders of Nelson's day on their warships when navies of European countries were fitting modern breechloading guns. A further illustration of folly in the extreme is found again in Carlyon's work: "Trials at the British Musketry School in Kent during 1907 showed that at 600 yards two Maxim machine guns could wipe out a battalion (roughly 1,000 men) advancing in the open in one minute if the troops did not go to ground. *This trial offended Edwardian sensibilities.* Infantry and cavalry: that's what warfare was about. Hundreds of years of tradition said this was so . . . What sort of world was that for a chap who liked to wear spurs and a plumed helmet? And how could war be 'manly' if the hero was a machine? . . . In 1916 [generals] in France were still ordering infantry to advance across open ground towards machine guns."[10] Sir Ian Hamilton, the Allied commander in chief at Gallipoli, was sent home after the failures on the peninsula. Not only was he part of an arrogant, poorly planned campaign, but he was too much of a gentleman to be the authoritative and ruthless leader that was desperately needed to achieve success from the shambles that evolved. The whole British campaign at the Dardenelles

7. Carlyon, *Gallipoli*, 89.
8. Spilsbury, *The Thin Red Line*, 108.
9. Spilsbury, *The Thin Red Line*, 28.
10. Carlyon, *Gallipoli*, 198.

brings to mind the popular adage "failing to plan means planning to fail," a typical example of the vanity of the times.

Not only in war but in other fields, British arrogance illustrated an almost complete disregard for the dire consequences that entailed. In periods between wars, the British navy in particular, promoted navy men to be explorers. When we look at the race for the South Pole between Robert Falcon Scott and the Norwegian Roald Amundsen, we come across two completely different approaches to attaining the prize. Roald Amundsen was a driven, meticulous explorer who had been reared in the snow and cold of his native land, was an experienced survivor of such conditions, and an expert sailor in the icy conditions of northern seas. His research into the construction of suitable ships and the building of adequate shelters in the ice and snow was continuous. Before his successful drive to the Pole, Amundsen had already sailed in Arctic seas and wintered in the Antarctic trying out his skiing and sledging skills whilst there. He investigated the diet necessary to prevent the dreaded scurvy, he experimented with dog teams, he mastered the building of igloos, he dressed in furs like the Inuit of the north. Scott, on the other hand, had never seen snow before his first expedition to the Antarctic in 1909, could not master skis, and dressed in navy-issue woollen clothing. He failed to seal his fuel efficiently to prevent evaporation—unlike the Norwegian. Scott also could not adapt his thinking to habits of the huskies to gain the best results—in fact he thought it cruel to use dogs. British polar explorers in the north obviously were of the same mind—they preferred to use the men to haul the sledges irrespective of the fact that these men needed to conserve all their energy for the expedition itself. In a new idea, untried, Scott took with him Shetland ponies (and some dogs, whose idiosyncrasies he failed to master). He also took motorized sledges but decided against taking a mechanic to maintain them. Amundsen's rigid planning extended to reducing his pack of huskies systematically for food for the men and the remaining dogs. Scott would not shoot a struggling pony because it was not the Christian thing to do—an action that indirectly but ultimately contributed to the demise of him and his men.

Amundsen set out for the Pole from a base camp set amidst some dangerous ice formations. Scott left from a base some ninety-three miles further from the Pole, a position that had been recommended by the librarian of the Royal Geographical Society as the most advantageous starting point. This was where the experience of Amundsen surmounted the risks he took, whereas the arrogance of Scott succumbed to the risks he took—"I don't hold that anyone but an Englishman should get to the South Pole."[11] Robert Scott was the product of the thinking of the British navy. In the preceding years there had been a continuing effort to find the Northwest Passage—the magical route to supposedly enhance trade and commerce. From Frobisher in 1577 right through to the beginning of the twentieth century, Englishmen endeavored to break through the impenetrable ice of the Arctic to find the elusive passage. It was a saga of endless failures to the point where, even when the last link was discovered in 1850, the men who found it were encased in the Arctic ice for a further four winters. Ironically it took Amundsen, between 1903 and 1906, sailing in a converted herring schooner, to navigate through and establish that, because the passage was so shallow it would only accommodate a small ship, the Northwest Passage would consequently be useless as a trade route.

The failure of all the expeditions could be attributed directly to navy thinking. After the Napoleonic Wars the navy turned to exploration to make use of its superior fleet and manpower. However, though they were heroic and adventurous, these navy men found it impossible to accept that there were ordinary men of experience who could greatly help them in their quest for new lands and new seas. One of the best examples of this was the rejection of input from William Scoresby Jr., one of the most experienced Arctic sailors in the land. Besides his gifts in the field of linguistics, history, navigation, mapping, and theology, he was a whaler.

> But he was a persona non grata to the British Admiralty, precisely because he was a whaler. In 1817, after returning from a whaling expedition, he contacted Sir Joseph Banks, the influential head of the Royal Society, to tell him that the ice that normally closed the wide straits between Greenland and Spitzbergen was gone. It was an opportune moment to reinaugurate the search for the Northwest Passage, which greatly interested Scoresby. He offered his services to Banks. The Admiralty turned him down . . . It would become one of the most fascinating and ironic notes in British Arctic exploration that the Navy never would learn from their supposed inferiors, no matter how expert they were, simply because they were, in Navy eyes, inferiors. They had the same attitude toward the Inuit, who had survived for thousands of years in Arctic conditions. The Navy refused to adopt any of their ways. Dozens of ships were lost and hundreds of men died

11. Langner, *Scott and Amundsen*, 1.

as a result. This was a breed of men whose heroism was matched only by their arrogance.[12]

In his quest for the Northwest Passage, John Franklin returned to England a hero after his 1819 expedition, because he and most of his men survived by eating the leather of their shoes. But they had been forced to do this to survive because Franklin had not planned efficiently; he had gone too far afield without supplies and had struggled to return, losing eleven men to starvation and even murder in the process. But, as Anne Fadiman states, "Englishmen admire heroic failure."[13] Whilst the native Inuit survived around him, Franklin, on his second expedition of 1845, lost two ships, his own life, and those of his 129 men. When some remnants of the journey were discovered amongst the dead some fourteen years later, it was revealed that the men, when forced to abandon the ice-crushed ships, dragged with them monogrammed silver cutlery, clothes brushes, slippers bound in silk ribbon, watches, some small devotional books, a copy of *The Vicar of Wakefield*, a backgammon board, button polish, towels, soap, toothbrushes, combs, twine, nails, saws, files, bristles, wax ends, sailmakers' palms, etc.—in other words a vast collection of some useful but mostly useless items. There was also a quantity of guns, knives, and gunpowder for hunting purposes but no real survival gear. As Fadiman notes, "These men may have been incompetent bunglers, but, by God, they were gentlemen."[14]

A further example of the arrogance and lack of empathy of the higher echelons of British society is sadly seen in the last days of the war during the onset of the Russian Revolution in Petrograd. Lady Georgina Buchanan, wife of the British ambassador, Sir George Buchanan, watched the carnage from her "vantage point in the corner drawing room ... [she] had found it all rather thrilling: 'One really almost felt one was in the front trenches.'" Meanwhile her husband, refusing to take his family to the safety of the cellars, stood on the balcony with members of his staff. "Sir George later recorded that he had spent 'an exciting morning' watching, till around 1.00 p.m."[15]

This was the scenario when Great Britain entered World War I—the war to end all wars—overconfident to the point of arrogance, gentlemen

12. Brandt, *The North Pole*, 63.
13. Fadiman, *Ex Libris*, 19.
14. Fadiman, *Ex Libris*, 19.
15. Rappaport, *Caught in the Revolution*, 221.

to the point of buffoonery, and ill-equipped and ill-prepared. The youth of England, golden and promising, was to be sacrificed along with the youth of those colonies who still saw England as the home country. There were 60,000 casualties in the first morning of the Somme offensive; 20,000 of these were fatalities. The plan was to bombard the Germans for some five days, destroying their trenches and barbed wire so that the British could just walk in to defeat what was left of the enemy. However, the German trenches were some thirty to forty feet deep and so survived the barrage. A party of soldiers was sent in on the eve of the battle to check if the barbed wire had been destroyed. When they reported back that all was still intact their report was discounted.

From a Small Skirmish to a Great War

Kaiser Wilhelm II continued on his usual erratic course—advancing his troops on France and then ordering a retreat, whilst at the same time planning to wage war on Russia. Both King George V and Tsar Nicholas II vainly attempted to defuse the situation. But Austria, sure of the support of Germany, was determined to avenge the assassination of Franz Ferdinand and this reignited all the Balkan countries once again. Now they were fighting with larger powers as their allies.

No longer was the hostility between just two protagonists.

By the action of the Kaiser in invading France through Belgium and thus violating that country's neutrality, Britain was forced to declare war on Germany by international treaty rights. A recollection of Margot Asquith sets the somber mood:

> I looked at the children asleep after dinner before joining Henry in the Cabinet room. Lord Crewe and Sir Edward Grey were already there and we sat smoking cigarettes in silence; some went out, others came in; nothing was said.
> The clock on the mantelpiece hammered out the hour, and when the last beat of midnight struck it was as silent as dawn.
> We were at War.
> I left to go to bed, and, as I was pausing at the foot of the stair-case, I saw Winston Churchill with a happy face striding towards the double doors of the Cabinet room.[16]

---

16. Marlow, *The Virago Book of Women and the Great War*, 23.

Some weeks later Japan, seeking fulfillment of imperial ambitions, declared war on Germany under the 1905 alliance it had with Britain—thus opening up fields of conflict in Asia and the Pacific. The Ottoman Empire entered the fray as an ally of Germany when it noted the early Teutonic successes and the battlefields spread all over Turkey, Palestine, Egypt, and North Africa. Turmoil ignited in South Africa when the Union took arms to support Britain with remnants of the Boer War beginning more conflict in the area. India reacted to the British, attacking the Islam nation of Turkey.

Within months kings, tsars, and emperors were no longer the powerful autocrats of the past—the new rulers were the politicians and the soldiers. It began for the Australians with the futility of the Dardenelles where so many died, some never even reaching land—and for no gain. "Looking down from the hill, a Turkish officer said the shore was strewn with corpses 'like a shoal of fish.' A British airman looked down on a sea 'absolutely red with blood.' The stain, he said, spread for 50 yards from the shore."[17]

---

17. Carlyon, *Gallipoli*, 196.

2

The Start of the Great Adventure

Soldiers from all over the British empire heeded the call to arms and were sent to the Dardenelles, Egypt, Palestine, and the Western Front . . . some were sent straight into the fray whilst others waited in isolated outposts . . . perhaps savoring the respite from the future battle but eventually becoming bored and desperate to get to the real fighting. In this war, "thousands of Australian and New Zealand boys lied about their ages, forged a parent's signature and went off to fight in a war on the other side of the world. They found they could die as well as any man, but they would never grow old. Like Peter Pan's lost boys, they have remained forever young."[1] John Smith was fourteen, Frank Day was just eleven. Day stowed away on outgoing vessels on two occasions. Both times he was discovered and sent back to Australia. On the second voyage he had managed to get to Egypt. "There was also fifteen-year-old Jack Harris from Sydney, who died at Lone Pine, eighteen hours after arriving on Gallipoli . . . And there was Leslie Thomas Prior, from Melbourne . . . He died at Bullecourt, a battle that should never have happened, three months after his fifteenth birthday. He was the second-youngest Australian to die in the First World War, and the youngest to be killed in action."[2] They all went willingly, to embark on the great and terrible adventure.

---

1. Byrnes, *The Lost Boys*, 8.
2. Byrnes, *The Lost Boys*, 10.

Part One: The Great War

Journal of George Samuel Halsall—Palestine

One country lad, George Halsall, who was old enough to enlist, went with his mates from Euroa and Longwood in Victoria and, in late 1915, found himself on a ship bound for the Middle East. He kept a diary for his family back home.

Wednesday, 27th September, 1915

Left Port Melbourne pier at two forty-five for some foreign country. There were about five thousand people there to see us off and they gave us a great send off. We passed through the Heads about eight o'clock but the sea was very smooth and the Ulysses did not rock much—she is a great old boat!

> Being amongst reinforcements for the 13th Light Horse Regiment in Egypt. The first wave of the 13th Light Horse had left Melbourne for the Suez on May 28, 1915, the main body on the HMAT *A34 Persic* with a small rear party leaving in June on the HMAT *A44 Vestralia*. After initial basic training in Egypt the regiment was sent to help relieve the exhausted troops in Gallipoli. Landing in Anzac Cove on September 11, they were destined to take over the defenses on the ridge to the southeast at a locality later called Lone Pine. They were joined by the 6th Infantry Brigade and, in a short time, became accomplished soldiers, burrowing in trenches, lugging supplies and water up to the front line, and capitalizing on their skills as riflemen for, in Gallipoli, much depended on the expertise of the snipers on both sides.

Thursday, 28th September

Still going strong. Was called up at six o'clock for breakfast—porridge, beans and bread, butter and jam—quite a luxury. There are a lot of blokes sea-sick and one of my mates got the measles. The sea was nice and smooth in the morning but it got pretty rough near evening. It knocked all the plates and cups off the table. Went on deck until eight o'clock and then went to bed.

> The men were not the only ones who had to adjust to ship travel. Horses were swum through the sea and led up ramps then down into stalls in the hold of the ship. These stalls were narrow and each was separated by a single rail. In these the horses had to stand for the whole journey so extra care was required to ensure

their survival—watered from canvas buckets, fed from bales of hay, and each day their legs were massaged, often under great difficulty in rough seas, to ensure they coped with the continuous standing. Many had continual sores from their flanks rubbing on the rails. Those who tended to them had to take frequent breaks so that the fetid air did not make them ill.

Arrived at Fremantle on Tuesday, 2nd November.

Arrived at Suez Canal about 7.30 on Monday, 22nd November—all going strong.

Temporarily in hospital with bronchitis—returned to regiment on 20th December.

> The men of the original 13th Light Horse Regiment who survived the horrors of Gallipoli, were eventually evacuated from Anzac Cove on December 19, by the battleship HMS *Mars*. They spent Christmas on the island of Lemnos and returned to Egypt (and their horses) in early January 1916. They left Gallipoli with a great sense of disappointment at a task not accomplished, but they knew they had given it their all and lost good men in the process. However, the benefit of their experiences was conveyed in many ways to those recently arrived in Egypt yet to be blooded in this great enterprise. Refreshed and strengthened the Anzacs looked ahead with the expectation of defeating the Turk in the desert.
>
> During January there were reports received that approximately 25,000 Turks were in the Sinai/lower Palestine area. Although this figure was probably exaggerated, General Sir Archibald Murray, who took over the command of the Eastern Expeditionary Force on January 10, extended the defensive trenches from the Canal to twelve miles into the desert with the troops based in three sections—Suez, Ismailia, and Port Said with an added objective of advancing to El Arish. The Turks were not expected to become a threat until the winter months.

After Gallipoli—1916

> With the evacuation of the British from Gallipoli, the Turkish army was free to pursue its dream of capturing the Suez Canal, a venture that had failed for them in early 1915. The Turks felt triumphant—they had routed the enemy from the Dardanelles, they had protected Constantinople and all their sacred sites, they had successfully massacred the Christian Armenians, and were now on a crusade to annihilate the Christians in the remainder

of Asia Minor. In addition, Bulgaria had joined the Central Powers and Serbia had been overthrown—this meant a more certain containment of Russia. Under the continuing administration of the Germans, they were easily encouraged to turn to the Middle East, largely unaware of Germany's main motivation in keeping the British and their allies too busy to move all their troops to the Western Front. Thus, early in 1916, the British received the reports of a large Turkish army coming towards the Canal from Sinai. Many allied troops had left Egypt for France but there were some regiments left guarding the Canal. Even so, some of the soldiers in these regiments had managed, by one method or another, to obtain transfers to other regiments serving on the Western Front. Cooling their heels in the desert became frustrating for the ambitious adventurers. By this stage, those in command had gauged the attitude of Great Britain in that the main theater of war was France and that the army in the Middle East was merely guarding strategic outposts for the empire until matters in the area became clearer. Eventually the regiments with which they were left were the Australian Light Horse, the New Zealand Mounted Rifles, the British Yeomanry, and some Artillery. Even so, Ian Jones, in *The Australian Light Horse*, records that, "on a single day in May 1916, nine hundred light-horsemen applied for transfer to the infantry"[3] with the hope of going to France. Men even transferred to the Cyclist Battalion with the same objective.

Maintaining an army of men and horses was formidable but, amazingly, the horses themselves proved to cope better with the onerous tasks given them than the camels—in fact, the Australians noticed that the native camel-drivers seemed to have more stamina than their camels. The army had learned many lessons in the Boer War concerning the care of their horses. At one stage in the South African campaign they were losing five horses a day from starvation, disease, or exhaustion. There had been an almost casual attitude to the care of horses from horsemen used to turning their horses out into the paddock without grooming or hand-feeding. The horses in the Middle East campaign were acclimatized—a great deal of care was taken to exercise them gradually on their arrival in Egypt after their long trip by sea when they were, in almost all cases, permanently confined to horse stalls. There in dark, poorly ventilated holds, the men had slaved to ease their awful shipboard conditions. But, in the desert, they proved they had stamina and great hearts—sometimes lasting sixty hours without water

---

3. Jones, *The Australian Light Horse*, 45.

and carrying loads of up to 285 pounds. Australian horses, generally known as Walers—being stockhorses from New South Wales originally, but from all over Australia—were generally smaller and lighter than the typical British cavalry horses but were hardier and recovered more quickly from long, hard rides. The Light Horse also learned from experience that it was far better to travel at night when it was colder and the horses were less likely to suffer from thirst. The men spent a great deal of time grooming and watering them and learned the best way to balance the load to protect the horse's back. Often men had the same horse throughout the whole campaign and in these instances an enormous companionship developed between horse and rider. Other horses had been supplied to the army from outback stations and were "wild warrigals of the west." However, they became a challenge for the country-bred trooper whilst proving their worth in the extreme conditions of the desert.

Saturday, 29th January, 1916

Left oasis camp Heliopolis for a camp name Tel-el-Kebur at 10 a.m. on horseback. Had a good ride, saw some great sights and had good times chasing Arabs and getting buckshee [extra rations] *oranges and sugar cane. We had dinner on the Canal and moved off at two o'clock and then we stopped at a town named 'a' for the night. Arrived there about five o'clock then we made tea and had some great sport serving out the tea as everybody wanted to have a dip in our dixies—got rid of them alright and then the sergeants came along and told us we had to have breakfast ready at a quarter to seven so we had a bit of an argument with the mess orderlies about getting water to boil but we arranged about getting up at half past five in the morning to get it. Then we went to bed but had a hard job to get to sleep with the damn Arabs around the fire talking. I felt fit to get up and stick the bayonet through the devils.*

Heliopolis, the first mentioned camp, is a district of Cairo established by the Heliopolis Oasis Company. This company, beginning in 1905, was headed by the Belgian industrialist Édouard Louis Joseph, Baron Empain. The Baron, an amateur Egyptologist, originally came to the area to save one of his company's projects, the construction of the rail line between Matariya and Port Said but he lost the contract to the British. However, he stayed on in a country he loved and developed Heliopolis as a "city of luxury and leisure" with wide avenues, modern facilities, large hotels, and apartments as well as low-cost housing. He also established a golf course, a racetrack, and parks.

Sunday, 30th January

Got up at five thirty to get water for the tea; started across the desert and got lost but, after a bit of hunting about, we found a well and three of us pushed the old wheel round while the others filled the dixies, then we started back to camp. We had about one mile to go and we had had enough of it when we got there but that is all in soldiering. Had breakfast then we started off at nine, saw Arabs running along the top of the drain just like a circus. We had a great trip along the road, got a lot more buckshee oranges and sugar cane and plenty of lucerne for our horses. We passed through Chebini-el-Kanater, a rotten hole of a place—they live like rabbits—then we passed through another town named Inshas, only a small place. They go in for all irrigation about here; saw some bonzer beans off the road. Some of the damn places would make anybody think you would not go through one for anything! Then we arrived at another town named Bilbers—we went through just the other side and camped. It is a big town but a rotten hole. We had tea about eight o'clock and went to bed at ten. One of my hats fell in the channel!

Monday, 31st January

Got up at half past four and made breakfast then we started off again on our trip at half past eight. It was pretty foggy and some of the wagons broke down and we had to get off and wait—fixed them up alright and off we went again through a small town named Kafa-ayoub. Good country about there with irrigation around. We passed through a town named El-Zavura. There are a lot of palm trees there between it and the next town Kefr-El-ayad. Poor country here for about eight miles to El-seneka then it gets a little better. Some good crops and beans about here and a little sugar cane. We came to a little village named Zagazig then we had dinner between there and the next town—a bit of bully beef and bread just like a soldier always gets. Then we moved off again at two-thirty, passed through Zagazig being all desert from here to the camp and heavy on the horses. After their long trip we arrived in camp about five-forty tired, weary and hungry—had tea and up came my cousin Claude!

> Claude was the first of the Halsall family to enlist—at the age of twenty in 1915. He was attached to the 12th battery 4th Field Artillery Brigade and sailed for the Middle East on November 18, 1915.

We went down to the 2nd Brigade and saw some of our mates from Longwood and Euroa—Sgt Major Herbert Kong Meng, Private Clarence Wignell, Private Thomas Jones, Lance Corporal Leslie Grant, Lieutenant Frank Tubb and Private William Pezet. They all looked well and were pleased to see me as they were going to the front in the morning.

> These mates were part of the 7th Infantry Battalion. It was among the first infantry units raised for the AIF during World War I. Recruited from Victoria, with the 5th, 6th, and 8th battalions, it formed the 2nd Brigade. This Brigade was raised within two weeks of the declaration of war and embarked in October 1914 on HMAT *Hororata* for Egypt arriving in December. It took part in the Anzac Gallipoli landing on April 25, 1915, as part of the second wave and was then transferred to Cape Helles to attack Krithia. A great many men were lost in this attack. The 7th Battalion then returned to the beaches of Anzac Cove and consequently fought at Lone Pine. It was there that Frank Tubb's brother, Lieutenant Frederick Tubb, earned his Victoria Cross with another of the Longwood boys, Corporal Alexander Burton. Burton's VC was awarded posthumously. Frederick Tubb later rose to the rank of major and died, aged thirty-five, on September 20, 1917, from wounds received in the battle of Menin Road, Belgium. Frank Tubb survived the war earning a Military Cross at Pozières. Two other Tubb boys, Sapper Alfred Tubb and Lieutenant Arthur Tubb, also returned home.
>
> Some of the mates were old cycling enthusiasts with George, competing in country races as well as riding for pleasure. The father of Herbert Kong Meng, originally from the Malay States, was reputedly the first man known to bring a cargo of tea to Australia!

Tuesday, 1st February

Got up next morning and led the horses to water. Had about one mile through the sand as I had given up cooking but I wished I had taken it on as we only get half a loaf of bread a day and a little cheese and stew. A bloke would starve on it if he did not buy some for himself. Went to bed at nine o'clock but had to get up at ten to go on stable picket—had a shit of a job for four hours hammering in pegs but we had porridge at twelve o'clock and that helped us through.

> Early this month reports came in of 12,000 Turks at Jerusalem and 13,000 at Beersheba. There was evidence that plans were afoot to move onto Katia. A new railway was almost completed and there were armaments ready to be transported.

Wednesday, 2nd February

Got up next morning, had to go on picket all day until six o'clock—not a bad job of a daytime.

Thursday, 3rd February

Up next morning and went leading horses again. When I got back they wanted me to go cooking again for the officers and my mate and I took it on as it is a good job. We only have to cook for six officers and six batmen

Saturday, 5th February

Up at six o'clock, made coffee for the officers and then we got breakfast. They pulled down all the tents and took one blanket off each of us and at night it came on to rain. We got wet through washing up the dishes then Frank Huggard and I built a little house made of a few boards and a box but it kept the rain out—just the thing—a lot of the other blokes sat around the fire all night and never got to sleep. It is a rotten life, a soldier's life, he has to put up with a lot.

Sunday, 6th February

Up at five o'clock to get breakfast as we were going to move off at nine o'clock. Got a start about twenty minutes after packing up our transport but we had a rotten trip as we only had a ride on the wagons for a mile when they made us get off and walk as it was too heavy for the horses to pull. Had dinner about two o'clock then moved off again at three. Got a ride for about a mile and a half then we had to walk for the rest of the way. Pulled in at the station called Shamallia to fill the water tank; off again walking as usual and met some Arabs; tipped their baskets upside down and took twelve oranges and my mate Frank Huggard got six. They revived us up lovely for a while then we arrived at the camping place about eight twenty tired, weary and hungry after walking fourteen miles. Made tea and did not get to bed until eleven o'clock.

> Trooper James Francis Huggard was a farmer from Toolamba, Shepparton and served with the 13th Light Horse Brigade in the Middle East. He left from Alexandria for the Western Front on June 17, 1916. Frank was transferred to the 37th Battalion on November 20, 1917. On July 11, 1918 he was gassed whilst fighting and, as a result of this action, he was awarded the Military Medal for the conspicuous manner in which he conducted himself on the battlefield in the face of the enemy. Promoted to lance corporal, he was eventually discharged, as permanently unfit due to asthma and problems with his lungs, on April 3, 1919.

Monday, 7th February

Up at quarter to six and got breakfast. Off again at ten past eight but had to walk again as the road was very heavy. My mate and I had a fill of bully beef and a biscuit for lunch at ten o'clock. As we were walking along we arrived at a town called Aboa Souair about twenty past eleven for dinner and stopped there for the night to give the horses a spell. I was not sorry as one of my feet was getting sore. Went over and had a look at the town. It is a rotten hole of a place. Got some tomatoes and eggs for tea and my mate and I got some coal off the engine driver in exchange for a tin of bully beef as we had little wood to boil the billy. Then we went to bed and had not long got in when a damn big rat ran over my arm and head and over my mate's head—then we got to sleep.

Tuesday, 8th February

Up again next morning at half past five. Got breakfast and off again at eight o'clock, walking again and they were making the pace pretty solid. My mate and I crossed over onto the railway line and it was a lot easier walking on the line. Some Arabs wanted to buy our pocket knives off us. I wanted five for mine and they would only give me one and a half so I told them to 'banshee' and then we walked along the line for about half a mile. The road took a turn so we had to go back to the road and it was pretty solid tramping in the sand. We came to a small bridge across the canal about five feet wide and eighty feet long and I had a rest on it for about ten minutes. There was a small boat just beside it and I wished we could get in it to ride down the canal but we got on the wagon for about a mile then we got off and walked along the canal 'til we got near another bridge. Then the Captain came over and told us we were on the wrong track! As we were coming over to the right road he gave us an orange each, took the horses out and gave them a drink and then off we went again. We crossed over the line and had dinner at a camp named Nefisha; saw a chap from Euroa named Hartley [possibly William Hartley]. Off again at one o'clock, struck a good road about a mile down so we got on the limbers and rode all the way. Went through Ismailia at two o'clock—it is a pretty town in places—they have some bonzer camps there. I only wish we were there. Going through the street, my mate Frank Huggard, got a loaf of bread and three oranges for nothing then we came to some Arabs fishing and we got some nice fish and cleaned them in the canal while we were waiting for the horses to cross the bridge. We had to push our transport across the bridge as the horses are frightened to cross it and some of them fell in the day before. We went straight into camp, arrived there at twenty past eight and then we went to bed very tired on it after having to walk about thirty-four miles out of the thirty-eight so you can guess we were tired on it.

> General Murray had notified the War Office that he was proceeding with preparations to occupy Katia.
>
> Evidently the horses were afraid to cross the bridge because it was a "floating" bridge. These appear to have been a row of boats lashed together supporting a roadway. There were also pontoon bridges, which swung open for boats to pass through. After proceeding up the Suez Canal on the desert side the men then had further trouble controlling the horses because of the camels of the Camel Corps that joined with them at the camp.

Wednesday, 9th February

Got up next morning at twenty past six and I was not sorry we had come to the camp to have a spell off the track. It is a rotten place to get water. I could not get any water 'til after eight o'clock to make the tea so we took fine care we got water the night before after that. Cooking is a lot better than having to drill!

Thursday, 10th February

Up at six and got breakfast and then had to shift our cooking place to the other side of the tents near the officers' tents. Had roast beef and potatoes and boiled cabbage for dinner so we are getting plenty to eat. We see plenty of camels going past the camp. I saw two hundred go past today, the most camels I ever saw. They were all carrying water for the soldiers in the trenches.

Friday, 11th February

Cooking as usual and I am having a good time and plenty to eat.

Saturday, 12th February

Cooking and we were paid one hundred and fifty-one piastres and half. We were all glad to get it as we were all short of money.

> Piastre is a monetary unit of Egypt, Lebanon, Sudan, and Syria, the hundredth part of a pound.

Sunday, 13th February

Cooking and we were watching the Church Parade. It looks very nice. I only wish I could go myself but we cannot go and leave the cooking.

> On this day the regiment was broken up with three divisions given the task of patrolling the desert west of Suez with their headquarters at Serapeum.

Monday, 14th February

Cooking and we have to wait on the officers now as the batmen have to go back into the lines and learn a bit of drill. They were a lazy lot—they want a bit of shaking up.

Tuesday, 15th February

Still cooking, the only trouble is that had very little wood so we have to share a little here and there.

> During this period General Murray was struggling to achieve his objectives due to a serious lack of transport facilities. At the same time the Russians were fighting well, had captured Erzerum, and were causing problems for Turkey's armies.

Wednesday, 16th February

Up at ten to six and had the billy boiled by five past, a record for the fire. Had breakfast and then I went to Ismailia for tucker for the officers. Had to walk all the way—it was about four miles. I crossed the canal in a punt—the first time I had ever been on one. I saw a balloon on the way and got to the store at half past ten and then off back again. Just got back in time for dinner. Frank and I had to get afternoon tea for three nurses in the afternoon and the Major told us that they said we were good cooks so that is a feather in our caps.

> This was probably Major F. H. Hutchings as Major E. F. D. Langley had been transferred to the Anzac Provost Corps on February 1.

Thursday, 17th February

Cooking as usual but it took my mate one hour and a quarter to boil the billy this morning and the officers wanted their drink of tea—I bet they were cursing us. At night we went over to the canteen and some blokes pulled a cask of jam out and my mate got six. He gave two to me and I put them under my coat and we went off back to the camp and put them in our box—not a bad haul as jam is pretty scarce here. We went to bed at quarter to nine as we have to get up early in the morning.

Friday, 18th February

Up at half-past five and got breakfast and dinner then went to Ismailia for some food. It is a pretty long walk but it is good for a bloke as he does not get much exercise cooking. I received ten letters and was more pleased to get them than anything else. We would give five bob to get a letter from home.

Saturday, 19th February

Cooking again as usual and the wind blowing like anything, nearly blowing the fire out. It is not much sport. Wrote one letter home and have about a dozen more to write.

> First troops, including a section of the Camel Corps, left the infantry defenses to proceed to Katia. [TYPESETTER, THIS NOTE HAS A SPACE ABOVE AND BELOW]

Sunday, 20th February

Up about twenty to six, made breakfast and then got the dinner on. We were issued with our iron rations so as we could move off at a minute's notice. We also got issued with presents sent from Australia and they were lollies, fruit, milk, honey, sauce and cigarettes which were very nice to get. We could not go out as the officers were away and we had to stop in and get them their tea. It was about eight o'clock when we went to bed. We got a nice reward from the officers—they gave us one hundred piastres each.

Monday, 21st February

Still cooking for officers. They are a fine lot of men and very easy to please. One of them, Lieutenant O'Hara-Wood is a great tennis player.

> Hector (Pat) O'Hara-Wood became an international tennis player after the war, following the example of his brother Arthur who was the Australian men's champion in 1914. Arthur was killed in the war in October 1918, but Pat lived to 1961 and, with his wife Meryl, was an eminent part of the Australian tennis world.

Tuesday, 22nd February

Up at a quarter to six still cooking. Frank went to Ismailia and I had to get the tea ready. When he came back about five o'clock he was so very hungry he nearly ate all the custard and fruit while I was serving the tea!

Wednesday, 23rd February

Still cooking—it is a bonzer job, the only thing we fight about is who gets the porridge and the eggs that are left. My mate and I have sent twelve letters home so they will be all pleased when they get them. I cooked a jam saurbish for the first time—it was very good but the officers did not fancy it too well so my mate Frank and I ate it and we were not very hungry for tea.

Thursday, 24th February

Cooking as usual and I went into Ismailia for food for the officers. When I was there I went through part of the gardens. They were very nice. I also saw the balloon rise from the ground for the first time—it was just the thing to see it go up. Got back at five o'clock and then got their tea.

Friday, 25th February

Still cooking and it is warming up. I cooked some pancakes for dinner and they were just the thing! The officers came back. I was cooking 'til about three until I had run out of flour and eggs so they must have liked them. A silly old drunk fell over just by our fire and the doctor wanted them to put him in the guard tent but the warrant officer did not!

We got paid after tea—I got fifty piastres and we will be able to save our money here as there is nothing to spend it on.

Saturday, 26th February

Still cooking but having a good time as we get plenty to eat and not much to do. I received two Euroa papers and was glad to get them to see some of the news about Victoria. We received a nice donation of one hundred piastres each given by the officers. They must think we are good cooks and I bet we will do all we can for them. Had a piece of cake from Australia, also some lollies and dates—they taste twice as good as what you get here.

Sunday, 27th February

Got breakfast. We have one more to cook for now as the other officer is back from the school. I had just got the meat on when we had to go out on Parade as they suspected a spy in our regiment but they were not successful in finding him in our lot and good job too! Got dismissed then we got dinner and after we are having a spell as it is a rotten, windy, dusty day and dust is getting into everything.

Monday, 28th February

Up at half-past five, got some cocoa for the officers and then we got breakfast and after breakfast I made a pudding. It was my first and it turned out a bonzer. They all enjoyed it. I know I did myself as I had nothing else to eat—only pudding for dinner. There was a bit of fun in the guard tent at tea-time. They had a drunk in and he bolted out and the guard after him with fixed bayonet. He was getting away from them but tripped over his own boot and they caught him and then he was going to kill the lot of them. He had the guards a bit frightened but one of them quietened him down and he was alright after that and a good job as I think he would have killed some of them if they had of kept on bossing him.

Tuesday, 29th February

Still cooking but the only thing about it is that we are still short of wood. It would be a bonzer job only for that. One of my mates, Harry Forbes, went to hospital after being sick for over a week. We all got issued with cigarettes and they are just the thing as we are all short.

> Trooper Henry (Harry) Forbes was from Barham in New South Wales. He was later killed in action on April 25, 1918 at Villers-Bretonneux.

Wednesday, 1st March

Cooking for officers. I was issued with new trousers and socks and it was about time as the ones I have on me want a wash badly.

> During the month of March, General Sir John Maxwell, commander of the forces in Egypt, returned to London, leaving General Murray to assume control of all the troops. This meant that Murray was now also responsible for the internal security of Egypt and the equipping and training of men in that area—men destined for other war fronts.

Thursday, 2nd March

Cooking and it was rotten as a sand storm came on and nearly put our fire out. The sand got in our eyes and we could hardly see. I don't want any more days like it.

Friday, 3rd March

It is just as bad—the sand is getting into everything and we are eating bread and sand instead of bread and jam.

Saturday, 4th March

Up at half-past five. It is not so bad but the sand storm came on again about nine o'clock. It knocked off after dinner and I had a ride into Ismailia for food. As I was going in the horse fell with me but I did not get hurt. The road is like glass, too slippery for me to ride home on.

Sunday, 5th March

Up at five o'clock as we are shifting camp to a camp named Moascar. We left our post at ten o'clock but we did not have to walk this time as they gave us a horse to ride on. My mate, Frank Huggard, struck a beauty—it bucked like blazes, but I don't think any horse could shift him. It quietened down after a bit but there was some commotion along the track as the road is still as slippery as glass and there were many falls. One chap named Stobaus was taken to hospital.

> Private Robert Stobaus was a twenty-three-year-old from Carlton, an inner suburb of Melbourne. It is often assumed that the

men of the Light Horse were mainly country born and bred. Even in official records, it is noted that the Light Horse was comprised almost wholly of men from country areas, most of whom bred and owned the horses they rode in their regiments. The horses and men together were often part of a reserve company who annually trained together in the Australian bush. However, this may not be a completely true depiction, for example, the 13th Light Horse could not be accurately described as a regiment of bushmen. "From the trades and callings recorded in the embarkation rolls, fewer than a third followed rural occupations such as farmer, shearer, stockman, boundary rider, station overseer, farm labourer, pastoralist or grazier. The larger grouping worked in urban trades such as clerk, butcher, carpenter, painter, driver, labourer, agent, mechanic, chauffeur, gardener or jockey. The officers however, were more rural based, two-thirds being farmers, graziers or pastoralists, one was a doctor, one a veterinary surgeon and the remainder followed various urban occupations."[4]

This is, of course, a breakdown of only one regiment but certainly the statistics are worthy of note as the majority of reporting on World War I assumed that the Light Horse, in general, was composed of men from the bush. There are four later significant writers of the Light Horse who vary in their opinions on this matter but, suffice to say, a significant percentage of the men were country folk.

We arrived into camp at one o'clock, it is a rotten trip shifting about as we have to carry all the officers' cooking utensils. We were just about knocked out when we finally got fixed up then we cooked the officers some dinner about two o'clock. It is not as good a camp as we left as the sand is up to your boot tops but you have to put up with a lot when you are soldiering. They say we are going to France and a good job if we do.

Monday, 6th March

Up at six o'clock for breakfast. It is a sandy rotten hole! I went to Ismailia for food for officers and it was very hot—I think it must have been about one hundred in the shade and I had to walk nearly all over Ismailia to get all the food I wanted as I could not get it all at the one place. They are rotten shops; I don't think they

---

4. Hunter, *My Corps Cavalry*, 12.

keep anything much. Got back just in time for tea and I was ready for it too.

Tuesday, 7th March

Up at five o'clock, got cocoa and toast for the officers and then we had to get breakfast. The only thing we cannot get enough of is water but I managed to get some today and I have done some washing. It was time I washed my clothes as I found fifteen lice in them the first ever I have had on me since I have been in Egypt.

Wednesday, 8th March

Frank Huggard went to Ismailia and I had to stay and do the cooking so I was kept pretty busy. He just got home in time to help me get the tea.

Thursday, 9th March

Still cooking for officers. At night Frank and I went and saw some mates that I knew. I saw Tommy Saxon, Joe Saxon, Archie Gascoyne, Tom Mackrell and Tom Donovan. They all looked well and they were pleased to see me. It was a pretty long walk there and back and all the sand makes it hard walking but we are all used to it by now.

> Tommy and Joe Saxon were brothers from Euroa—Tom a printer, and Joe a grocer's assistant. The younger, Joe, was killed in action aged nineteen in France on August 4, 1916. Tommy was wounded in April 1917 and returned home in 1918. Their brother Will also served—in Gallipoli he and another Euroa local, Harold Weatherhead, had carried out continuous courageous work as stretcher bearers. Both Thomas Mackrell and Archibald Gascoyne, also Euroa lads, were killed in action in France—Tom near Pozières in July 1916 and Archie in May 1917. It was learnt that Archie was blown up and unconscious for some two hours afterwards in August 1916. He thereafter battled shell shock, evidently with little sympathy from various hospital and army doctors, and eventually returned to the battlefield in April 1917.
>
> Those at home found it extremely traumatic to deal with the death of a loved one. It was much worse when a soldier was missing presumed dead or in any other situation when a body

could not be found or identified. Wives, sweethearts, and parents grieved for the rest of their lives without having the memory of last hours spent together, as in illness, or a nearby grave to visit. In the case of Tom Mackrell it was not until March 1931 that the remains of an Australian soldier were identified as that of Thomas Mackrell and he was buried in an official war grave in France. In 1946 his sister was writing to ask for a copy of his will and in 1967 his niece was requesting an Anzac medal for which the family felt he was entitled. Uncertainty about the fate of a soldier, as was the case with the missing in action, or even the obvious inability to view the remains of those officially listed as killed, caused many to hope against hope, sometimes for forty or fifty years.

Friday, 10th March

I made a blancmange for dinner and it was very good. I made a plum pudding for tea and it too must have been good as they came back for a second lot. I received fifty piastres but as there is nothing here to spend it on it will go in the kitty for when we get to France.

Saturday, 11th March

Still cooking and in the afternoon went to Ismailia for food for the officers. It was a rotten day, the wind was blowing, it was dusty then it started to rain but this cleared the dust. I got a goose for three shillings on my way back and I killed it after tea.

Sunday, 12th March

We gave the officers a surprise! We gave them roast goose for dinner and they told us it was a good dinner we got for them. They gave us fifty piastres each that night so it was just the thing to look after them well.

Monday, 13th March

Got up about ten to three and got breakfast as we were shifting camp and had to move off at five o'clock. We had to pull up the horse lines and then we were marched to the station as we were going by train. We left Moascar at half past ten and we arrived at Tel el Kebir at half past twelve. Got to the camp at one o'clock and at two o'clock Eagle and Sloan and I went over to the old battle field about two miles away and I got a bullet and a piece of old rifle and an old shell. I saw a lot of old skeletons there. I just got back as the troop arrived from Moascar and we had a bit of trouble getting their tea as none of the cooking utensils had come. But worst of all none of our blankets had arrived so I had to sleep with one of my mates, Eagle. He was one of the lucky advance guards and he had his blankets. They had a good bit of trouble with the horses at night as none of their lines had come and they had them all tied together and they nearly all got away two or three times. We did not get much sleep that night.

> Chester Eagle was a twenty-year-old fireman from Barham in New South Wales. By March 1916 his brother Edward had also joined up—both survived the war. Chester was wounded on two occasions whilst serving on the Western Front. Sloan was Albert Sloan, a twenty-year-old farmer from Rainbow and had just been released from hospital suffering from mumps. He went on to serve in the Australian Provost Corps and the Field Artillery Brigade, finishing his war duty in 1917 as a driver in France.

Tuesday, 14th March

I did not get up till after six o'clock and our dixies did not come 'til about eleven o'clock so we could not get much of a dinner for the officers but we had to do the best we could.

Wednesday, 15th March

Up at half past five, we shifted our fire to the other end of the lines in the officers' area and near the mess shed. The Arabs started to build fire also—it does not take them long to put one up when about one dozen get at it. They had it finished at six o'clock.

Thursday, 16th March

Up at twenty to six and my mate, Frank Huggard, went to the doctor's as he was sick with influenza. The doctor told him he had to have two or three days spell so I had to get another mate to help me but he does not know much about cooking.

Mr Lydiard went to the hospital suffering with pleurisy.

> Lydiard returned to his unit from hospital on March 26. Captain G. E. Lydiard is addressed as "Mr" here probably because he was known to George. He was a thirty-six-year-old grazier from Euroa who served in Gallipoli, Sinai, and later proceeded to the front at France, honorably leading his squadron at the Hindenburg Outpost Line in 1918 after being promoted to Major in July of that year.

Friday, 17th March

Got up at quarter to six and made tea for officers. We had to fly around as the General was going to inspect us all and we had to have the place clean and we did it too!

I received ten letters last night and I was very pleased to get them and to hear how they are getting on in Australia.

The Arabs started to put up a kitchen for us to cook in and a safe to put things in. We want it badly to put everything away from the flies as they are getting very troublesome.

Saturday, 18th March

Still cooking. I went and did some shopping in the afternoon and it was dusty and windy. The dust used to nearly blind me at times— you have to put up with a lot here especially if you are a cook.

Sunday, 19th March

Cooking as usual. We had a pretty easy day as it was Sunday and we gave them cold meat for tea with blancmange and fruit but that is pretty good to get out here.

Monday, 20th March

My mate went to the doctor again but I don't think the doctors know too much especially some of them as they don't seem to give him much relief. I had to get another man, named Eric Walters, in his place. He is a good bloke too and a bit of a cook.

> The assessment of Lance Corporal Eric Walters was not misguided—he went on to receive the Distinguished Conduct Medal on the Somme in September 1918. He came under heavy machine-gun fire whilst out on mounted patrol, dismounted

and, with one other man, succeeded in knocking out the enemy machine-gun. The next day on a similar patrol he was badly wounded in the legs and eventually invalided to the UK.

Tuesday, 21st March

Still cooking. Frank went to the hospital with Eric in his place. We had a hard day's work carrying water all the afternoon. We had about half a mile to carry it. They christened the mess shed and they gave us a bottle of beer but, as I am a teetotaller, I gave it to a mate.

Wednesday, 22nd March

We had a busy day today cleaning up for the Prince of Wales came to inspect us. I was very pleased to see him and he is a fine looking young fellow. We got word to shift tonight so we started packing up some of the things because we have to move out at seven o'clock.

Thursday, 23rd March

Up at ten minutes to five; got the officers their breakfast at six as they had to move off at seven. Then we had to pack up all the food and crockery—got them packed—then we had to wait for the wagons. We did not get a start until five past three and the sweat poured off me when we were loading the train as we only had five minutes to put the stuff on. We arrived at Moascar about seven o'clock, unloaded the train and arrived at camp post at eight. Then I had to boil the dixie to give the officers some tea. Went to bed at twenty past ten, tired and sleepy.

Friday, 24th March

Up at six o'clock but could not boil the billy as there was no axe to cut the wood. We only had a poor dinner today as we only had bully beef and fish and a few vegetables. That is the first time I have had bully beef for about two months so I cannot groan about the food. I am living like a fighting cock.

Saturday, 25th March

Still cooking for officers but the only thing about it is that we can't get any meat so we have to live on fish and bully beef.

We started a cricket team, the troops are playing against one another for the championship of the squadron.

Sunday, 26th March

Up at twenty past six as it was Sunday and we can lay in a little longer but no meat again only vegetables.

We played the third troop today and we beat them. I carried my bat out for five runs. Now we are playing the first troop for the final and they have got four of us out for six so we don't seem to have much chance. I was there for over half an hour when they caught me out. It was too dark and you could just see the ball. They called me a champion stonewaller.

Monday, 27th March

Up at half past five—it is pretty early to get up every morning but you get used to it. We finished our game of cricket and were beaten by sixteen runs. I took four wickets for four runs, not too bad an average. Now the sergeants have challenged the privates and they have got five of us out for twenty-five. I was still in myself with six runs when stumps were drawn.

Tuesday, 28th March

Up at a quarter to six; got tea for them and then got breakfast. Just near dinner time Frank Huggard arrived from the hospital with a big swag up—nearly enough for two men. Had dinner and then went and finished our game of cricket. We beat the sergeants by three runs but they got us all out in the next match for sixteen runs so we gave them that game and now we have started the final. They have eight of us out for twenty-four and I am not out so we might give them a good go for it again.

Wednesday, 29th March

Still cooking and we got issued with beef at last after a week without it so we had a good feed. We did not finish on the cricket today as it was too hot and they all got inoculated and their arms were sore!

Thursday, 30th March

I did not get up until after six. We got the dinner on and a dust storm came and blew down our mess hut. My mate was in it and it knocked him off the stool but he did not get hurt. They had to get a fatigue party to put it up. We got fifty piastres that being my pay so I do not have much to throw away between each pay.

Friday, 31st March

Up at a quarter to five to get breakfast for Mr Lydiard [Captain] then after breakfast I had to go to Ismailia for some sweets as there were five nurses coming to tea and we had to have something nice and we did too. We had the table laid in fine style. It made a bloke think of home when you see some Australian ladies and they said that they really enjoyed an outing. They had a ride back in a limber and I bet they had a rough ride.

> A limber was a horse-drawn vehicle consisting of an axle, pole, and two wheels. It was used to tow a field gun.

Saturday, 1st April

Still cooking and we had an easy day. The only thing was we had to wait a long while for tea as they had to water their horses at the canal and had to take them across on the punt—it takes a long while that way.

Sunday, 2nd April

Sunday, and we played a cricket match against the sergeants and they got us out for fifty-six after having eight down for twenty-four. Myself and Page made a good stand for the last wicket and just about pulled the game out of the fire as we had three of them out for seventeen.

Charles Page was a stationer from Melbourne who went on to serve in France and then return home to his wife.

Monday, 3rd April

We were supposed to have finished our match but I think we had the sergeants frightened. We could not get them to finish it. Got issued with eleven tins of milk and some cocoa and tobacco. It all comes in very handy. The best of all was that I got two letters from Australia—that is what we look forward to most.

Tuesday, 4th April

I had to get up at half-past four to get cocoa for the officers as they have started early morning parades but we get a good rest in the day now. I made three puddings—one for the officers and two for the sergeants and they all turned out bonzer. I am becoming a good cook now. It only takes a bit of practice!

Wednesday, 5th April

Still cooking and my mate went to Ismailia again for some biscuits and cake as there were two nurses coming in the afternoon and we had to get them afternoon tea. Played a challenge cricket match for fifty piastres between eleven and fifteen a-side and the fifteen team won.

Thursday, 6th April

Still cooking. Two anti-aircraft guns arrived at the camp, the first I have ever seen. They belong to the Fifth Division and they would be just the thing to fetch down aeroplanes.

Friday, 7th April

Still cooking and my mate and I got our photo taken at the fire. I think it will be a good photo.

Saturday, 8th April

Cooking for officers still and I had to go to the doctor with indigestion—I suppose with eating too much pudding! We had General Murray inspect our camp and he was well satisfied with the way it is kept.

Sunday, 9th April

Still cooking and I made three puddings—two for the sergeants and one for the officers. We had another General through the lines, General McKay and the lines were a credit to the Fifth Division Calvary. We got fifty piastres given to us today by the officers and we also had cigarettes issued to us.

Monday, 10th April

Still cooking for the officers and my mate and I had our photo taken—pretty good for a new chum photographer.

Tuesday, 11th April

My mate had a day's leave to go to the rail-head to see some of his mates in the 8th Light Horse and he arrived home about half-past five just in time for tea—and I was also issued with a new pair of boots and a dixie.

Wednesday, 12th April

Up at five o'clock to get tea for the officers as they like their morning drink and I also gave one to the quartermaster—that is the man to look after and he will give you anything you want! Mr Lydiard got his commission today for he is a Captain now. Well done George and a good bloke too.

Thursday, 13th April

Up at seven o'clock as it was my turn to sleep in and I had to go to Ismailia to get biscuits and cakes for the nurses as they were coming out but it turned out a rotten day, the worst I have ever seen in Egypt. The sand is something awful; it nearly blinds you at times.

I don't want to see many days like that so I will be glad when they send us to France or somewhere else out of this place.

> British pilots had reported that a group of Turks were attempting to sink a well at Jifjafa, which was situated fifty-two miles east of the Suez Canal. A squadron of Light Horse, including troopers from the 13th and officers and men from the Australian and British Engineers, were organized to advance into the desert to the enemy outpost.

Friday, 14th April

Still cooking for officers. It turned out a good day. The rain had laid the dust and we played a cricket match in the afternoon—an eleven against fifteen and I was playing in the eleven. I carried my bat that afternoon after being there for almost one and a half hours for four runs and we had four wickets down then we got them out for fifty-two.

Saturday, 15th April

Up at five o'clock but I did not feel too good as I had a bilious attack. We finished our match in the afternoon and we beat the fifteen by nine runs after a ding dong go.

Sunday, 16th April

Up at half-past five. Got the officers their morning drink. I could not sleep in as I had to get up—the band was playing and it was just the thing. The best band I have heard for a long time. We did not play any more cricket today as it was too hot.

Monday, 17th April

Up at five o'clock—still the same old game, cooking, and it turned out a very hot day. I went for a swim in the evening in the canal—it was just the thing, it freshened you up and makes you feel fit for anything.

Tuesday, 18th April

Still cooking and we played a game of cricket in the afternoon. I made top score for our side and took two wickets for five runs but we got beat by about eight runs after a ding-dong go.

Wednesday, 19th April

Cooking and I am making them a plum duff for dinner as it has turned out a nice cool day, it turned out a bonzer. We played a cricket match in the afternoon—Lieutenant Davies' team against Lieutenant Woods' team. They got us out for thirty-nine and they made sixty-seven in the first innings and eighty in the second so we have a big job in front of us to beat them. I got two hundred and fifty piastres that was our pay. It will come in very handy.

Thursday, 20th April

Up at five o'clock and my mate got up early too to go and have a look for some money where they made a raid on the gamblers and I picked up fifty piastres and my mate only got one—not a bad morning walk. I only wish I could pick them up every day. We finished our match in the afternoon and Lieutenant Woods' team won.

Friday, 21st April

Still working for officers—we did very little else as it was too hot to play cricket and as it was also Good Friday we had a holiday.

Saturday, 22nd April

Up at half past four, got a drink of tea for the officers. We also had goose for dinner as General McKay was going to inspect them at seven o'clock and we had to get everything nice and clean. I also saw Lieutenant Colonel Maygar and he looks well on it. Best of all I received two parcels—one from my auntie and the other from home which I was very pleased to get.

> Lieutenant Colonel Maygar hailed from Ruffy, not far from Creightons Creek, which was the original home of the Halsalls when they came out from Halsall in Lancashire in 1859. Maygar was the most highly decorated of local men from the area.

> He had had an illustrious career in the Boer War, where he was awarded the Victoria Cross for gallantry at Geelhoutboom. He was the first Victorian to receive the Victoria Cross.

Sunday, 23rd April

I did not get up until almost seven o'clock as it was Sunday and there is not much to do. The Army Medical challenged us at cricket and we beat them by fourteen runs—the first time they have been beaten since they have been in Egypt—so that is a feather in our cap.

Monday, 24th April

Up at five, got them their breakfast. I also got ten letters and some papers—that is what we look forward to most—then I went to Ismailia and got some presents to send home. I spent 250 piastres so I had some nice gifts to send and I bet they will be pleased to get them. There is not much else to do with your money, it is a lot better sending things home than gambling or drinking, etc.

Tuesday, 25th April

We had a holiday today as they were keeping up Anzac Day. We played cricket all day, the Cycle boys played us and they gave us a beating. I gave them a lot of trouble to get me out. I suppose I was batting for over two hours for eleven runs, not too bad a performance for me.

> In addition to motor vehicles, bicycles were used for transport of equipment and other military needs throughout the war in all fields. There were also donkeys and mules used for the same purposes.

Wednesday, 26th April

Still cooking and it turned out the hottest day we have had since we have been in Egypt. It just put me in remind of a summer day in Australia—the hot winds would nearly burn your face. I don't want many more days like that.

Thursday, 27th April

Up at five o'clock but it was a lot cooler day and a good job too. I put in a lot of time writing letters. I wrote eight so I did a lot of writing!

Friday, 28th April

Still cooking but I would like a change back in the troop again as I am getting tired of cooking. I received three letters today and I was pleased to get them as they were from home.

Saturday, 29th April

It was all go today as we are going to be inspected by the General and we had to have everything clean and so we did. He told us we were the best lot of cavalry he had seen and that is a feather in our caps.

Sunday, 30th April

Up at six to get tea for the officers and after breakfast I went to the doctor as I was not feeling too well and he gave me a day off.

Monday, 1st May

I did not get up very early. I went to the doctor's again as I did not feel too good and I had another day's spell. I got one letter and three papers and that was the best of all as we are always looking forward to mail from home.

Tuesday, 2nd May

I got two more letters this morning and they were both from home. I went to the doctor's again but I feel a good bit better today and think I will start work tomorrow.

Wednesday, 3rd May

I did not go on cooking as I did not feel too good and I thought I would have another day off. Got paid at night 150 piastres so I have a few bob in my pocket now.

Thursday, 4th May

The officer told me to have two or three days off till I got quite better so I took him at his word.

Friday, 5th May

I wasn't feeling too good again so I went to the doctor and he told me that I had indigestion and he gave me a tonic and I felt a lot better after taking it.

Saturday, 6th May

I started cooking again today as I was feeling a lot better and could eat some hard food at last so that tonic was good stuff that the doctor gave me.

Sunday, 7th May

Up at half-past three as we had to get breakfast early for the officers as they were going out on a route march and I went to bed after they left and did not get up till half past eight the latest I have got up since I have been here.

Monday, 8th May

Still cooking and I am getting tired of the job especially here. I won't be sorry when we get a shift to France.

> Many of the Light Horse stationed in Palestine were becoming frustrated at the lack of action. Even though they had proved their fighting ability at the Battle of Romani, men were convinced that where they were was just a "sideshow" and they saw the real war being fought in the fields of France. In fact, in one day in May 1916, as noted earlier, 900 light horsemen applied for a transfer to the infantry with the objective of embarking for the Western Front. Some even enlisted in the Cyclist Battalion and the Flying Corps to this end. There was also an instance of a light-horseman convalescing in England, obtaining an offer of a commission in a British Regiment. Only the 13th and part of the 4th Light Horse eventually went to France. The remainder stayed in Palestine until 1919. They were engaged in strategic battles and many raids and skirmishes over this time, one being the Battle of Beersheba

on October 31, 1917. During this battle, Lieutenant Edward Ralston, the commanding officer of the 12th Light Horse Regiment wrote to the mother of Trooper Ernest Craggs the following words on the death of her son: "The day before the fight, he was laughing and joking as usual and was full of spirit all through the long night ride. He rode into action just behind me and the last I saw of him, he was standing in his stirrups and cheering."[5] Ralston was wounded at this point and Sergeant John Bailey went on: "He and I were wounded at the same time, he was hit in the head and the chest. I helped him under the cover of his horse which was killed. I held the poor boy's hands while he passed away. He only lived about ten minutes after he was wounded and did not have any pain, Thank God."[6]

Lieutenant Colonel Leslie Maygar VC (Boer War) was awarded the Distinguished Service Order in 1917. Maygar, leading the 8th Light Horse, another of the Light Horse regiments left behind in Palestine, was wounded by an attacking German aircraft at Beersheba. His horse bolted with him into the night and by the time he was found he had lost too much blood and died the next day. He was buried in the Beersheba War Cemetery. As noted earlier, Maygar hailed from Ruffy and told the volunteers from the district, of which George Halsall was one, that he himself had to live up to his VC and they must expect to be in the thick of it with him. If any of the men thought or felt that their hearts were in the wrong place, they should drop out then and there. But all the men decided they were going to take the risk.

It should always be remembered that the men who commanded the Australian brigades and regiments in Egypt and Palestine proved to be fine leaders, in particular those at the very top—Major General Sir Harry Chauvel, Brigadier General Charles Fox, and Brigadier General Granville Ryrie. Each of these men had vastly different qualities of leadership but all bore testament to the admirable Australian army practice of promoting men by sheer ability, devoid of any social or political influences, unlike the practice of the British army of the time.

Brigadier General Granville Ryrie, aged in his fifties, was a large man (over sixteen stone), but rode a horse more lightly than any other man, and was capable of climbing palm trees to reach the succulent dates.

---

5. Australia. Department of Veteran Affairs, *The Australian Light Horse*, 44
6. Australia. Department of Veteran Affairs, *The Australian Light Horse*, 44

The Start of the Great Adventure

Tuesday, 9th May

The only thing we were doing today was cooking and it is getting blooming hot for that job now.

Wednesday, 10th May

Still cooking and I went for a swim in the afternoon and it was just the thing to freshen a bloke up a lot.

Thursday, 11th May

Still cooking is the only thing I can say today as there is very little doing but the best of all I received four letters from home and that is what we look forward to most.

Friday, 12th May

Still cooking and we had a busy night in front of us as they were going out sham fighting and the first lot left at a quarter to twelve and the next lot at half past two so we did not get much sleep but you have to put up with a lot in soldiering.

Saturday, 13th May

Up at half past four, got cocoa for the officers.

3

The Horrors of Reality

THE JOURNAL OF GEORGE Samuel Halsall now ceased, as probably the experiences on the Western Front were too traumatic to chronicle, George eventually ending up with severe shell shock. The keeping of diaries on the Western Front was also strictly prohibited, although many soldiers did, as illustrated by following excerpts from V. C. Walker. Also the journal George wrote whilst in Palestine had been posted back home before he left for France. From the boredom of waiting endlessly in Palestine, the Great Adventure became a lifelong nightmare.

Excerpts from the journal of V. C. Walker

At the end of May, preparations began to move the 13th Light Horse and part of the 4th Light Horse to France. V. C. Walker, a corporal in the 13th Light Horse recorded the following in his journal:

> 1/6/1916—*Regiment commences moving to Ismalia, trucked horses on train to Alexandria*
> 2/6/1916—*Loaded horses on ship Kingstonian*
> 3/6/1916—*Sailed from Alexandria escorted by Royal Navy*
> 7/6/1916—*Still at sea, very rough, many horses very sick. Disembarked horses at Marseilles. Entrained horses and train left for War Zone*"[1]

---

1. Hunter, *My Corps Cavalry*, 33–34.

In July, the 13th Light Horse Regiment transferred to the village of Contay and a squadron was involved in the attack on Pozières on July 23. In August the men were in Flanders and by October they had returned to the Somme. In a complete contrast to the blazing sun and endless sand of the Middle East, the Regiment was now in the midst of bitter cold and unrelenting rain.

> *30/10/1916—15th British Corps Cavalry move out of forward zone and 13th Light Horse take over their positions*
>
> *31/10/1916—Enemy shellfire stirs up ground very muddy. Our horses and transport in 2 feet of mud. Infantry muddy up to waist. Regiment ordered to protect Fricourt, which Germans are shelling heavily. German planes [word uncertain] our positions. Conditions bad. Few casualties and several horses killed and wounded.*
>
> *1/11/1916—Aerial attacks repeated. Infantry cut overcoats off to waist length as mud is already thigh high and very heavy on troops.*
>
> *6/11/1916—Another heavy bombing attack from German Air Force. Our horses scared badly and difficult to control.*
>
> *8/11/1916—Heavy bombardment. Australian and British artillery now re-enforced, reply with heavy shelling of German forces. The noise is terrific. German Air Force continue attack on our position for several days".*[2]

The Germans called this "terrific noise" *Trommelfeuer* (drumfire). During the early stages of the war the Germans had superior gunpower and many more shells. The constant intense bombardment beginning like a giant kettledrum and gradually becoming louder and louder to an almost unbearable pitch and depth, resulted in strong men shaking uncontrollably, unable sometimes to stand or walk, and often on the verge of weeping like children. C. E. W. Bean describes the effect of two giant German howitzers:

> The shells from these guns are beginning to fall more thickly. Huge black clouds shoot into the air from various parts of the foreground, and slowly drift across the hilltop. Suddenly there is a descending shriek drawn out for a second or more, coming terrifyingly near, a crash far louder than thunder, a colossal

---

2. Hunter, *My Corps Cavalry*, 36.

thump to the earth which seems to move the whole world about an inch from its base: a scatter of flying wood splinter, whirr of fragments, scatter of falling earth. Before it is half finished, another exactly similar shriek is coming through it. Another crash—apparently right on the crown of your head, as if the roof beams of the sky had broken in. You can just hear through the crash the shriek of a third and a fourth shell as they come tearing down the vault of heaven . . .[3]

As well as the poor young bodies torn apart by this seemingly endless shelling, there were also cases of bodies found without a visible mark of injury—the shaking and vibration causing a fatal concussion when the brain was pummeled inside the skull. In the same way endless shelling with oxygen sucked violently from the surrounding air caused "lung shock," where lungs collapsed or bled internally.

A letter published in a British newspaper told of wounded men, "lying in the shell holes among the decaying corpses: helpless under the scorching sun and bitter nights, under repeated shelling. Men with bowels dropping out, lungs shot away, with blinded, smashed faces, or limbs blown into space. Men screaming and gibbering. Wounded men hanging in agony on the barbed wire, until a friendly spout of liquid fire shrivels them up like flies in a candle."[4] Continual horrific sights resulting from the whining, shrieking, bursting shells increased the trauma for each and every soldier. Mates were blown into unidentifiable pieces, some were decapitated, others with a torso and head seemingly untouched but the lower part of the body obliterated. Lieutenant John Raws records a journey through the trenches: "The ground was covered with bodies in all stages of decay and mutilation and I would, after struggling free from the earth, pick up a body by me to try to lift him out with me, and find him a decayed corpse. I pulled a head off—was covered with blood. The horror was indescribable."[5] Nor were these experiences isolated: always the crises were ongoing: "This officer survived the almost total destruction of his battalion three times in heavy fighting . . . he was in a dugout that received a direct hit . . . then he was buried by debris for several hours."[6] Eventually, after being rescued at the end of the day, he suddenly collapsed and cried uncontrollably for a week.

3. Bean, "Trommelfeuer," 7.
4. Gilbert, *A History of the Twentieth Century. Volume 1*, 457.
5. Downing, *Breakdown*, 219.
6. Downing, *Breakdown*, 103.

The Horrors of Reality

As dusk crept over the muddy terrain his mind struggled to summon up visions of home—the myriad colors of each day's sunset in the diminishing sounds of the bush—in doing so, he saw that even amidst the unspeakable horror of the trenches, the disappearing sun spread its light on the horizon... sometimes dull grey, sometimes sharp grey, casting forth violet hues with a vainly infinitesimal glimmer of hope of a better morn. But still he dreamed of the vibrant red of a sun diffusing over the heavens into a glorious golden red and eventually a pinkish primrose—colors that seem impossible to be captured by human design and colors that were rapidly fading into the far recesses of his memory. These poignant dreams of home were becoming harder and harder to hold on to in the midst of mud and blood, of broken bones and rotting corpses. What he daily lived with now were not dreams, but constant nightmares blackening his heart and his soul, destroying his hope of return—a return not only to a distant land but to a hope of a future in that old home—to soft balmy breezes drifting through the gully, filled with aromas of eucalyptus and wattle and the sound of the currawongs and the magpies as they weaved and soared through the bush. He remembered the feeling of the promise of refreshment in the clear waters of the channel at the end of the day.

> I feel my legs moving one after the other
> I smell the eucalyptus trees among the bush
> I taste the water running down my throat
> I hear the birds above and around me
> I see my home and I'm almost there.[7]

Although in the trenches and taking part in the attack on Pozières, for the next few months most of the duties of the 13th Light Horse comprised traffic control—a difficult task with new troops marching to the front and exhausted men stumbling back to some kind of temporary respite from the battle. The regiment also carried out dispatch riding, acting as orderlies at headquarters, escorting prisoners of war, and providing work parties. In fact, some of the men with farming experience were employed in the harvesting of French crops when the French farmers were fighting elsewhere. Although it may sound idyllic, they were naturally under constant fire from German guns whilst attempting to complete this task.

---

7. Halsall, "Untitled," 1.

In February 1917 the Allies planned an advance through Bapaume towards Cambrai in pursuit of retreating Germans. The Light Horse was sent ahead to find any gaps in the rear guard of the enemy, an exercise initially hampered by heavy fog and then prevented from any worthwhile achievement by barbed wire, heavy bombardment, and never-ending machine-gun fire. At the end of the day of this advance, February 24, George Halsall was admitted to a field hospital, "sick" rather than wounded—suffering badly from shell shock—a state often viewed unsympathetically as LMF—lack of moral fiber! However, at this stage of the war, attitudes were changing and men affected by the constant shelling were somewhat carefully analysed. Special centers, less than twenty miles from the battle lines and therefore hopefully away from the noise of the front, had been set for this purpose. (This was probably a futile aim as the noise of shelling could often be heard across the Channel in London and other eastern cities.) Medical treatment, social activities, and entertainment ensued. After a prescribed length of time, any who were still suffering were sent back to England and others, deemed fit, were returned to the trenches.

Incontinency, constant trembling, stammering, hallucinations, jerking and shaking comparable to epileptic fits, and always the terror of returning to the front were experienced by the "so-called" milder cases.

In his book on shell shock, Taylor Downing records:

> The men showed no visible signs of physical wounds. They had not been hit by machine gun bullets, nor had they been struck by shrapnel. They did not have damaged limbs. They had no apparent wounds to the head... But they all seemed to display similar strange symptoms that mystified the MOs. Most were suffering from peculiar forms of paralysis. Many were described as having 'the shakes.' Some could not stand up or walk normally. A few did not appear to speak coherently and were stammering badly. Others had been struck completely dumb and could not speak at all. Most appeared to be in a state of stupor and a few had completely lost their memory. Others seemed to find it difficult to see clearly. Many had lost their sense of taste or smell. Some vomited repeatedly... One MO described what he had witnessed: 'The eyes pop out of their sockets, the expression becomes fixed and glassy; the facial skin loses all of its red colour, the skin becomes yellow, the cheekbones protrude. The lips are shut tight and sticky spittle tacks up the tongue to the

roof of the mouth. The heart works in short, convulsive beats, breathing becomes slower."[8]

With the worst cases sent back to military hospitals in England, of these the dangerous cases were sent to asylums as soon as they reached the shores of the home country. In the early stages of the war on the Western Front, the military authorities were startled with the shell shock phenomenon and completely at a loss at how to separate the genuine cases from the shirkers or malingerers. The initial reaction was harsh—soldiers were to be made an example for others. Lieutenant General Sir Aylmer Hunter-Weston regarded such men as depraved. They should be made an example of and court martialed. In addition, just as the Australian Diggers were not keen to have conscripted men in their battalions because they might be unreliable in times of danger, so the men in the trenches who were allowed to go unpunished for supposed "shell shock" would then be a source of danger for their comrades. Lieutenant Colonel Viscount Gort "bluntly stated that shell shock 'must be regarded as a form of disgrace to the soldier'. Those still suffering from it 'were probably bordering on lunacy before the war began.'"[9] Thus, in the early years of the war, punishment was immediate and severe—more than 400 soldiers were shot at dawn after court martials, with little or no legal representation and no right of appeal. When medical officers were called to give evidence, that evidence was largely disregarded—in fact, "troublesome" MOs were sent back home. The commander in chief, Sir Douglas Haig, refused to overrule any verdict, reasoning that any decision reversed would send the wrong message to the troops and encourage malingerers and cowards. Victory would be jeopardized! Where there was good morale, discipline, and fine leadership in battalions there appeared to be less instances of shell shock. But with the constant arrival of new recruits under the control of officers not long out of public schools, the ideal was impossible to attain. Fortunately, by the latter years of the war a more sympathetic approach evolved, although the treatment that unfolded in the military hospitals was based solely on the type of soldier, generally: "the cure for 'rankers' . . . was discipline, punishment and electricity: for officers, it was therapy, discussion and hypnosis."[10] One "ranker" became mute through his experiences. The treating psychologist, Lewis R. Yealland reported:

8. Downing, *Breakdown*, 78–79.
9. Archer, "Shell Shock," 13.
10. Archer, "Shell Shock," 18.

> Many attempts had been made to cure him. He had been strapped down in a chair for twenty minutes at a time, when strong electricity was applied to his neck and throat; lighted cigarette ends had been applied to the tip of his tongue and hot plates had been applied to the back of his mouth. But all these methods proved to be unsuccessful in restoring his voice. I talked to him sternly about his duty and his family. In the electrical room lights were turned out and the doors locked. The patient was told that he would not leave the room until he was cured, and strong currents were applied for long periods of continuous treatment until he was permanently cured.[11]

One wonders how his life progressed when he was discharged!

On March 9, 1917, George Halsall became a patient in the Colchester Military Hospital, one of several army hospitals in England during this period, which indicates his state of health was more involved than a minor case of shell shock. His medical condition was listed as tachycardia, a condition generally attributed to old age, with symptoms of hypertension, abnormalities of heart valves, atrial fibrillation, and dysfunction of the heart's natural pacemaker. He was told it was a result of shell shock. He returned to Australia in August 1917, unfit for any more war service.

Experiences of Soldiers

Men and boys from the British Isles, though perhaps not seeing the venture onto the battlefields of France as a "Great Adventure" like those thousands of miles away in the colonies, nevertheless found no hesitation in their decision to go. A great many came from the public schools and universities, or from families with military traditions. But for the ordinary man the reason was similar to many who had previously enlisted in the British army and served in places like India and the Sudan. The consequences of unemployment and the need to support large families led men to qualify for the "King's shilling." "[Robert] Money argues that maybe the ranks are better used to harsh conditions. Sharing one room in a Glasgow tenement slum with eight siblings, a midden for a lavatory in the courtyard use by nine other families, while your father knocks seven bells out of your mother every night . . . a wet trench with your mates is not the horror it seems to others. A wet trench is an escape from the Poor

---

11. Archer, "Shell Shock," 18.

House. And you are with your mates. Your mates is all this war will leave you with."[12] No doubt this was the case for some—in the beginning.

Six Weeks: The Short and Gallant Life of the British Officer in the First World War, by John Lewis-Stempel, takes its title from the average life expectancy of the subaltern, the most junior officer on the Western Front.

Of these young men, many went straight to the fighting trenches of France from their public schools, experienced only by participation in school cadet corps, but nevertheless shaped by years of tradition, discipline, and rigor throughout their school lives.

Lewis-Stempel writes the following about these officers, and includes the two ranks above them, the lieutenants and the captains: "Together they were the single most important factor in Britain's victory on the Western Front. They led gallantly in battle, the first over the top, the last to retreat—and as a result suffered something like a holocaust."[13]

In the same work we read a comment by Private Burrage, who had a dim view of officers: "I who was a private, and a bad one at that, freely own that it was the British subaltern who won the war."[14] Gunner Needham wrote to Richard Talbot Kelly's father: "I am your son's servant and I am sure you must feel proud to be the father of so brave and sporting a young officer. We are all very proud of him and hope we always have the luck to have him with us."[15] Too young for cynicism, too eager for the glory of battle, and wholly committed to love and serve those under him, the young subaltern was something the inflexible German army did not have. He listened, he counseled, and he guided the men under him, experiencing the same horrors as they did, yet leading by example and rarely letting them see he too was afraid—all this with many men who were years older. He honored his country and kept in the forefront of his mind the lessons learned from his revered school—"tell Eton/Harrow/Uppingham I didn't let them down," were often the last words on a dying subaltern's lips!

No doubt, boys straight from school to the fields of France had ingrained in their minds and hearts a famous poem of the times. In 1897 Henry Newbolt wrote the poem "Vita Lampada" about a schoolboy cricketer facing his fears when fighting the war in Africa:

---

12. Davidson, *A Doctor in the Great War*, 239.
13. Lewis-Stempel, *Six Weeks*, 7.
14. Lewis-Stempel, *Six Weeks*, 6.
15. Lewis-Stempel, *Six Weeks*, 163.

There's a breathless hush in the Close to-night—
Ten to make and the match to win—
A bumping pitch and a blinding light,
An hour to play and the last man in,
And it's not for the sake of the ribboned coat,
Or the selfish hope of a season's fame,
But his Captain's hand on his shoulder smote
'Play up! play up! and play the game!'

The sand of the desert is sodden red,—
Red with the wreck of a square that broke;
The Gatling's jammed and the colonel dead,
And the regiment blind with dust and smoke.
The river of death has brimmed his banks,
And England's far, and Honour a name,
But the voice of schoolboy rallies the ranks,
'Play up! play up! and play the game!'

This is the word that year by year
While in her place the School is set
Every one of her sons must hear;
And none that hears it dare forget.
This they all with a joyful mind
Bear through life like a torch in flame,
And falling fling to the host behind—
'Play up! play up! and play the game.'[16]

Some thirty years after penning these words, Newbolt was still being asked to recite it. He had grown to loathe it, calling it a "monster." After seeing the loss of so many boys who were yet to experience life beyond the classroom, the pain and futility may have been too hard to bear.

Adversely there is plenty of evidence of blundering generals and brigadiers sending countless soldiers into unnecessary carnage in all the avenues of war. A few of those in charge of the British army were long past the age of soldiering but brought back to service in 1914. Some had been stationed at outward posts of the empire and had not even ever experienced battle. Lieutenant General Sir Aylmer Hunter-Weston, the "Butcher of Helles," wreaked havoc at Gallipoli until he was recalled after his complete breakdown. He refused to attack under the cover of night in case the men became lost!—nor at an early time in the morning because of the inconvenience to the routine of the day. The transferring of

---

16. Newbolt, "Vitaï Lampada," lines 1–24.

the wounded to hospital ships at Anzac Cove resembled the chaos of the Crimean War. Lord Kitchener had gained renown because of his actions at Khartoum. However, he was secretive and tended to make up plans on the spur of the moment.

Field Marshal Sir Douglas Haig, head of the British Expeditionary Force in 1916, committed huge numbers of British troops to the Battle of the Somme, which resulted in some 420,000 casualties; a similar exercise at the later Battle of Passchendaele drew the wrath of the British public. (Haig commented at one stage that it was a good blooding for the troops!)

At the first day of the Battle of the Somme: "The one Dominion force in action that day, a Newfoundland battalion, was almost wiped out. Of the 810 men who went into the attack, 710 were either killed or wounded. 'It was a magnificent display of trained and disciplined valour,' one of Haig's staff informed the Newfoundland Prime Minister, 'and its assault only failed of success because dead men can advance no further.'"[17]

For all the "blunderers" there were also many admirable men who rose to prominence in all the theaters of war and inspired those in the ranks with their tactics, their courage, and their leadership. Some Australians and New Zealanders featured amongst these, particularly at Gallipoli, although Antill and Godley were not good examples. Major General Alexander Godley was a pompous man, as was his wife a vainglorious woman—she was upset because injured soldiers did not sit up to attention in their beds when she visited the hospital. But it seemed as if the newer leaders were much more flexible, more aware of the huge responsibility of protecting their men and, not weighed down by military practices of the past, methods that were used in wars incomparable with wars of the new century.

From the very beginning the campaign in the Dardanelles suffered from poor British leadership. In the Suvla Bay operation, for example, "The most abject of all was the corps commander, Lieut.-General Sir Frederick Stopford . . . a general whose closeness to his men could not be assessed since he had never commanded troops in battle . . . Stopford was so feeble that he was unable to lift his own despatch case into the train when he set off for Gallipoli."[18] He had been in retirement since 1909 after serving in Egypt, the Sudan, and South Africa as an ADC. On arrival to the peninsula he was filled with pessimism, failed to carry out

17. Gilbert, *A History of the Twentieth Century. Volume 1*, 409.
18. Laffin, *Damn the Dardanelles*, 128–29.

an adequate reconnaissance of Suvla Bay, and made little attempt to train his men for scouting and fighting under the cover of darkness. On one of the few occasions that the commander in chief, Sir Ian Hamilton, left his command ship, the *Queen Elizabeth*, to visit his brigadiers, "Stopford decline to accompany him—about 400 yards—because his leg was troubling him."[19]

An instance of pure stupidity on the battlefield in France was related by the sister of a young Scottish soldier, David Finlayson. He was instructed to take orders to a section stationed in front-line trenches, having to traverse perilous trenches and open land to reach this unit. When he arrived, the captain said he would only accept written orders before he could act. David then returned, attained the orders in writing and took them once again to the unit in question. On his return to the dispatch headquarters he was killed by a sniper's bullet. Corporal Arthur Cook, 1st Somerset Light Infantry recorded:

> During the night I went into no-man's land, taking another man with me, searching for dead bodies. I found four but their condition was too bad to move, so I collected their paybooks which I handed into the orderly room for identification purposes, making sure their identity discs were left on the body. The stench of these bodies when I turned them over was horrible, and the gases inside gave forth a belching noise... They took particulars of the dead men in the orderly room, then calmly sent for me and ordered me to return the books to the bodies.[20]

There were conflicting attitudes to the enemy, often changing with circumstances.

With some soldiers there was no mercy shown to the Germans. A captain in the trenches wrote to his family in obvious delight when he managed to shoot a German sniper in no man's land. He judged the experience to be more exciting than receiving a letter from home! Private Ernest Deighton, fighting in the Somme, was devastated when his pal Clem Cunningham was killed by German machine-gun fire:

> I were so wild when I saw that Clem was finished... I got up and picked up my rifle and got through the wire into their trench ... I had this Mills bomb. Couldn't use my arm, I pulled the pin with my teeth and flung it down and I were shouting at them,

---

19. Laffin, *Damn the Dardanelles*, 138.
20. Van Emden, *The Soldier's War*, 198.

> I were that wild. 'There you are! Bugger yourselves! Share that between you!' Then I were off! It were hand to hand, I went round the traverse and there was one—face to face. I couldn't fire one-handed, but I could use the bayonet. It was him or me— and I were first! Jab! Just like that! It were my job. And from there I went on. Oh, I were wild.[21]

But with a sense of comradeship in the hardships endured, Private Frank Williams, 88th Field Ambulance, Royal Army Medical Corps wrote: "Attended two services and enjoyed good sermons . . . Whilst in church some of our largest guns opened out—up to six-inchers. The ground has begun to tremble now and the bombardment seems increasing in intensity. Though our heavy batteries have not fired a shell, the crashing roar of some of the reports made me pray for the Germans."[22] From many other accounts it appears those of the enemy who were wounded greatly aroused the compassion of the British Tommy. Many acknowledged they were only fighting for their masters just as the British were. In fact, one soldier felt that the average German was almost a brother in arms, fighting in a war that no longer held much meaning to the individual warrior. As Van Emden relates in *The Soldier's War*: ". . . in September 1917, the Reverend Bere, serving at a Casualty Clearing Station (CCS), noted that 'On Saturday a British Tommy stuck a knife into the shoulder of a Fritz during a hand-to-hand fight. The Tommy was wounded too. They came here together in the same ambulance and smoked each other's cigarettes on the way.' Duty done, honour satisfied, there was no reason for continued animosity."[23]

The horrific experiences of soldiers in the field stayed with them forever. Private Harry Patch, 7th Battalion, Duke of Cornwall's Light Infantry, was haunted by the following memory:

> I can still see the bewilderment and fear on the men's faces when we went over the top. C and D company was support, A and B had had to go at the front line. All over the battlefield the wounded were lying down, English and German all asking for help. We weren't like the Good Samaritan in the Bible, we were the robbers who passed by and left them. You couldn't help them. I came across a Cornishman, ripped from shoulder to waist with shrapnel, his stomach on the ground beside him

21. Macdonald, *Somme*, 72–73.
22. Van Emden, *The Soldier's War*, 186.
23. Van Emden, *The Soldier's War*, 88.

in a pool of blood. As I got to him he said, 'Shoot me,' he was beyond all human aid. Before we could even draw a revolver he had died. He just said, 'Mother.' I will never forget it.[24]

All through no man's land there lay decomposing bodies of men, boys, and horses—British, German, French, Australians, New Zealanders. There was nothing glorious in this scene of mutilation. Private John McCauley, 2nd Border Regiment recalled: "My nostrils were breathing in the foul air of rotting flesh, and the stench of stagnant water in shell holes, and I dropped back into the trench with a horrible feeling of fear and nausea. That sense of fear clung to me from that day forward and stayed with me to the end of the war."[25]

The constant monotony of shelling, machine-guns, mud, cold, and starvation in trenches surrounded by rotting corpses and screaming wounded had taken its toll so that life was pointless and death almost an attraction. One of the soldiers felt that survival was a death in itself. He wasn't the same person who had ventured into this scene of horror and revulsion. In fact, his whole being, his body and his soul, had been stolen from him for ever. He had lost all his courage, his pride, his perseverance, his ambition, and his joy in life itself. Strength had descended into weakness; peace into anxiety. He no longer saw himself as a real man in the post-war world—all his manhood had been squandered on the bloodied fields of France.

What thoughts were pounding in soldiers' minds as they crouched in muddy, bloodied trenches awaiting the call to "go over the top" and attack? Was it to be compared with Dante's *Inferno*?

> My fears, at this, were somewhat quieted,
> though terror, awash in the lake of my heart,
> had lasted all the night I'd passed in anguish.[26]

... waiting amongst the mud and corpses, dreading what would rise up from this hell on earth:

> Snow, massive hailstones, black, tainted water
> pour down in sheets through tenebrae of air.
> The earth absorbs it all and stinks, revoltingly.
> Cerberus, weird and monstrously cruel,

---

24. Arthur, *Lest We Forget*, 290.
25. Van Emden, *The Soldier's War*, 91.
26. Dante, *The Divine Comedy 1: Inferno*, Canto 1:19–21, 3.

> barks from his triple throats in cur-like yowls
> over the heads of those who lie there, drowned.
> His eyes vermilion, beard a greasy black,
> his belly broad, his fingers all sharp-nailed,
> he mauls and skins, then hacks in four, these souls.[27]

. . . trapped in the blast and fire from shells and incendiaries:

> For flames were scattered round among these tombs.
> The pits were therefore so intensely fired,
> no tradesman needs his brand iron half so hot.
> The covers of the tombs all stood half-raised;
> and out of each there came such cruel lamenting
> these must have been the cries from pain within[28]

. . . hearing the shrieks of the wounded and dying:

> Sighing, sobbing, moans and plaintive wailing
> all echoed here through air where no star shone,
> and I, as this began, began to weep.
> Discordant tongues, harsh accents of horror,
> tormented words, the twang of rage, strident
> voices, the sound, as well, of smacking hands . . . [29]

Many soldiers implicitly likened such a war to this vision of Dante's hell. Over the top and into the enemy's barrage—did they see the edge of the world as they fell? ". . . they found themselves facing great golden gates. And for a moment none of them was bold enough to try if the gates would open—'Dare we? Is it right? Can it be meant for us?' But while they were standing thus, a great horn, wonderfully loud and sweet, blew from somewhere inside that walled garden and the gates swung open."[30]

The futility of fighting for a few yards' advancement and often being driven back that same few yards weeks or months later, all with the needless sacrifice of so many young men, is reflected on by Donald Hankey when he surveyed the fields of dead with their limbs and bodies torn and contorted beyond recognition. He had heard all the grand motivations to seek glory in the name of King and country. But he could only see

---

27. Dante, *The Divine Comedy 1: Inferno*, Canto 6:10–18, 49.
28. Dante, *The Divine Comedy 1: Inferno*, Canto 9:118–23, 79.
29. Dante, *The Divine Comedy 1: Inferno*, Canto 3:22–25, 21.
30. Lewis, *Chronicles of Narnia: The Last Battle*, 763.

the true horror of it all: "Indeed it is an evil harvest, sown of pride and arrogance and lust of power."[31]

German and British with Faith in their Cause

September 17th, 1915.

Dear Parents,

I am lying on the battlefield badly wounded. Whether I recover is in God's hands. If I die, do not weep. I am going blissfully home. A hearty greeting to you all once more. May God soon send you peace and grant me a blessed home-coming. Jesus is with me, so it is easy to die.

In heartfelt love, Eduard[32]

I once quoted this letter at a seminar on World War I, held by the Presbyterian Church in New South Wales. I introduced my little spiel by stating that both my father and father-in-law served in this war and that my father was the one who cleaned up when I was ill from childhood migraines—he had been in the Ambulance Brigade and one of his duties was to clean up after nurses when they often became ill after assisting at field operations. I then moved on to my main motive of expressing the view that the adage of "God is on our side" was shared by both British and German soldiers and that here was an example of a German soldier who had a vibrant living faith that did not desert him even amidst the horror of the battlefields. When I resumed my seat there was a very obvious silence. Eventually someone commented on the great job that nurses did in World War I and how often we all forget this. Nothing more was said and the discussion moved on. I had committed a huge "faux pas"; I had provided evidence that there were Christians fighting for the enemy—in a way, I had denigrated the sacrifice that so many of our soldiers had made for future generations.

But war is a great leveler of humanity—it does not take into account race, nationality, social status, sexual orientation, or military rank. And, as

---

31. Gilbert, *A History of the Twentieth Century. Volume 1*, 410.
32. Witkop, *German Students' War Letters*, 155.

in Paul's words, Christianity is also a great leveler of humanity: "There is no longer Jew or Greek, there is no longer slave or free, there is no longer male and female; for all of you are one in Christ Jesus." (Gal 3:28 NRSV)

"'Which side is going to win, Padre?' we asked. 'Whose side is God on? The Germans say God's with them.' We had discovered that the Germans had the words 'Gott mit uns' (God with us) on the buckles of their belts. We got into a bit of an argument among ourselves about that one until the padre intervened. 'God is not on anyone's side. He's with everyone.'"[33] Many soldiers didn't pause to ponder on this great truth—during the worst of the cold they would call out to the Germans, "we've got mittens too!"

My letter from a German student was not an isolated example. It comes from a collection of German students' war letters. Another student, Johannes Haas, wrote to his mother from Champagne on March 3, 1916:

> Dear Mother, don't be unnecessarily anxious. It is quite quiet where we are. And even if we ever do have to go into the thick of it, I feel just as my dear little brother did. His gallant words—"Then you must be proud that you have been permitted to give me to the Fatherland"—come straight from my heart, too. And God only knows whether he intends me to be united with Konrad in a French grave, or whether He is preserving me for some other purpose. For God is the God of History, and in a small way we are all His co-workers in the History of the World. That is a sublime thought! . . .[34]

Just over two months later, on May 13, 1916, Haas is before Verdun:

> My dear, good, old Parents,
>
> Here we have war, war in its most appalling form, and in our distress we realize the nearness of God. Things are becoming very serious; but I am inwardly unalarmed and happy. 'Let me go, I long to see my Jesus so.' It must be splendid to see God in all His glory and His peace, after all that, with human misunderstanding, one has longed and struggled for! I think often and joyfully of the next world. I do not fear the Judgement. I am indeed a poor, sinful creature, but how great is God's mercy and

33. Ramsay, *Hell, Hope and Heroes*, 186–87.
34. Witkop, *German Students' War Letters*, 206.

the Saviour's love! So, without fear or dismay, I do my duty to the Fatherland and to my dear German people. I thank you, dear Parents, for having led me to the Saviour; that was the best thing you ever did. I love you tenderly. God be with you!

Hans.

June 1st '16.

Dear Parents,

I am lying on the battlefield, wounded in the body. I think I am dying. I am glad to have time to prepare for the heavenly homecoming. Thank you, dear Parents. God be with you.

Hans.[35]

    Not only were many of the combatants committed to a cause that was felt to be ordained by God, but both nations of Britain and Germany saw World War I as a holy war. Britain faced it in terms of an imperial theology, whereby it was her Christian duty to protect both her empire and those countries oppressed by the invading armies. Germany, on the other hand, was coming from a background of the Lutheran doctrine of the state, a doctrine that had been vaguely gleaned from a short treatise by Luther and developed (based purely on individual interpretation) and politicized in the period of the so-called German Awakening. Consequently, in Germany a two Kingdoms doctrine evolved in the late nineteenth century whereby Christianity was entirely spiritual and personal. The secular state was a separate kingdom which, although having been set up by God and serving God's purposes, operated independently of Christianity. The believer was bound to submit to the law of the state. According to the state, war was a vital part of God's sovereign plan and World War I was necessary to defend the sacred German culture against western barbarianism and to cleanse the nations by sacred and apocalyptic violence.

---

35. Witkop, *German Students' War Letters*, 207.

The Horrors of Reality

On June 30, 1916, a British soldier, Jack Engell, wrote the following missive to his parents:

> I'm writing this letter, before the most important moment in my life ... Tomorrow morning I shall take my men over the top ... I took Communion yesterday with dozens of others who are going over the top tomorrow. I placed my soul and body in God's keeping, and I am going into battle with His name on my lips, full of confidence and trusting implicitly in Him. I have a strong feeling that I shall come through safely, but nevertheless, should it be God's holy will to call me away, I am quite prepared to go and [you] will know that I died doing my duty to my God, my Country and my King.[36]

Engall was killed in action on the Somme, July 1, 1916.

Brian Calkin entrusted a last letter to his father's office manager at Lloyd's Insurance brokers. In it he wrote: "It will comfort you to know that I am not in the least worried or concerned about what may happen to me, but am perfectly happy to leave the issue in the hands of God. My only concern is for you all, should I be taken. Do not, I beg of you, be unhappy, for I am, and you are, convinced that I shall be happier with Him."[37] As a young boy, Calkin had been a chorister and soloist in the St Paul's Cathedral Choir. He had sung for the King of England and the Kaiser of Germany in Westminster Abbey on the occasion of the coronation. In 1914 he falsified his age and enlisted in the Queen's Royal West Surrey Regiment. After four years of fighting he was killed, aged twenty, in July 1918.

Both the German soldier and the British soldier were issued with a prayer book. The German prayer book was entitled *Mit Jesus in der Feld*, the British prayer book *With Jesus in the Field*. Strangely both books contained the same illustration of the Christ. It would be interesting to query whether they both came off the same printing press, or at least printing presses with branches in both countries. On discovering a similar prayer book to his, Private Sydney Fuller, 8th Suffolk Regiment, came to the conclusion "that the whole war was a horrible mistake."[38]

Even before World War I there were conflicting views on who was "on the Lord's side" in battle. Bert Brocklesby from South Yorkshire recalls:

---

36. Lewis-Stempel, *Six Weeks*, 190.
37. Nicolson, *The Perfect Summer*, 264.
38. Van Emden, *The Soldier's War*, 265.

> I got what was perhaps my earliest lesson in international pacifism from a young German, Walter, who had left his own country to avoid being conscripted and had settled in Conisbrough as a pork butcher. He became unpopular during the Boer War because he was able to see the issues with an unbiased mind. One day—I was about eleven years old—I saw him working in the yard below a room where we played. I called out "pro-Boer!" and dodged out of sight. He came upstairs to where we were playing and asked me if the Methodists were praying for victory. I said they were. He then told me that Paul Kruger was a Christian; did I suppose *he* was praying for victory? I supposed so. "Well," he remarked, "that puts God into a fix, doesn't it?" And he left me to think it over. I remembered the wordplay when 14 years later we were again praying for victory . . .[39]

Naturally there were many who could not reconcile their conception of God to their present situation. They were torn between the commandment, "Thou shalt not kill" and the sacred duty to fight for their God and country. Lieutenant John Bellerby, 1/8th West Yorkshire Regiment (Leeds Rifles), came to this conclusion: "I was cured of any belief that it was admissible to appeal to the Almighty."[40] Bellerby saw himself as an executioner flouting God and his commandments. God was a god of love who could not logically become involved in the systematic destruction of human beings. Therefore, he found it impossible to pray to this god of love on the battlefield of hate.

In his work *The Lost Boys*, Paul Byrnes records that the commander of the landing of the army in Gallipoli, Sir Ian Hamilton, thought differently about the involvement of a "God of love." On the night of April 24, 1915, he wrote in his diary: ". . . 'God has started a celestial spring-cleaning, and our star is to be scrubbed bright with the blood of our bravest and our best.' [Byrnes then commented that] God had not started any of this, but He was already getting the blame. And yet Hamilton's belief that a blood sacrifice was somehow overdue was common, and not just among the British. German and Turkish officers had similarly romantic notions: if God want war, who are we to say no? And God—whichever god—was always on their side, even if he required

---

39. Smith, *Voices Against War*, 24.
40. Van Emden, *The Soldier's War*, 265.

their blood. In this way, war became not just inevitable but necessary, to wipe out the dross, as well as the bravest and the best."[41]

When Vera Brittain went to France to nurse the wounded and dying, the first ward she was assigned to was for German soldiers. An extract from her chronicle recalls:

> Another badly wounded boy—a Prussian lieutenant who was being transferred to England—held out an emaciated hand to me as he lay on the stretcher waiting to go, and murmured: "I tank you, Sister." After barely a second's hesitation I took the pale fingers in mine, thinking how ridiculous it was that I should be holding this man's hand in friendship when, perhaps, only a week or two earlier, Edward up at Ypres had been doing his best to kill him. The world was mad and we were all victims; that was the only way to look at it. These shattered, dying boys and I were paying alike for a situation that none of us had desired or done anything to bring about.[42]

These words express the turmoil Vera felt as she battled to cope with all her harrowing and conflicting experiences. Where was reason; where was God in all this? After the war, she felt compelled to write *Testament of Youth*, "to understand how the whole calamity had happened, to know why it had been possible for me and my contemporaries, through our own ignorance and others' ingenuity, to be used, hypnotised and slaughtered."[43] A whole generation of youth had been lost to the world to satisfy the ambitious desires of a few. Vera Brittain's daughter, Shirley Williams, says in the preface to her mother's book, "It was hard for her to laugh unconstrainedly; at the back of her mind, the row upon row of wooden crosses were planted too deeply."[44]

The Lost Generation—Romanticism vs. Reality

An incredible legacy that has been left to future generations is the enormous amount of literature that emanated from World War I, both during the conflict and in the years following. During the onset of hostilities, we find a somewhat stirring "call to arms" against a heinous foe with

---

41. Byrnes, *The Lost Boys*, 54.
42. Brittain, *Testament of Youth*, 376.
43. Brittain, *Testament of Youth*, 471.
44. Brittain, *Testament of Youth*, 10.

lines of idealistic, romantic verse lauding the heroic sacrifice. As the war progressed, poetry (and prose also) reflected changing attitudes to the war and became a steady progression to works that depicted the distress of enforced endurance and expressed feelings of horror and revulsion, futility, despair, and even pacifism. Phrases from both spectrums—the desire for death and the fear of death—are prevalent.

From Rupert Brooke's famous poem "The Soldier":

> If I should die, think only this of me;
> That there's some corner of a foreign field
> That is for ever England. There shall be
> In that rich earth a richer dust concealed;
> A dust whom England bore, shaped, made aware,
> Gave, once, her flowers to love, her ways to roam,
> A body of England's, breathing English air,
> Washed by the rivers, blest by suns of home.[45]

From W. N. Hodgson's "England to her Sons":

> Sons of mine I hear you thrilling
> To the trumpet call of war;
> Gird ye then, I give you freely
> As I gave your sires before,
> All the noblest of the children I in love and anguish bore.
>
> Free in service, wise in justice,
> Fearing but dishonour's breath;
> Steeled to suffer uncomplaining
> Loss and failure, pain and death;
> Strong in faith that sees the issue and in hope that triumpheth.
>
> Go, and may the God of battles
> You in His good guidance keep:
> And if He in wisdom giveth
> Unto His beloved sleep,
> I accept it nothing asking, save a little space to weep.[46]

From Siegfried Sassoon's "Counter Attack":

> . . . Bombing on the right
> Down the old sap: machine-guns on the left;
> And stumbling figures looming out in front,

---

45. Hudson, *Poetry of the First World War*, 18.
46. Hudson, *Poetry of the First World War*, 12.

The Horrors of Reality

> 'O Christ, they're coming at us!' Bullets spat,
> And he remembered his rifle . . . rapid fire
> And started blazing wildly . . . then a bang
> Crumpled and spun him sideways, knocked him out
> To grunt and wriggle: none heeded him; he choked
> And fought the flapping veils of smothering gloom,
> Lost in a blurred confusion of yells and groans . . .
> Down, and down, and down, he sank and drowned,
> Bleeding to death. The counter-attack had failed.[47]

And Arthur Graeme West's "The Night Patrol":

> Only the dead were always present—present
> As a vile sickly smell of rottenness;
> The rustling stubble and the early grass,
> The slimy pools—the dead men stank through all,
> Pungent and sharp; as bodies loomed before,
> And as we passed, they stank; then dulled away
> To that vague foetor, all encompassing,
> Infecting earth and air.[48]

Arthur Graeme West was the son of a retired missionary widower and grew up in a gloomy, narrow-minded atmosphere only relieved when he was sent to boarding school after his father remarried. West enlisted in a wave of patriotism but quickly began to feel disillusionment at army training camps. He loathed the regulated army life and, even before going to France, he began to question the reasons for war, his belief in the cause he was now committed to follow and, ultimately, his personal faith. Wounded in France and hospitalized in England, he became influenced by the writings of Bertrand Russell. He consequently embraced pacifism and, like Siegfried Sassoon, came to the momentous decision to renounce the war after his experiences in France. However, he could not bring himself to send his missive to the army authorities and returned to the fray where he fell in April 1917, killed by a sniper's bullet. West saw the earlier poets' sanguine view of war as senseless:

> GOD! How I hate you, you young cheerful men,
> Whose pious poetry blossoms on your graves
> As soon as you are in them, nurtured up
> By the salt of your corruption, and the tears
> Of mothers, local vicars, college deans,

---

47. Hudson, *Poetry of the First World War*, 47.
48. West, *Diary of a Dead Officer*, 151–52.

> And flanked by prefaces and photographs
> From all you minor poet friends—the fools—
> Who paint their sentimental elegies
> Where sure, no angel treads; and, living, share
> The dead's brief immortality.
> 									Oh Christ!
> To think that one could spread the ductile wax
> Of his fluid youth to Oxford's glowing fires
> And take her seal so ill! Hark how one chants—
> 'Oh happy to have lived these epic days'—
> 'These epic days'! And he'd been to France,
> And seen the trenches, glimpsed the huddled dead
> In the periscope, hung in the rusting wire:
> Chocked by their sickly foetor, day and night
> Blown down his throat: stumbled through ruined hearths,
> Proved all that muddy brown monotony,
> Where blood's the only coloured thing. Perhaps
> Had seen a man killed, a sentry shot at night,
> Hunched as he fell, his feet on the firing-step,
> His neck against the back slope of the trench,
> And the rest doubled up between, his head
> Smashed like an egg-shell, and the warm grey brain
> Spattered all bloody on the parados:
> Had flashed a torch on his face, and known his friend,
> Shot, breathing hardly, in ten minutes—gone![49]

The romantic notion of the splendid warrior marching off with song and bravado soon gave way to the reality of an endless war stuck in mud-filled trenches existing alongside the dead corpses of former comrades and the live bodies of feeding rats. In fact, Charles Hamilton Sorley, in a critique of Rupert Brooke's poetry states:

> He is far too obsessed with his own sacrifice, regarding the going to war of himself (and others) as a highly intense, remarkable and sacrificial exploit, whereas it is merely the conduct demanded of him (and others) by the turn of circumstances, where non-compliance with this demand would have made life intolerable. It was not that 'they' gave up anything of that list he gives in one sonnet: but that the essence of these things had been endangered by circumstances over which he had no control, and

---

49. West, *Diary of a Dead Officer*, 148–49.

he must fight to recapture them. He has clothed his attitude in fine words: but he has taken the sentimental attitude.[50]

On the earlier idealistic poets Sassoon wrote: "For the soldier is no longer a noble figure; he is merely a writhing insect among this ghastly folly of destruction . . . He does not cry for wisdom . . . I want to find someone who has some faith in the war and its purposes. But they see nothing but their own tiny destinies."[51]

Once the reality of battle burst into the life and soul of the young adventurer or the zealous patriot, most participants in World War I felt like the young German, Gerrit Engelke:

> But spare me, Death.
> I am still young—
> My work has not been done,
> The future is still unknown—
> So spare me, Death.
>
> Some time later, Death.
> When my life has been lived, has burned away
> Into my work, and I
> Have nothing left to say -
> Then take me, Death.[52]

Death carried Engelke off in the last year of the war.

---

50. Murray, *The Red Sweet Wine of Youth*, 66–67.
51. Murray, *The Red Sweet Wine of Youth*, 110–11.
52. Engelke, "To Death," 65.

4

The Role of Christianity

THE MAIN PART CHRISTIANITY played in all wars was the dispatching of chaplains to the war front. The chaplain in World War I, or the padre as he was then commonly known, entered a type of battlefield of his own. He was often only just tolerated by many of the officers, handy to provide cups of tea to the wounded and organize games and concerts for off-duty combatants, but not to become a nuisance in the war arena. In their favor, it should be acknowledged that the vast majority of chaplains had never acted in this capacity before. They came straight from their pulpits where they preached to "the converted," often just to congregations of good-living, well-intentioned people who went to church each Sunday because it was the acceptable social thing to do. Now they were thrown into a mire of challenges and confusion. From preaching the typical Sunday sermon, what did they preach to soldiers about to face the most horrific and life-changing events of their lives? Add to this the fact that these men were forced to endure sermons under duress when they would rather be trying to forget what was happening all around them. The church parades were a bane for most soldiers because they were compulsory. Private William Knott, an evangelical Christian, abhorred the idea of worship by order of the military: "Some of these Church Parades are the great hypocrisies of the British nation and I trust we shall soon be privileged to gather again with people who congregate to receive blessing and help not because they are driven to it like slaves."[1]

---

1. Brown, *The Imperial War Museum Book of the First World War*, 245.

A sermon on the power of suffering could be well received by many, making their experiences be placed in some perspective, but then rejected as sanctimonious by others, especially those who were yet to endure the "baptism of fire." As Robert Graves commented in his book *Goodbye to All That*, a chaplain, "just before the Loos fighting, preached a violent sermon on the Battle against Sin, at which one old soldier behind me grumbled: 'Christ, as if one bloody push wasn't enough to worry about at a time!'"[2] One soldier enjoyed a sermon on tithing because it took his mind off the enormous horrors awaiting him on the morn—perhaps that was the intention of the preacher? The Reverend Victor Tanner preached a sermon in which he tried to help men come to terms with why so many very young died on the battlefield. He pointed out that Jesus was only thirty-three but had completed his life's work. God had a plan for each man: "He has an appointed task for each man's life and if that man is called upon to lay down his life in fulfilment of his duty we may be sure that his work on earth is finished."[3] Before the landings at Anzac Cove, The Reverend James Green preached on Josh 3:1–8 using the text of verse 5: "sanctify yourselves; for tomorrow the LORD will do wonders among you." Another used the story of the ten lepers cured by Christ when only one came back to thank the Lord. He suggested that perhaps those who survive the battle don't think to thank God for deliverance when so many around him do not survive. Dependent on the words he used, of course, this is something like telling a child to behave correctly. This is how some soldiers viewed the chaplain anyhow—they felt they were inhibited and had to behave if they were billeted with them. Being "unchurched" they did not see the value of such men although, in many cases, this may have been because of the chaplains themselves.

Naturally, many chaplains were not necessarily good preachers, even in their home parishes, and certainly not in this unknown, demanding atmosphere. The one aspect of church parades that was successful, however, was the lusty singing of well-known hymns. Even today, community hymn-singing of gusto definitely stirs the soul and brings all sorts of feelings to the fore. Some were able to exemplify the relevance of Christ in chance conversations:

> It has been a strange Holy Week, but I have never realized the Passion so vividly before and the meaning of the blood shedding.

2. Graves, *Goodbye to All That*, 159.
3. Brown, *The Imperial War Museum Book of the First World War*, 248.

> O'Neile, the dear little padre, gave me a most beautiful meditation on the sorrowful mysteries as we sat on two heaps of coal in the cellar on Tuesday night. The Passion is reproduced in the life of nearly every soldier. 'He went forth bearing the Cross for Himself', my text last Sunday morning. There is the Cross, the soldier's pack (O'Neile says the pack weighs the same as the Cross), and the Crown of Thorns—the tin hat—and of course the Agony, the loneliness of the soldier wounded, helpless until he is picked up . . . The seven words—the first thing the boys ask for is a drink, so the cry 'I thirst'—and the 'bloody sweat' and the falling beneath the weight of the Cross, and then the picture of home and mother flashing before him at the 4th Station; the splendid women of Jerusalem—the good nurses; the Simon of Cyrene, compelled to bear the Cross—so like the good but unbelieving doctors, who seem often so unresponsive spiritually but so splendid in relieving the actual Cross-bearing . . . And the stripping of the garments—the undressing of the wounded; and the hanging on the Cross—the sick-bed and the theatre and the stretcher.[4]

In fact, often much more effective work was probably achieved in one-to-one talks with the chaplains. Soldiers could see that it was the courageous who often fell in battle and the weaker men who made sure they survived in one way or another, and they questioned the justice of this. Men also came to the chaplain immersed in guilt at their actions in battle—how could they justify thrusting a bayonet into the stomach of the enemy—a man against whom they had no personal hatred but merely belonged to a nation at war with his nation? Some of these questions sent men to the edge of insanity and chaplains were also known to succumb to breakdowns after continually trying to pastor to soldiers with these horrific, soul-destroying problems. But many men, even those who had previously led a life full of Christian beliefs and practices, became hardened by the experiences of battle—their emotions were almost paralyzed, enabling them to concentrate on killing Germans. These too, often sought out the chaplain on a casual solitary basis: "I have often felt when officers or men seem to be deliberately inflicting upon me all their war callousness, that they were trying to thaw themselves out a little at the fires of humanity they expected me to keep burning."[5] The chaplains who were able to experience these intimate moments were those who

---

4. Macdonald, *The Roses of No Man's Land*, 253.
5. Henderson, *Khaki and Cassock*, 78.

concentrated on establishing an easy, approachable footing with the men, rather than those who retired well back from the trenches and waited for men to seek them out.

One of the tasks to which the chaplains were dedicated was in helping with the dying and the wounded, both in assisting stretcher-bearers and medical people and in just being with the casualties. There were even cases when harassed medical staff had chaplains carrying out medical procedures when great waves of wounded arrived at the casualty stations. The Roman Catholic priest concentrated on his sacred duty to give soldiers the Last Rites, being constantly at the front, disregarding his own safety to give succor to the dying. At the Gallipoli landings, chaplains were instructed to wait until the following day—the Roman Catholic chaplain, Father John Fahey, went with the men on the 25th. As Robert Graves comments, "Jovial Father Gleeson of the Munsters, when all the officers were killed or wounded at the first battle of Ypres, had stripped off his black badges and, taking command of the survivors, held the line."[6]

Even if not a Roman Catholic, many a priest would minister to a man in his last moments on earth. They constantly frequented the tents where soldiers who were beyond medical help lay alone in their pain and distress. Roman Catholic soldiers were not ashamed to acknowledge their faith when a priest appeared, whereas soldiers of other denominations kept their counsel. The men admired the Roman Catholic chaplains because they shared their hardships and sufferings and were scathing of the chaplains who stayed behind the lines:

> For Anglican regimental chaplains we had little respect. If they had shown one-tenth the courage, endurance and other human qualities that the regimental doctors showed, we agreed, the British Expeditionary Force might well have started a religious revival. But they had not, being under orders to avoid getting mixed up with the fighting and to stay behind with the transport. Soldiers could hardly respect a chaplain who obeyed these orders, and yet not one in fifty seemed sorry to obey them. Occasionally, on a quiet day in a quiet sector, the chaplain would make a daring afternoon visit to the support line and distribute a few cigarettes, before hurrying back. But he was always too much to the fore in rest-billets. Sometimes the colonel would summon him to come up with the rations and bury the day's dead; he would arrive, speak his lines, and shoot off again . . . The colonel in one battalion I served with got rid of four new

---

6. Graves, *Goodbye to All That*, 158–59.

> Anglican chaplains in four months; finally, he applied for a Roman Catholic, alleging a change of faith in the men under his command . . . Anglican chaplains were remarkably out of touch with their troops.[7]

Nevertheless, there were many chaplains of the Protestant denominations who did wonderful work and were much admired and loved by the men. Notable Australians were the Salvationist, William McKenzie; the Presbyterian, The Reverend Andrew Gillespie; and the Anglican, the Reverend William Dexter. Gillespie died at Gallipoli, but both McKenzie and Dexter were able to serve the whole war. "Fighting Mac" McKenzie was always there with the men and, due to many daring and caring actions:

> His life soon assumed legendary proportions, and rumours abound that he even led charges, armed only with a shovel. When the troops begged him not to expose himself to danger, he responded: 'Boys, I've preached to you and I've prayed for you, and do you think I'm afraid to die with you?' The Diggers loved him to a man, and described him as 'big-hearted,' 'incorruptible,' 'considerate of the feelings of the individual,' 'one of the bravest of the brave,' 'a friend of sinners,' and 'a man of deep mysticism combined with unalterable common sense.' Scores found Christ through his ministry, and hundreds were buried with tender affection under his ministry. The death, gore and indescribable misery affected McKenzie deeply, and he lost five stone during the Gallipoli campaign.[8]

It needs to be remembered that chaplains were, in most cases, under orders not to proceed to the front lines. They were considered a danger to the fighting men and a hindrance in time of battle. Many brigadiers directly enforced this regulation. There was also the possibility that, if a chaplain was killed disobeying such an order, his pension would not be honored to his dependents at home. Those chaplains who disregarded such orders were welcomed by the men who were undergoing the extreme fear of unimaginable wounds and constantly existing under the shadow of death. Kenneth Henderson felt it essential to be in the depth of this earthly hell as, "The one great advantage of a padre's position is . . . the fact that he is the one unofficial element in a stern, hard, official world—the one embodiment of peace, goodwill, and the half-forgotten decencies of life."[9]

---

7. Graves, *Goodbye to All That*, 158–59.
8. Linder, *The Long Tragedy*, 131–32.
9. Henderson, *Khaki and Cassock*, 145.

He discovered also that men were terrified of experiencing ghastly wounds but had a fatal acceptance of the possibility of death:

> To some this fate is the providence of God; to others it is merely fate; to very few it is chance . . . There is somehow linked to it [the belief held] a real belief that those who have 'gone west' are not far away; they are absent, detached for duty elsewhere. The veil of eternity is very thin . . . The dead still seem to belong to the battalion. This feeling is linked with that idea of destiny, and only needs the natural extension to the idea of God calling His own around Him, tested by the fierce trial of this life for the fellowship of service in the life to come.[10]

How Did the Christian Soldier Reconcile the Things He Had to Do?

Lieutenant Colonel Alexander White wrote home from the first Anzac battlefield: "Dear little wife and kiddie I seem so far away from you all; I do not want to speak about the war; it's horrible. If I let myself think too much about it my nerves will go. Have seen things and done things I want to forget."[11] Not only were dreadful actions perpetrated in the actual battle but there were occasional other deliberate crimes carried out against the enemy. Soldiers who were assigned to escort prisoners of war sometimes allowed their anger at the loss of fellow combatants to come to the fore. A couple of grenades solved the problem and a report to headquarters that the prisoners were killed by a German shell was accepted. Fortunately, this did not seem to occur too often.

Wilfred Owen, the World War I poet, attempted to compose a Christian response to war:

> Already I have comprehended a light which will never filter into the dogma of any national church; namely that one of Christ's essential commands was: Passivity at any price! Suffer dishonour and disgrace; but never resort to arms. Be bullied, be outraged, be killed; but do not kill . . . Christ is literally in no man's land. There men often hear His voice: Greater love hath no man than this, that a man lay down his life—for a friend . . . Thus you see how pure Christianity will not fit in with pure patriotism . . .

---

10. Henderson, *Khaki and Cassock*, 151–52.
11. Carlyon, *Gallipoli*, 396.

This practice of *selective ignorance* is, as I have pointed out, one cause of the War. Christians have deliberately *cut* some of the main teachings of their code.[12]

In contrast, Kenneth Henderson writes:

> I felt very pessimistic and 'blue' about my work at first, but grew more and more optimistic as time went on. Sometimes, when rather depressed, a talk with a stretcher bearer in a sap, or a casual conversation on the road, or a quiet and fervent evensong with twenty or thirty men in a barn or dug-out, would make me feel that, after all, the Church was founded on a rock, and that the gates of hell could not prevail. When you find religion in the army it is the real thing—awful in its quiet sincerity.[13]

To him there were only two interpretations of the war: "the victorious suffering and pain which God is sharing, the struggle for the world's future in which He is our fighting comrade—or hell, however well-regulated for some people—on earth."[14]

How Did the Chaplain Play a Convincing Role as Theologian?

Possibly the most effective strategy to be a convincing agent of God's compassion is to practice "agape" love in God's name, rather than trying to influence soldiers by sermonising both formally and informally. He should always demonstrate practical "agape" Christianity by self-sacrificing love and care extended day and night to the suffering and the dying. Personal affinity with a soldier was the ultimate:

> Each man must build for his soul an abiding fortress. The frail and defenceless body may be crushed; but that his soul should come out on top, in the fiercest struggle with circumstance that can be conceived, is the first demand that a man's ordinary day's work makes upon him. He has discipline and comradeship to sustain him, but the ordeal is very fierce. So most men, consciously or otherwise, try to find an eternal citadel in the midst of their stormy experiences, within which, in weariness of the

---

12. Murray, *The Red Sweet Wine of Youth*, 148.
13. Henderson, *Khaki and Cassock*, 146.
14. Henderson, *Khaki and Cassock*, 147.

body, in the strain and storm of nerves, they can with steady will and clear purpose go forward to their day's work.[15]

Probably it was as difficult for the padre to find some meaning to the deep quagmire of battle as it was for the ordinary soldier. But, by tackling the problem on a personal level, he could bring some comfort to those who toiled in the trenches. Whatever perils the body experiences, nothing could touch the soul living under the shelter of God, the father and the creator: "He will cover you with his pinions, and under his wings you will find refuge; his faithfulness is a shield and buckler." (Ps 91:4 NRSV) Certainly it appears that the clergy on the home front, generally out of touch with the horrors, could live with the righteousness of their cause. However, there were possibly some chaplains in the field who found it difficult to reconcile their experiences to their dogma. Cast into a battlefield without any preparation for a vastly different type of pastoral work than they had ever encountered, the military chaplains desperately needed a theology of war.

John A. Wood, a professor of religion, in his study on war in the Bible, specifically the concept of "holy war" states:

> I entered this project with a deep ambivalence about war. I was and am strongly attracted to the power and beauty of the pacifist tradition but cannot embrace it fully because of the compelling logic and realism of the just war tradition. Now, after examining the biblical materials I now know the source of some of this ambivalence. It is evident to me that the people of the biblical era, whose situation differed greatly from mine, also experienced profound ambiguity about this issue and this ambiguity is faithfully recorded for us . . . I undertook this study because I had to and because war has never ceased to trouble me. I now see that it never ceased to trouble the people of the Old and New Testaments.[16]

In his work, Wood lists the names of innumerable theologians who struggle with the concept of God as a warrior sanctioning warfare for the Israelites. But God is also a god of justice and righteousness; a god of power and might; a god of splendor and majesty; and a god of love for his people. He is the divine sovereign in control of the world he created. Wood emphasizes that control means that there must be an order in God's world: "God's people are to receive his gifts but are also to be

---

15. Henderson, *Khaki and Cassock*, 147–48.
16. Wood, *Perspectives on War in the Bible*, 7–8.

responsible in his world."[17] God is a god of grace but that grace has to be responded to with gratitude and honor.

The people who are destroyed in battle by the Israelites are a wicked pagan people who continually reject God as their god. The Canaanites, for example, practiced a pornographic nature-worship and developed a barbaric mythological tradition. The Israelites, in comparison, God's chosen people, were to be dedicated to living a life of purity, worshipping the one true God and following his ethical laws and commandments. As mentioned elsewhere, God also allowed pagan nations to defeat Israel in war to fulfill his righteousness when he found his people repelling his gift of grace, deserting their holy commitment, and sinning against him with idols and alien gods.

God has created a world that was besieged by the evil one. He allows humankind to have free will. Therefore, God now has to act in a world that is no longer perfect. He uses his holy wars to achieve his purposes. "In a complex and sinful world could there be any other way? Since so much of history is the history of warfare, if God is involved in history, he must be involved in some degree in warfare. There is no escaping this conclusion given the Biblical understanding of the nature of God."[18]

Christianity—the Church at Home

At home in Britain there was initially a considerable anti-war lobby and many people were individually petitioning for peace. Women from a number of countries came together to make their voices heard. As early as 1915 the Women's International League for Permanent Peace was formed and met at The Hague. However, for the second meeting of this body, British delegates were prevented from attending because their travel documents were canceled. The authorities in Britain were anxious to curtail the activities of such organizations. Nevertheless, in July 1916, the first women's mass anti-war demonstration in Britain was held in Glasgow. Participants were quickly labeled as cranks and traitors.

As the war progressed and reached stalemate after stalemate with the accompanying loss of thousands of young men, statesmen and politicians from both sides raised the possibility of discussing a peaceful solution but never with success. Germany, in particular, but others also in the

---

17. Wood, *Perspectives on War in the Bible*, 165.
18. Wood, *Perspectives on War in the Bible*, 169.

Central Powers, were loathe to relinquish their territorial gains. Wealthy industrialists in Germany were clapping their hands with glee at all that had been attained in resources, whilst others looked to expanding Germany's agricultural holdings. Germany had no intention of pulling out of the war even to the point of taking advantage of the strong unrest in the country of its enemy. Russian prisoners of war, for example, were routinely screened to ascertain any who were of a revolutionary bent—men who had possibly been involved in the industrial risings of 1905 onwards. Any detected as such were supplied with money and false papers and sent back to Russia to hopefully reactivate their revolutionary past. At the same time, approaches to Germany from its main ally, Austria-Hungary, for peace negotiations were immediately rejected.

In Britain even the churches were supportive of the government's decision to declare war on the Central Powers—the coalition of Germany, Austria-Hungary, Bulgaria, and the Ottoman Empire: ". . . as church historian John Moses has pointed out, there was in place in 1914 a general theology of empire in British ecclesiastical thought which made it fairly easy for British churches to join in the war fever of the period. Brooke Foss Westcott, the scholarly Bishop of Durham, for example, had advanced a systematic analysis of the nature of the use of force in civilized society which insisted that Christians must acknowledge war as an ultimate means for maintaining a righteous cause."[19] People looked to the authorities of the day for guidance—churchmen (from the bishops to the local curate), university professors, and other academics, and leading politicians such as W. E. Gladstone. Not only a statesman, but a scholar and a churchman, Gladstone maintained that "power brought with it the responsibility to protect the weak."[20] The starving children of Belgium was a popular admonishment to Empire children who would not eat their meals (as was an admonishment to Australian children of the starving Korean children during the 1950s).

In the church an imperial theology of the great British empire took hold. Clergymen who had no experience of war, pontificated personally and in the pulpit, on the glory of sacrifice. As A. B. Baker recalls:

> A few days later I had a letter from our curate. In it he talked about war as a noble discipline. He said it purged men of selfishness, and by its pity and terror brought men nearer to God. I felt

---

19. Linder, *The Long Tragedy*, 26.
20. Linder, *The Long Tragedy*, 26.

sick for a second time. He put with his letter a printed Prayer for Victory and told me to say it every night. I remember that my prayer in the dug-out had been just this, said over and over again: 'O God, stop this war; stop it, and let me go home.' At home the curate had been rather a hero of mine. He wasn't my hero any more.[21]

Meanwhile, at the outbreak of hostilities Australians seemed united. Both the major political parties immediately pledged their support of Britain at such a time. The press emphasized how important it was for Australia to step into the breach. There had been some who had spoken out against the Boer War and had, as a result, been ostracized so most people were reticent to speak out against this war. The clergy also was also immediately supportive seeing it all as a noble cause to go to the aid of the mother country in her hour of need. For God to have ordained such a war to occur he must have some great plan and would ensure that his purposes would be fulfilled. Ministers were almost joyous in pronouncing a time of great revival when all the sins of society would be destroyed and the people would be purged from their evil pastimes. A cleansing fire would reinvigorate the country. In these times a great number of the population of Australia was happy to claim religious affiliation with a specific denomination even if only with the commonly used "C of E" by those who never darkened the church door. But even non-churchgoers looked to the clergy for direction and so such men were in a position to wield a great deal of influence on matters of importance. There developed a type of patriotic church service devoted entirely to the war and people flocked to these with enthusiasm. Although there were some fine churchmen in the history of Australia, unfortunately quite a number of religious leaders had come to the Antipodes to make their mark, not having the gifts to make a climb in status in the home church. Their skills were often poor in learning and expression, as Manning Clark notes in his *History of Australia*:

> Lowther Clarke, the English-born Anglican leader in Melbourne since 1902, became the nation's spokesman at a service of intercession on the first Sunday of the war. He was, perhaps, not the most qualified person for the task; his own dean described his cathedral sermons as 'Sunday School talks delivered in a somewhat portentous and pompous style . . . Clarke gave a rather dull performance; he preached from the text *'Be still and know that*

---

21. Baker, "The story of a W.A.A.C.," 397.

I am God' which emphasised that God was in control, that the believer would not despair or be concerned unduly. He was optimistic: 'these days will bring their own blessing... they will teach very many better than they know it now the value of religion.'[22]

The denomination that had suffered greatly in this regard was the Roman Catholic Church, often being burdened with priests whom the Irish Church wished to be rid of, particularly rebel priests who were involved in the battle for Home Rule in the years before World War I. On the whole the Roman Catholic Church did not wholeheartedly support sending men to the war and was slow to appoint chaplains to accompany the troops. Older priests or priests unpopular with the hierarchy in the church were the ones eventually sent. However, most proved to be effective pastors to the soldiers. Father O'Dwyer, the rector of Xavier College in Melbourne, was a rare Catholic imperialist. There was also great prejudice against the RCs (as they were called) resulting in fewer Roman Catholics in government at any level, and little representation in the positions of leadership in the professions. Generally, they were treated as second-class citizens. The Roman Catholics also had their own school system to protect their children from being indoctrinated by Protestant influences. During this period Protestants resurrected the tradition that Roman Catholics were unreliable in support of the country because they looked for authority to a foreign Pope.

But, in time, even as the men at the front began to question the whole morality of their being there, people at home began to lobby for peace. Nevertheless, the churches as a whole continued to support the war, still seeing it as a crusade for Christ. In Australia, when World War I had begun, the Church of England synods, the Assemblies of the Presbyterian Church, and the Conferences of the Methodist Church had passed resolutions in favor of striving to win the war. Boys in Protestant colleges were led to believe that "death on the battlefield was the way to life everlasting."[23] Some historians have concluded that the Australian clergy were enthusiastic in supporting the war because they saw it as a means of demonstrating their relevance to the people. Anglican theologians, in particular, believed the empire was the framework from which Christianity could be preached and thus it was vital to safeguard its existence. So

---

22. McKernan, *The Australian People and the Great War*, 16–17.
23. Clark, *A History of Australia*. Volume 6, 6.

zealous in support of the empire were some clergy that German Lutheran pastors were ostracized and interned.

Conscription of men for the fighting forces or for war work became a necessity as thousands more men were sacrificed on the battlefield. This was a particularly contentious issue in Australia. As the war progressed, Prime Minister Billy Hughes greatly upset his Labor colleagues when, on an extended visit to Britain in 1916 he said, "The war has saved Australians from physical and moral degeneracy and decay,"[24] "and that those who opposed war were 'foul parasites.'"[25] By this stage Australians at home had come to realize that their beloved husbands and sons were not engaging on the great crusade for God and Empire but were embroiled in a desperate bloody battle, losing their physical and mental health, if not their lives, amidst the carnage and mud of a far-flung foreign field. But Hughes's priority was no longer to the Australian Labor Party but to victory at any cost. The fallen must be replaced and the voluntary system could not suffice. But conscription was against the Labor thinking of building a great Australia through peaceful means—"the Trades and Labor Council passed resolutions against conscription and the Australian Workers' Union condemned it."[26] So incensed was the Political Labor Leagues of New South Wales that it expelled Hughes from the Labor Party, opposed all Labor members who voted to support conscription, and refused to support any candidates in favor of conscription. Labor saw any compulsion as anti-British and something masterminded by the capitalist press.

The Australian churches became strongly involved in the conscription issue. The Anglican synod in Melbourne enthusiastically supported conscription; the charismatic Roman Catholic Archbishop of Melbourne, Daniel Mannix, condemned it. Australian Roman Catholics were slow to support the same British who were acting with brutality in Ireland. Sectarianism came to a head in country areas where the bush culture epitomized the brave digger—opponents of conscription were assaulted and Roman Catholic schoolchildren were persecuted. Some Roman Catholics felt that conscription denied free will. However, the Roman Catholic Archbishop of Sydney, Michael Kelly, did support the issue, becoming a leader in the Universal Service League.

---

24. Clark, *A History of Australia. Volume 6*, 22.
25. Clark, *A History of Australia. Volume 6*, 1.
26. Clark, *A History of Australia. Volume 6*, 30.

The Role of Christianity

The Presbyterian Church in Melbourne, meanwhile, discussed the attitude of Mannix, criticizing his views as "diabolic, dastardly, disloyal utterances."[27] Yet the Director of Home Missions for the Presbyterian Church, Donald Cameron, felt that Presbyterians were evenly divided on the issue. The Methodist Church leaders disclaimed their right to interfere in political matters and saw conscription as more of a moral issue, which should be decided on individual conscience. They encouraged members to vote with a conscience for conscription yet not generally condemning those who disagreed. Interestingly, an Adelaide Methodist minister, Albert Morris, who preached against conscription was the center of much anger and unhappiness when the church transferred him to a country backwater. The Anglican synod in Sydney followed the lead of their Melbourne brethren claiming it was immoral to desert the memory of those who had fallen in the cause of freedom. Some Protestant ministers advocated that Christ himself would support conscription; others that conscription was incompatible with Christian beliefs. Basically, the Roman Catholic Church saw the issue as a political one; the Protestant churches recognized it as a moral question. In all walks of life "families were divided, churches were divided, parties were divided; friends for a lifetime found they were on opposite sides."[28]

We see an age-old problem—Christianity is a way of life—not just something to be observed one day of the week. Therefore, preachers must be relevant to life—"in the world" but "not of the world." They must preach from God's inerrant word honestly, but they must be involved theologically in the matters of the world. How the churches approach this problem differs in different periods of history. Some lost their theology whilst others became lost in their theology.

Both the referenda of 1916 and 1917 in Australia were defeated. The second campaign was particularly divisive. Riots and violence became so commonplace that some people feared a civil war. In the end most clerical leaders gave support for the Yes vote but evangelicals, for example, maintained a silence. The wedge between Roman Catholics and Protestants grew even wider as Mannix grew more militant; the discontent of the laboring classes deepened with strikes by workers and prosecutions by Hughes (who had formed a new national government with the Liberals), and groups like the Women's Peace Army were persecuted when

27. Main, *Conscription*, 86.
28. Clark, *A History of Australia*. Volume 6, 37.

they protested about food prices and other problems affecting the people on the home front.

It is interesting to look at the attitude of the soldiers in the trenches with regard to conscription. They too took part in the referenda. Whilst it was generally felt that those at home who refused to volunteer were getting off "scot free," not having to risk their lives and suffer the horrific hardships of war, neither did they want men to be forcibly sent to the front. It was recognized that conscripted men, under duress to join in the fighting, could not be relied upon to be part of a coordinated unit. In every attack each man had to play a vital part overcoming his personal fear and supporting his comrades no matter how impossible the situation became. There was a justifiable doubt that conscription would work.

Meanwhile the slaughter continued unabated.

5

Brutality, Survival, and Grief

WOMEN EMBARKED ON MANY roles in World War 1. The predominant career was that of nursing where such "Angels of Mercy" endured and persevered to bring comfort and healing to soldiers whose bleeding, battered bodies and shattered, desperate psyches needed so much. Reading Vera Brittain's *Testament of Youth*, or her war diaries, *Chronicle of Youth*, we have a first-hand account of the loss of a fiancé, a brother, their close school companion, and a comrade in arms of her brother. Vera was a VoluntaryAid Detachment (VAD) nurse who served in London, Malta, and France, nursing British and allied soldiers and, at one stage, German wounded. Her writings bring the reader poignantly close—too close—to the terror and tragedy of war and one can fully understand why she dedicated the rest of her life to a vibrant peace campaign. She experienced, as did many others, the loss of her generation with its accompanying constant pain of grief. Her *Chronicle of Youth* contains a preface by her fiancé's sister, Clare Leighton, who writes:

> As I write this I find myself back in childhood. It is a cold morning in January and I am in the garden of our cottage in Sussex. My father is with me. I carry two heavy kettles. They are filled with boiling water, for we are about to bury the tunic—blood-stained and bullet-riddled—in which Roland has been killed ... Father watches the windows of the house, for my mother must not see this tunic that Father has hidden from the packages of

Roland's effects returned from France. I am to thaw the frozen earth so that it may be buried out of sight.[1]

Vera Brittain continued her nursing of the wounded throughout the heartbreaking losses of those she so dearly loved.

Wartime nurses in World War I were exposed to the greatest horrors imaginable. They served sometimes only a short distance from the front and were under constant bombardment and the threat of emergency evacuation daily. Without the wonders of modern medicine and with somewhat rudimentary anesthesia practices, they labored with doctors in appalling situations, endlessly having to choose which soldiers to treat and which ones to leave to die. Amputations were continuously undertaken because, by the time men reached the casualty stations and operating tents, gas gangrene had set in and threatened the very existence of the patient. The mud the men lay in whilst awaiting rescue was permeated with corpses, rats, and flies although in some cases the activities of maggots did help to clean a wound. A soldier who lost both arms and legs in addition to his eyes had a nurse write to King George V requesting some type of euthanasia but his plea was rejected. We don't learn of his fate when he returned home but his life must have been an unceasing torment.

On a hospital ship lying off Gallipoli, an Australian nurse Kath King wrote: "I got such a nice boy in haemorrhaging and was taken to theatre, operated on, returned to the ward with my hat pin through his neck ... he died suddenly in about half an hour after returning to the ward ... The ward was frightful, with patients dying almost as quickly as they are admitted."[2] (Possibly the hat pin was being used to staunch the bleeding.) On the Western Front, Alice Ross King, reporting on 500 admissions to her ward, wrote: "I have one man who is quite mad. He got into the 4th line of German trenches and went to take some prisoners. They cried mercy and while he hesitated one threw a bomb right into his face. The fire enveloped him and he says he lay grovelling in the earth. For two days he was not picked up and today when we took his dressings down his eyesight was not gone. He wept for joy."[3]

Many of those nursing had only basic training as VADs, and although as such they were not qualified to carry out a lot of nursing work, circumstances often called on them to do so—particularly as dressings

---

1. Brittain, *Chronicle of Youth*, 9–10.
2. Rees, *The Other Anzacs*, 62.
3. Rees, *The Other Anzacs*, 172.

had to be changed daily and there were just not enough doctors and nurses when literally thousands of wounded arrived at the same time. In the midst of all this carnage many medical breakthroughs were made guided by desperate necessity. There were, even from early days of the war, a number of teams from leading American medical schools, including Harvard, coming to the Western Front. Amongst them were men interested in research and consequently new procedures were tried—blood transfusions being a major lifesaver. Where gas gangrene was in its early stages, a type of antiseptic irrigation was used with success, whereby the Carrel-Dakin solution was syringed through tubes. The British also were not backward in trying new methods—the government immediately sent medical personnel to investigate the horror of gas when it was first used. Later in the war incredible work was developed by a sculptor and member of the Royal Academy, Captain Derwent Wood, RAMC, in the field of face reconstruction. He worked with photographs of soldiers taken before they left for the Front, with the aim of having a finished product that was as close to the original face as possible.

No doubt an extremely hazardous war service was that of the stretcher-bearer—at the front with the combatants, but unarmed. Here was someone continually in perilous situations dragging the wounded from no man's land and dressing wounds whilst under a heavy barrage: "One soldier had been shot through both legs and was left lying on the battlefield for three days. Then, while his legs were being bandaged, a shell exploded near him, killing the dresser and wounding the soldier in the chest."[4] To reach the field hospitals ambulance men carried stretchers through acres of glutinous mud. In fact, the mud was so bad that to pull a person from it was sometimes impossible. There was even a case of a soldier breaking his back in the process of being pulled free from its tenacious hold. When stretcher-bearers put down their load to change positions the wounded panicked that they were going to be left.

> However, thousands of wounded were still stranded in no-man's land, crawling around, hands waving, crying out for help, but no one could get to them. About midday both sides' guns abruptly stopped and the most eerie stillness fell over the whole section of the front. All that could be heard were the cries of the wounded out in no-man's land . . . Hour after hour they called out the names of their mates, many of whom were probably dead. Then

---

4. Rees, *The Other Anzacs*, 173.

a couple of brave souls couldn't stand it any longer. Risking almost certain death, they started out to help them.[5]

The Other Side—Angels of Death?

Hatred and brutality are the cause, the execution, and the result of war, exercised by all combatants at one time or another and in one way or another. Some proponents were worse than others; many were extreme but, conversely, many died because they could not bring themselves to commit brutal acts even to defend themselves. Others who originally thought themselves incapable of carrying out such horrendous acts became hardened to it all as the war progressed. Generally, the Turks respected the Red Cross and allowed the enemy to tend to their wounded unmolested. Yet Turkey was responsible for the almost complete annihilation of the Armenian nation. When this horror occurred, in most instances, nations of the world stood by, refusing to intervene for various diplomatic reasons.

The Armenian population of Turkey had already suffered massacres of their peoples when, in 1909, they supported the government of the "Young Turks," hoping that they would be granted more freedoms and rights under their rule. But their hopes were dashed when Muslims slew several thousand Armenian Christians, a repeat of the massacres from 1894 to 1896, conducted under the iron rule of Abdul Hamid. In 1915 when Russia invaded Turkey as part of the World War I strategy of the Allies, Armenians began to hope that finally they would gain some national rights. But Turkish soldiers shot dead many thousands of Armenian men, and drove women and children into the desert of Syria to die. The Armenians appealed to the Germans who, for diplomatic purposes, only made a feeble protest, which was ignored. Similarly, the United States refused to become involved. Eventually some few were rescued from the coast of Syria by the French navy. Well over a million people died of brutality or deprivation. The few that survived were forcibly converted to Islam. "The British, French and Russian governments, each of them at war with Turkey, issued a joint public denunciation . . . describing the killings as 'a crime against humanity and civilization'. The original phrase, drafted by the Russians, had read 'a crime against Christianity and civilization'. This was changed in order to spare the feelings of the Muslim populations

---

5. Ramsay, *Hell, Hope and Heroes*, 91.

in both British India and the French colonies."⁶ War brings countless examples of such dishonorable inaction.

In a former war—the Boer War in South Africa—in an effort to force the Boers to surrender, the British army was responsible for the first concentration camps. These were set up to imprison Boer women and children but the inmates experienced inhumane conditions. Twenty-eight thousand women and children died in these camps—more people than died in the actual fighting. An Afrikaner once related the history of his family. His grandmother was one of seven children imprisoned with their mother in a British camp. Aged eight, she and her baby brother were the only survivors. For the rest of her life she refused to speak English or to acknowledge that she understood English.

In World War I the Germans on land were responsible for a "scorched earth" policy whereby they destroyed everything in their path to prevent following armies or inhabitants of the land to benefit from food or other vital supplies. The deliberate destruction of Louvain, with all its historical and architectural treasures, was a crushing and seemingly unnecessary action. Anything in the German military path was destroyed—civilians, buildings, crops. On sea they torpedoed hospital ships and even passenger liners although, the sinking of the *Lusitania* is a controversial incident as, besides carrying over 1,000 passengers it also had in its hold armaments and ammunition contrary to maritime law. Nevertheless, this would give the Germans the right to board and search but not to sink on sight.

There were also innumerable cases of unnecessary individual cruelty. No nation was innocent. As mentioned beforehand it was often thought by soldiers that bringing back prisoners of war was an unnecessary burden and a grenade often solved the problem. Kitty Kenyon, a VAD at Camiers, had read where Germans had been killing British soldiers and, aghast, she was expressing her anger to a patient: "He fell absolutely silent, made no answer at all. It was as if a shutter had come down over his face, and I realized in a flash that he must have done the same thing."⁷

Men coped with their experiences in vastly different ways. Many quickly developed a callous attitude to death—from shaking the hand that was protruding from the mud and wishing the owner a "good morning"

---

6. Gilbert, *A History of the Twentieth Century. Volume 1*, 357–58.
7. Macdonald, *The Roses of No Man's Land*, 94.

to using another hand poking out from the wall of a dugout as a hook to hang items upon. A soldier taking part in a card game might fall dead from shrapnel but the game continued unabated. Soldiers used corpses as benches and commandeered articles of clothing to replace their own. Men gloried in the number of Huns they had killed but after the action experienced guilt and remorse to the point of being violently ill. Yet the next day they would be keen to be back in the fray. Then again, when injured himself, the soldier, particularly the Australian digger, often made light of it all. One man who lost one of his hands in shelling, whilst being helped back to the casualty station, kept asking passing soldiers, "Can you give me a hand, mate?", a typical Australian saying used macabrely. The callousness, the cynicism, the bluffing, was all part of coping with the endless horror of war.

Writing about the Australian soldier, Roy Ramsay points out that the well-feted attribute of the Aussie is the cult of "mateship," and this mateship was the glue that held Australian diggers together in the midst of the carnage of war:

> You didn't let your mates down, no matter what. The love of a soldier for his mates knew no bounds. Some gave their last piece of food, last mouthful of water or last cigarette and went without themselves. Some shared their gas masks at the cost of their own life. Some civilians who have no experience of war talk of the "glory of war." If there is any glory, which I doubt, it is the quiet bravery and mateship of the ordinary soldiers. It is in the lessons of life and compassion learned while facing imminent death. No one who hasn't been through it can understand it. That is why we found it hard to talk about it with our loved ones when on leave or after the war was over.[8]

The life and actions of the soldier at the front were little understood by noncombatants.

After the Bugle has Sounded

By September 1918, the Bulgarians were facing complete defeat and the Turks were losing their hold on Palestine.

> General Allenby advanced northward from Jerusalem, and within a week was in control of the Galilee. Among his tactics

---

8. Ramsay, *Hell, Hope and Heroes*, 171.

was the bombing and machine-gunning from the air of Turkish soldiers fleeing eastward along the precipitous slopes of the Wadi Fara... More than 86,000 machine-gun rounds were fired at men who had no means of firing back. Some of the Allied pilots who carried out these aerial attacks were so nauseated by what they saw of the effect of their shooting that they asked to be excused any further sorties.[9]

The General granted their request.

In contrast in these last days of fighting was the attitude of many of the American generals on the Western Front when the Armistice was signed on November 11, 1918. Signed at 5.00 a.m. in the morning, word was sent to all combatants notifying them that the longed-for Armistice would come into effect at 11 a.m. General Pershing was determined to continue the battle until the last minute, firmly believing that there should be no mercy shown and the German army should be pushed all the way back to Berlin so there would never be any question of its defeat. Due to the actions of an unrepentant Pershing and many other US generals, approximately 3,000 Americans were unnecessarily slaughtered during these last hours just for reasons of glory, promotion and, even in one case, so that the soldiers would have access to bathing facilities. Surely such leaders as these would have had to eventually answer to a higher authority. There was an investigation of such derelictions of duty but, as is often the case, no disciplinary action eventuated.

All through these years of war there was grief after each action—grief, sorrow, and guilt. Guilt was often the overwhelming emotion. The enemy was a soldier in similar circumstances—perhaps married with children—and now, due to the action of oneself, was now lying lifeless on the battlefield never to return to his family and home. The overall feelings when the war was over were life-changing and never-ending. There was no help for the returning combatant—no recognition of the extreme stress he or she had been under for so long—no realization that each had been forced to carry out legalized killing, committing acts that would have been punishable by death or incarceration in normal times. In Australia some soldiers joined the Returned Services League (originally called the RSSILA—Returned Sailors and Soldiers Imperial League of Australia) immediately on returning home; others joined years later; some not at all. At least, by meeting with those who had suffered similar perils, endured common hardships, and committed all the destructive

---

9. Gilbert, *A History of the Twentieth Century.* Volume 1, 511.

behaviors that war required to survive, those who had served could open up and somehow assuage their sorrow and guilt. The ones who never joined and who never marched on Anzac Day tried, often unsuccessfully, to put it all behind them and dedicate themselves to a life with no past but one full of a future of hope.

Men managed their emotions in different ways and none were left without scars from those years of fear and struggle. A few managed to put memories behind them; others stored them inside sometimes with tragic results; some only stored memories of comradeship with war stories becoming the yarns of scallywags. However, many became completely different people. Wives related how a carefree larrikin returned as a constantly scowling old man never able to recapture the intimacy of married life. A common thread appeared to be a lack of communication regarding their war experiences—it was almost impossible to relate to loved ones' endangerments that they would never understand and, to admit to them some of the horrific acts they were forced to carry out in a different life.

Surprisingly a great number of men (and women) were able to forgive the Germans and the Turks and to remember how there was an uncanny bond between combatants—they certainly respected those of the enemy who behaved honorably and courageously. At one stage Australians and Turks fought together near the end of the war against the common threat of marauding Bedouins. Some were even able to forgive the blundering British generals of the early war, particularly when the great gifts of Monash as a leader came to the fore in the closing stages, seemingly proving that, finally, everybody was discovering how to beat the enemy efficiently. Possibly the politicians and the Kaiser who together plunged millions of people into chaos and death, were not so easily forgiven.

Obviously there were many "what-ifs," which could have saved more lives or at least hastened the end of the war, but few dwelt on them when they could finally put all behind them. The frustration of having, in France, an American army that was not immediately utilized had been a source of immense vexation. General John Pershing, the head of the United States Expeditionary Force, refused to allow the Americans to be amalgamated into other armies. They would only fight as an American army in its own right. When at last some units were integrated, an American commander prevented their involvement claiming they were not completely trained. To the glee of some attached to one of the battalions they were able to participate at Le Hamel because the order came too late for them to turn back. In fact, it was true that American soldiers were not completely trained, as they were not prepared for trench warfare. Pershing insisted on training his men in open-field conflict despite knowing the situation at the front.

All the rehashing of World War I was eventually left to the historians, and the surviving combatants tried to resume some sort of peacetime life after four surreal years. Picking up the threads of a former life was impossible for many. Enid Stoker, a VAD serving in the Anglo-Russian Hospital in Petrograd:

> ... was shocked by the level of suffering endured by the wounded—shocked in equal measure to her admiration of their stoicism *in extremis* and their simple peasant faith, expressed in frequent prayers before the icons that hung in the corners of their wards. They sang a lot and played the balalaika and had a childlike gratitude that touched her, but some of their stories were heartbreaking. She remembered one young soldier, Vasili, from Siberia who had had both legs amputated. One day he was lying on the top of his bed with his stumps on a pillow, 'when an old peasant came into the ward. He had travelled, goodness knows how, nearly a thousand miles to see his son,' as Stoker recalled. But as soon as he saw him, he began to shout, 'the tears pouring down his cheeks,' Stoker was dismayed to be told by their interpreter that the old man was cursing the boy: Why hadn't he *died*? Then they would have got a small pension for him—now look at him, a hopeless burden. How could he work on the farm now? Just another useless mouth to feed and they were nearly starving already.[10]

There was now a whole lost generation. The future of the nation was now devoid of its youth; the young men of great promise for the future; the hoped-for fathers of the next generation; the vanished lovers and husbands.

In her grief, Vera Brittain penned these poignant words in "The Superfluous Woman":

> Ghosts crying down the vistas of the years,
> Recalling words
> Whose echoes long have died,
> And kind moss grown
> Over the sharp and blood be-spattered stones
> Which cut our feet upon the ancient ways.

10. Rappaport, *Caught in the Revolution*, 35–36.

But who will look for my coming?

Long busy days where many meet and part;
Crowded aside
Remembered hours of hope;
And city streets
Grown dark and hot with eager multitudes
Hurrying homeward whither respite waits.

But who will seek me at nightfall?

Light fading where the chimneys cut the sky;
Footsteps that pass,
Nor tarry at my door.
And far away
Behind the row of crosses, shadows black
Stretch out long arms before the smouldering sun.

But who will give me my children?

At home, women who had been left widows, mothers who had lost their beloved sons, and young girls who would never have the fulfillment of a married life, struggled to cope. Seventy years later think upon the elderly lady in her room in a hostel. She wears a blue sapphire ring on her left hand. There are no photographs of children and grandchildren as in other rooms. Her only photograph sits on her bedside table. It is of a very handsome World War I soldier.

Here was a scenario never experienced on such a grand scale before—the loss of beloved menfolk with no last words, no funerals, no burials, no proper mourning. Soldiers had died far, far from home and the vast distance compounded the grief of those left behind. All the customary forms of bereavement were impossible plus, in the society of those times, it was not acceptable to openly grieve—excessive mourning was thought to be insincere. Relatives wanted and needed to know how their soldier died and where his body was buried. They wanted details, which the army could seldom supply. Officers had the onerous task of writing to families of their men but these letters generally hid the real situation in an attempt to comfort the recipient. Occasionally padres or nurses wrote to families and were sometimes able to pass on some dying words in their missives. The great distance between the homeland and the battlefield compounded by a lack of real information made the heartache more intense and more incomprehensible. Today we see flowers tied to lampposts where someone has died in a traffic accident. But for many mourners during World War I there was nowhere to place the flowers.

Mothers, in particular, never recovered from their grief, but sometimes a visit by the mate of a dead boy did help to ease the pain. Frank Tate wrote of such a visit he made in 1915:

> As I sat at the bedside unfolding the narrative, the frail little lady, sitting bolt-upright, surrounded by pillows, watched me intently. Her eyes were fixed on mine as she listened with rapt attention to every word, as though, indeed, she had been living for this very moment . . . As the precious minutes passed, I became increasingly aware of the importance of what was taking place. This was, I felt, a direct personal report to an adoring mother who, for many months had been yearning for news, for some personal details, however small, concerning the son whose loss she was mourning so deeply and at such a cost . . . With a deep sigh and a fervent "Thank you," Dick's mother sank back into the pillows, saying, "I am happy now," and closed her eyes.[11]

In contrast, a mother who had lost four sons was presented to Queen Mary who expressed her thanks for the nation at the sacrifice she had made. The reply was not what the Queen expected—there had been no sacrifice as she had not given her sons willingly! Mrs Amy Beechey was a widow from Friesthorpe in Lincolnshire. She had eight sons and six daughters. All but two of her sons enlisted. In large families it is often the case, even in modern times, to find that the mother is often so embroiled in daily tasks that it is not always possible for her to build very close relationships with each of her children. A young man, one of eight brothers, related that his closest family relationship was with the brother with whom he shared a bedroom. No doubt all the Beechey brothers were extremely close and one of them, Frank, was a dear favorite with all his sisters. The death of the five brothers in the war resulted in their graves being spread over the globe. In 1917 a poignant effort was made to symbolically reunite them all. Crosses fashioned by stonemasons in Friesthorpe were placed on each of the graves. Barnard, the eldest, was killed in France but his body was never located. His cross was placed on the grave of a Lincolnshire soldier "known only to God" in a French cemetery. The cross for Charles was placed on his grave in a war cemetery in Dar es Salaam. Frank's cross was placed on his grave in a French cemetery.

---

11. Ziino, *A Distant Grief*, 16.

Harold, an Anzac having previously emigrated with his brother, Chris, to Western Australia, died in France, but his cross has been placed in St. George's Cathedral in Perth, his adopted home. His brother Chris, who had serious war injuries, was able to return to Perth. Leonard who died from poison gas in France, has a cross on his grave in Rouen. A final cross has been placed in the little church in Friesthorpe.

The other major problem in burying the dead was the number of bodies that could not be identified. With the wound of loss so close in time, the army hierarchy and also the serving soldier chose not to tell those who were grieving the exact circumstances of death and the horrific conditions in which they died. A great loss did not need to be compounded by relating every gory detail—and the details were gory. Men did not die peacefully in another's arms—they bled to death with loss of limbs; they lay in the trenches with their bodies split and their inner organs spilling out on the earth; they died in excruciating pain. Sometimes there was no body at all—men were often blown into unidentifiable pieces. They often died after lying for hours and days in no man's land, unable to be saved and taken to safety. Thus, in many arenas it was not possible to recover corpses for burial and these lay rotting for weeks and months, gradually sinking into the constant mud and sludge and being eaten by rats. In fact, only marginally more than half of the dead were buried in identifiable graves. Unidentified bodies numbered more than 180,000 and then there were the bodies that were never found. Even today French farmers are unearthing further remains.

From quite early on in the war, governments had realized the importance of finding the dead on the battlefields, identifying each one and giving proper burial in a designated cemetery. This was not always possible—when the Australians silently left Gallipoli under darkness they were loathe to leave their fallen comrades, especially those lying exposed on the hills. It wasn't until Turkey withdrew from the war that work there could begin. Feelings about the Turk ranged from one extreme to the other—at times he was an honorable foe; at other times a savage heathen desecrating bodies and obliterating any traces of a grave. There had been generally a respect from the diggers for their enemies at Gallipoli, especially when they found how poorly dressed and ill-equipped the Turks were. In 1934 a compassionate message was conveyed to those who were bereft by the Turkish President Mustafa Kemal, now known as Atatürk. His words were engraved on the Memorial at Anzac Cove:

> Those heroes that shed their blood and lost their lives . . . you are now lying in the soil of a friendly country. Therefore rest in peace. There is no difference between the Johnnies and the Mehmets to us where they lie side by side here in this country of ours . . . You, the mothers, who sent their sons from far away countries wipe away your tears; your sons are now lying in our bosom and are in peace. After having lost their lives on this land they have become our sons as well.[12]

On the Western Front, burials were carried out in recognized cemeteries behind the lines from 1916 onwards. Here we find officialdom at its best and at its worst. The work was constant well into the next decade and, in most cases, meticulous. Unfortunately, the individual's need was often overlooked. Sir Frederic Kenyon, the Director of the British Museum, was an advisor on the layout and design of cemeteries. He did attempt to satisfy the needs of the bereaved but felt the overall and deeper need was for the empire: "The sacrifice of the individual is a great idea and worthy of commemoration; but the community of sacrifice, the service of a common cause, the comradeship of arms which has brought together men of all ranks and grades—these are greater ideas."[13] The world of today wants us to look at "the big picture," but when generals look at the "the big picture" they tend to dismiss the massive loss of life as subordinate. The road to victory must tolerate the deprivation of human life no matter how great it might be. This is a horrific concept but surely with the right men "at the top" the loss could be mitigated. Only an experienced battle leader would know. Certainly, many historians have opinions on the subject.

As a substitute for the Australian grave, the idea for memorials evolved. War memorials became the surrogate grave and the ceremony of unveiling such became the surrogate funeral service. Nevertheless, many mothers expressed the feeling that they would prefer a photograph of their son's grave in a foreign land and there were sometimes officials and individuals who were able to fulfill this need. The memorials sprang up in the cities and in suburbs and country towns, listing the men from that particular locality. This helped in a small way to bring them home. Memorial days were annual events, for example, Armistice Day on November 11, when schools, businesses, and even people in the streets stood silently for one minute at 11 a.m. Small wooden crosses were planted in

12. Westminster Abbey, *A Service of Commemoration and Thanksgiving to Mark ANZAC Day*, 2019, 12–13.

13. Ziino, *A Distant Grief*, 110–11.

church gardens amidst flowering poppies. Anzac Day became a strong institution. Today there is the often voiced criticism that Anzac Day commemorates the glory of war, particularly when the participants drink to excess and enjoy a game of "two-up." Returned soldiers find solace in Anzac Day, whether they march or not. For one day of the year they renew a mateship that they can find nowhere else. To try and relieve the constant pain of loss, a few Australians were able to afford a pilgrimage to Gallipoli or the Western Front in the 1920s but many of these relatives were utterly confounded by the impossibility of locating one grave or one body amongst the fallen thousands. Many became distressed where there was no grave, whilst others often chose a grave with the inscription "Known only to God," praying that it might contain the remains of their loved one. Comfort and consolation were their reward.

All these observances and the establishment of memorials were driven by the inconsolable grief of World War I—all hopefully would recognize the devastation to the world and its people, both victor and vanquished alike, and help to visualize a better life for both in the years ahead. It was to be a memorial to what had gone before and a beacon to a future with no more wars. When King George V toured the cemeteries of France and Belgium in 1922 he said:

> Never before in history have a people thus dedicated and maintained individual memorials to their fallen, and, in the course of my pilgrimage, I have many times asked myself whether there can be more potent advocates of peace upon the earth through the years to come, than this massed multitude of silent witnesses to the desolation of war. And I feel that, so long as we have faith in God's purposes, we cannot but believe that the existence of these memorials will, eventually, serve to draw all peoples together in sanity and self-control, even as it has already set the relations between our Empire and our allies on the deep-rooted bases of common heroism and a common agony.[14]

To visit Verdun today you can almost hear the echo of those words when you stand outside the Douaumont Ossuary and survey the multitude of graves. Yet if you venture into the tranquil forest around the town you will find a clearing, just below the remains of a World War I trench, where fourteen resistance fighters were shot by the Nazis during World War II. The forest is silent and still, as if it senses your sorrow—a sorrow

---

14. Ziino, *A Distant Grief*, 117.

that should have ended for all time in 1918. Yet, in the midst of a huge memorial to death, it happened again.

6

A Peace for the World?

Was the aftermath of this "Great War" a promise of lasting peace? In fact, in some ways, war never ceased—anti-war feeling and, in some cases, pacifism, was strongly evident in those countries that had been victorious in World War I. The killing and bloodshed continued almost unabated in many of those countries that were the vanquished. As German soldier Ernst Jünger commented in 1918: "This war is not the end but the beginning of violence. It is the forge on which the world will be hammered into new borders and new communities. New moulds want to be filled with blood, and power will be wielded with a hard fist."[1]

The year 1919, the first year of peace, saw German soldiers still fighting from the Baltic to the Black Sea. They were attempting two things: "to contain Bolshevism and to secure the eastern border with the newly formed Polish state."[2] In Germany itself a socialist democratic republic had replaced the monarchy: the Kaiser and his family were now in exile. But almost immediately Bolshevik adherents attempted to proclaim a German Soviet Republic—the resultant battle in the streets of Berlin saw the deaths of 1,200 revolutionaries and the execution of its leaders. The 1920s were a continual battle for supremacy amongst various factions. Although now a republic there were a few who vainly dreamed of restoring the monarchy whilst many of the population were either partly or wholly involved in some form of communistic belief. With the harsh penalties of the Treaty of Versailles and the continual refusal of France

1. Bessel, *Violence*, 103.
2. Palmer, *The German Wars*, 143.

over the following years to lessen the reparations due to the victors, conditions in Germany steadily worsened—exorbitant inflation; famine that brought starvation on an unprecedented scale; loss of primary resources and industry; confiscation of extensive areas of arable land; and high unemployment—all contributing to bringing the nation to a desperate level.

Germany was rife for a war of revenge. Conceivably bordered by future enemies and weakened by the Treaty's demands, the Germans could not even rely on diplomacy or agreements with other nations. No nation was prepared to be involved and Germany had little to offer in its present state. Nevertheless, the Germans, having a long militaristic culture, were the first of all the former combatants to study World War I in depth and to attempt to learn from it for the future. They meticulously listed what they saw as successes and published an army manual with discussions and directions for operations and maneuvers.

Reichswehr was the 100,000-strong army that Germany was permitted under the Treaty of Versailles. A prohibition from increasing this army or from manufacturing armaments made Germany vulnerable to the newly established nations on its borders—Poland and Czechoslovakia. This factor became a challenge the Germans were determined to overcome to the point that, very early, Germany had in place a secret mobilization scheme. In addition, one of the ways the fighting force was inadvertently supplemented was by the establishment of the Freikorps, the Free Corps movement. Because of the volatile situation in German politics immediately after the cessation of war, volunteer groups of ex-soldiers were encouraged to join the Free Corps with the objective of keeping order in the streets. In many cases the regular army refused to fire on civilians causing unrest but the Free Corps, although not well equipped, were extremely disciplined and they came to be a dreaded body of enforcers. By 1921 the movement had grown to thousands in numbers and the Allies forced the German government to disband and disarm the corps although this decree was not embraced with much enthusiasm. Another militarized group at the same time was that organized by Ernst Röhm—when his Citizens' Militia was forced to disband, he retained his armory. Consequently, although Germany had an army restricted in numbers, it had access to a great number of trained men.

In 1926 a Russo-German treaty was signed in Berlin whereby each agreed to remain neutral if one was attacked. This of course upset other nations who worried, as it turned out with justification, that secret arrangements between the two countries may have been negotiated.

Germany was finding a way to build and strengthen its capacity for a future war. This was definitely the case. In fact, a small number of facilities were secretly set up in the Soviet Union. Much research and even military training were carried out. At four of these locations Russian factories manufactured weapons and munitions under the control of German personnel. There was also a chemical research center, a poison gas plant, and a flying school. After the war, investigation revealed that the majority of senior pilots in the Luftwaffe during World War II had been part of this "Russian" training in the late 1920s. Aircraft production also went ahead in secret. Factories were established clandestinely by Heinkel and Dornier in Sweden, Italy, and Switzerland. In fact, in late 1923 the Norwegian explorer Roald Amundsen met with Claude Dornier to investigate the possibility of using his planes in Arctic exploration. A more open operation in Germany itself was the establishment of the airline Lufthansa in 1926, which came about from the merging of Junkers and DAL and operated for civilian purposes. But all of the aircraft manufactured were designed to be capable of immediate conversion to war machines. In addition, from the 1920s onward, Germany became one of the world's experts in wireless radio. On the home front, associations under the guise of "sporting clubs" trained young men in military programs. These grew in popularity and consequently in numbers.

In Russia various groups were fighting for supremacy. There were broadly Red Russians and White Russians. The Bolsheviks were being attacked by a number of anti-Bolshevik armies, none of which was united with each other and all with differing strategies for gaining power and governing. Because of this lack of unity in leadership and objectives it was a situation destined for failure. Originally some of the allies lent support to some of these groups, either with fighting men or armaments, but gradually support from outside Russia was withdrawn and the killing continued. Lenin, who had returned from exile in 1917, consolidated the power of the Bolsheviks and by 1920 he was pursuing a reign of terror executing his opponents, either openly, or through the first of the show trials, which were so prevalent in the later dictatorship of Stalin. These spuriously devised trials found people guilty without the presentation of any evidence and resulted in death, exile, or long periods of imprisonment. Lenin was greatly influenced by the writings of Carl von Clausewitz who professed that war was a necessary part of politics to be used to achieve an end that could not be attained by normal means. Lenin's philosophy went even further, stating that the terror that comes with war was also essential and to deny this was to be grossly dishonest. Lenin pursued specific classes such as the clergy and the middle class, hounding and killing thousands. After his death, Stalin grasped the leadership of the Soviet States. His policies were even more extreme than those of Lenin. He reversed many of the changes that his predecessor had made to Communism—the New Economic Policy, for example, which had introduced some capitalistic programs to help solve the widespread starvation of the people and the impending bankruptcy of the state. Stalin went far beyond the principles of the founders of Communism, closing Russia off from the rest of the world and eliminating any classes of people who were profiting in any way. The Kulaks, the more prosperous of the peasant class, were mercilessly slaughtered or left to starve to death.

In Italy a similar form of dictatorship to that of the Bolsheviks came about under the leadership of Benito Mussolini. Originally the followers of Fascism were loyal Italians who had experienced the horrors of the trenches of World War I and had no wish to see a repetition of such brutal warfare. There were also those who had not fought but endured loathsome wartime privations. Both groups wanted to have a say in future governments and former soldiers were often given important positions in political ministries. The movement grew in numbers and developed an evil doctrine. Its chief exponent, Mussolini, eventually became Italy's prime minister and, as a result, Fascism became another example of one man ruling with an iron fist and tolerating no opposition. Whilst the major countries in Europe were attempting to find ways to cement a peaceful stability on the continent, Mussolini took the opportunity to undermine the findings of a naval conference held in London. His attitude conveyed the extremes to which he was prepared to go: "words are beautiful things, rifles, machine guns, ships, aeroplanes and canon are still more beautiful."[3]

Another dictator of this time was a monarch who survived World War I with his throne intact. King Alexander of Serbia became the ruler of the newly created amalgamation of the Balkan countries containing Serbs, Croats, and Slovenes—eventually known as Yugoslavia. He began his reign as a democratic ruler but, due to the constant conflict in his parliament, and the assassination of the leader of the Croat Peasant Party in 1929, Alexander abolished the constitution and set himself up as an absolute ruler. Any person who attempted, in any way, to overthrow the rule of the king was to be condemned to death immediately. Attempting

---

3. James, *Europe Reborn*, 138.

to bring Serbs, Croats, and Slovenes together as one nation with dissolution of their historic borders and rights resulted in terrorism, arrests, imprisonment, and executions.

There were ongoing conflicts all over the globe. In Jerusalem there was the struggle between Arabs and Jews—the British Mandate for Palestine had been established after the fall of the Ottoman Empire at the end of World War I as a homeland for the Jews. There was always going to be contention between the Jews and the Arab Muslims especially in the matter of Jerusalem, which both parties held to be crucial to their religion. Killings were frequent and it seemed to be an unsolvable situation.

In the years following World War I there was a steady growth of nationalism in India. At the same time there was a ruthless struggle between Muslims and Hindus with hundreds of people killed in the continuing clashes. Mahatma Gandhi, an Indian who was trained in law in London, became the leader of the Indian National Congress in 1921 and led nationwide campaigns to ease poverty, to excise discrimination, to establish women's rights, to enable different religions to live and work together, to improve the lot of the "untouchables" and, ultimately, to bring an end to British rule in his country. He encouraged the people to be involved in passive resistance to achieve these aims. Unfortunately, it would be a long time before Gandhi saw success and the following years saw his recurring imprisonment as the British refused to relinquish their control. Lives were lost on both sides no matter how hard Gandhi tried to continue on a peaceful endeavor.

Mongolia had, for many years, been much influenced by Russia but, in 1919, China found the initiative to force out the Bolsheviks and the Cossacks and took over the control of Mongolia, redrawing the boundaries on the world map. Also unhappy with gains that Japan had achieved through the Treaty of Versailles, China made a strong attempt to drive out any pro-Japanese parties in the country. Here, in the 1920s, there was a repetition of the hatred of all foreigners, which had been so strong in the early 1900s and, once again, the Christian missionaries were the main casualties. Eventually in this period the whole of China was in turmoil with many warlords trying to gain control of various provinces. By 1926 it had developed into a struggle for power between the north and the south with numerous battles and much bloodshed. Out of all this emerged an adherent to Communist doctrine, Mao Tse-tung, who eventually became a great leader or a cruel dictator, depending on which historian you believe. But for many long years, between the two wars, there was a continuous civil war and even conflict in his own Central Committee of the Communist Party before Mao consolidated his seat of power. Meanwhile, in 1931, the Japanese invaded and occupied Manchuria in the north, claiming to be protecting the Japanese still living in that region.

In Ireland the establishment of the Irish Free State did not satisfy those who yearned for an independent united Ireland. It even came to a point where Roman Catholics and Protestants were becoming more militant and the battle for Home Rule involving the Irish Republican Army and the British "Black and Tans" dragged the population down into a mire of assassinations destroying families, most of who just wanted peace and a life without fear.

Thus, out of the ashes of World War I arose a frightening world. Where monarchs had once reigned, came an age of dictatorships. King, Kaiser, Emperor, and Tsar may not have been worthy of their exalted status and, in many cases, had precipitated their own descent from lofty thrones, but dictators brought a new age of suppression and cruelty and eventually another world war. From the peace deliberations arose an attempt to prevent such an event. The League of Nations was formed with its principal aim being to maintain world peace and prevent wars through disarmament and negotiations in disputes between countries. It also aspired to protect minorities, improve global health, advance conditions for workers, safeguard refugees, and prevent the trafficking of humans and drugs. Initially it worked to ensure that prisoners of war were returned to their home country. All these were noteworthy yet perhaps idealistic ideals but, nevertheless, by the end of 1920 the League had achieved a great deal of success, particularly in arbitrating between various countries in their disputes over borders and territories. In contrast, by 1929 the League had much more difficulty when it was forced to re-examine the granting of past mandates.

The principal objective of enforcing disarmament was strewn with impassable obstacles. When detailed discussions began in 1929 it was found that this was going to be an impossible endeavor. Those countries that had been allowed to continue to arm themselves were obviously very reluctant to disarm, and those countries that had been forced to disarm by the Treaty of Versailles, were more than keen to rearm. Of course, trust was essential, but trust would prove to be unattainable. It has been seen that Germany, for example, was determined to rearm by fair or foul means—most commonly the latter—for fair means were never available to Germany at this juncture.

Part Two

World War II

> One thing I know is sure, and that's what I had remembered in my cell and scratched into the bricks of the Scheveningen prison wall. Jesus' last words before he returned to heaven were a promise. We all break our promises, but our Lord never does. He told us, "Lo, I am with you always."
>
> DIET EMAN AND JAMES SCHAAP,
> *THINGS WE COULDN'T SAY*, 1994[1]

---

1. Eman and Schaap, *Things We Couldn't Say*, 374.

7

From Humiliation to a Reich under Hitler

GIVEN THAT GERMANY WAS clandestinely rearming against the provisions of the Versailles treaty it was doing this to a background of massive and turbulent unrest amongst its own people.

A starving population, experiencing extreme bitter cold, often without proper shelter or economic means, became demoralized, surly, hopeless, and mentally depressed about the future. Suicide and abortion were on the rise. Hyperinflation gripped society. The professional class was slowly ceasing to exist as academics, teachers, doctors, and business executives left their positions and attempted to find laboring or farming work with its promise of a regular wage. Creativity and culture were fast disappearing due to people seeking first and foremost to just exist. Yet the Jazz Age had not bypassed Berlin and women there were wearing their hair short, smoking in public, and dancing the nights away challenging the puritanic Teutonic code.

The terms of the Versailles treaty were harsh—Germany lost its overseas territories and colonies to the victors and the French, in particular, were seen as being responsible for the destruction of the economy. They occupied the rich Ruhr Valley and reaped the industrial advantages. With other allies they consistently refused to extend any mercy to Germany, rebuffing German approaches to lower the rate and timing of the reparations to be paid. But the most contentious clause of the treaty, which at first the Germans refused to sign, was the fact that Germany and its people had to acknowledge that they, and they alone, must take responsibility for the war and its consequences. This collective guilt was felt by Germany to be wholly unjust. Dietrich Bonhoeffer, when speaking in the United States in 1930, expressed his assessment of Germany's guilt:

> Let me tell you frankly that no German and no stranger who knows well the history of the origin of war believes that Germany bears the sole guilt of the war—a sentence which we were compelled to sign in the Treaty of Versailles. I personally do not believe, on the other hand, that Germany was the only guiltless country, but as a Christian I see the main guilt of Germany in quite a different light. I see it in Germany's complacence, in her belief in her almightiness, in the lack of humility and faith in God and fear of God. It seems to me that this is the meaning of the war for Germany: we had to recognize the limits of man and that means we discovered anew God in his glory and almightiness, in his wrath and his grace.[1]

The new Weimer Republic, floundering amidst these overwhelming pressures, proved to be weak and indecisive. There was no one strong leader who had the courage to tackle the problems or even to bring some semblance of order to the Reichstag. In addition, a major development in reaction to Germany's situation was the rise of the Bolshevik movement with many people joining the fast-growing Communist Party and looking to the east for solutions. Into this time of turmoil stepped an angry, disenchanted, and poorly educated World War I veteran—Adolf Hitler. From the early 1920s Hitler had been working on the development of Nationalsozialismus (National Socialism). His small political party, the National Socialist Workers' Party, was the origin of Nazism. With meticulous care he designed the symbols that came to be known throughout Germany and the western world—the eagle, the swastika, and the many other party emblems, to be part of the distinctive uniforms worn by his adherents. Not only would he spread his message effectively by preaching and literature, but the Nazis would always be recognized constantly in the daily life of the nation. With impressive organizational ability and cunning manipulation of both the Reichstag and the people, Hitler ensured his party grew in numbers and power. By January 1933 he had become the chancellor of Germany. "The land of Goethe, Schiller, and Bach would now become led by someone who consorted with crazies and criminals, who was often seen carrying a dog whip in public. The Third Reich had begun."[2] Such was the strength of Germanic nationalism that

---

1. Bonhoeffer and von Wedemeyer, *Love Letters from Cell 92*, 268.
2. Metaxas, *Bonhoeffer*, 138.

this unbalanced man was able to draw the people into his quest for a Greater Germany with the acquisition of lands where German peoples had settled. Then, in 1940, he ventured further to overrun the hated enemy, France; the nation that had been the cause of abject humiliation:

> Hitler and Germany had waited twenty-three years for this triumphant moment, and if ever Hitler became the Saviour of the German nation, this was it. Many Germans who had reservations and misgivings about Hitler now changed their opinions. He had healed the unhealable wound of the First War and Versailles. He had restored a broken Germany to her former greatness. The old had passed away, and behold, he had made all things new. In many people's eyes he was suddenly something like a god, the messiah for whom they had waited and prayed, and whose reign would last a thousand years.[3]

---

3. Metaxas, *Bonhoeffer*, 363.

8

The Scourge of Nazism

CLAUDIA KOONZ, IN HER valuable study *The Nazi Conscience*, establishes how Hitler, at the beginning of his acquisition of power, was able to persuade a German nation to accept him as an absolute ruler ready to solve all the problems that the country faced. Being a gifted orator and ". . . always an astute reader of his audiences' desires, [he] heard Germans' hunger for a government they could trust and a national purpose they could believe in . . . Hitler transformed his followers' anger at cultural and political disorder into moral outrage. In place of the Weimer Republic, which he ridiculed as weak and feminine, Hitler promised the dawn of a resolute masculine order."[1] The primary continual thrust of his platform was the "Volk." This is a somewhat difficult word to translate and in German can mean "folk," such as a simple, uncultured people; the people in the ethnic sense; or the people of the nation. It was a type of combination of the three that Hitler intended, emphasizing the need for the German people to put aside personal ambitions, wealth, egotism, and selfishness to become one people, one "Aryan" race of pure blood, devoted to the community and thus to the German nation. In a further devious but clever interpretation, Hitler developed the Volk to encompass the "Nazi" conscience. Conscience became fluid—not bound by any already established moral laws but able to be adapted to a specific purpose; in this case, the purpose of building a strong and pure community. This was the way he was able to convince people to turn against Jews (and others) to prevent the contamination of true Germans. Thus, a greater

---

1. Koonz, *The Nazi Conscience*, 2.

and stronger nation would evolve. Koonz states: ". . . what is frightening about the racist public culture within which the Final Solution was conceived is not its extremism but its ordinariness—not its savage hatreds but its lofty ideals."[2] She uses an example of how a German, on seeing his Jewish friend transported, was not distressed that Jews were being victimized but upset that his friend happened to be a Jew. It can be seen how Germans were able to go beyond the personal and see a greater purpose in such horrific policies even condoning the euthanasia of the elderly, the demented, and the mentally and physically handicapped to prevent their genes from infecting future pure Aryans.

This study on the Nazi conscience fills a gap in the past research into Nazi ideals and practices. There has to be a greater explanation as to why some Germans constantly carried out ghastly acts and other Germans either acquiesced or ignored what was going on in the community. Koonz is enlightening and plausible in her conclusions. She details many of the devious methods used to "Nazify" the nation—from adapting the day-to-day culture for its own means, the use of specific words to transform thinking, the adaptation of new phrases "like 'Hitler weather' for a sunny day,"[3] to behind the scenes assault, extortion, and blackmail when open methods did not succeed. It was a slow but successful procedure. Those of the public who were not at first convinced were prepared to watch and wait because economic conditions were improving. Many clubs and societies for men, women, and even children were established to further the ideal of Nazi life through guileful education.

The most effective tool used to influence the masses was Nazi propaganda and Adolf Hitler perfected its use:

> Hitler was adamant that major principles of National Socialist ideology should be repeated relentlessly so followers would acquire a familiarity with them verging on religious certainty. In his words, the 'most brilliant propaganda technique will yield no success unless one fundamental principle is borne in mind constantly and with unflagging attention. It must confine itself to a few points and repeat them over and over.' The 'art of propaganda', in his view, consisted of 'putting a matter so clearly and forcibly before the minds of the people as to create a general conviction regarding the reality of a certain fact. It was through this process of propangandizing with a hammer, as it were, that

---

2. Koonz, *The Nazi Conscience*, 2.
3. Koonz, *The Nazi Conscience*, 73.

Nazism bridged the gap between theory and practice: by drilling his followers in ritualized, popular forms, ideological principles became a liturgy in action.[4]

Propaganda was daily used on radio, in newspapers, at lectures, and rallies not only by Hitler and Joseph Goebbels but through many other committed Nazis. Every proclamation was replete with constant repetition, an incredible use of synonyms, and abounding in imagery. There was little logic or reasoning, just a memorizing mantra. Walter Gross, who created the National Socialist Office for Enlightenment on Population Policy and Racial Welfare, used every process of crooked thinking to promote the cause: "He delivered a virtual sermon to women on the theme 'You are nothing. Your Volk is everything' and told them how fortunate they were to be 'little drops in the mighty bloodstream of the Volk.'"[5]

In 1939, a series of German propaganda talks and German press articles was compiled by W. G. Knop and published under the title *Beware of the English!* Given the fact that the German press, wireless services, and film industry were wholly controlled by Dr. Goebbels, Minister of Propaganda, these discourses form the almost sole view of the English by the general German public: ". . . this book reveals they are being doped day by day, month by month, year by year."[6] Hitler and Goebbels, by words, specifically captioned photographs, and cartoons, outlined the dangers of ignoring the devious intentions of Germany's protagonist. It is worthy of note that each previous propaganda campaign engineered by the government, "whether directed against Austria, Czechoslovakia, Spain, or Lithuania, has been followed by events which could not fail to keep the German public receptive and submissive to the next onslaught of its controlled Press and wireless."[7]

The thrust of the propaganda in *Beware of the English!* follows several criteria.

The prospective new leaders of England, namely Winston Churchill, Duff Cooper, and Anthony Eden, were proven warmongers dedicated to secretly rearming for war and influencing other nations to turn against Germany. These men wished to destroy the totalitarian regime, but Hitler asserted that he had been elected both by the democratic vote of the

---

4. Dennis, *Inhumanities*, 15.

5 ' Koonz, *The Nazi Conscience*, 114–15.

6. Knop, *Beware of the English!*, xi.

7. Knop, *Beware of the English!*, xiv.

people and the Reichstag. He further asserted that a democracy was a capricious system because it relied on the whim of whoever was at the head, whereas by totalitarian rule "our people, which under the leadership of Adolf Hitler has strained every nerve to rebuild its country and has proved itself able and willing to work."[8]

Hitler's system of government was not only strong and productive but had permanency. His dictatorial government was able to achieve the democratic rights of the people by studying and anticipating their needs. The problem was that when their needs were not appreciated by Hitler and Goebbels, propaganda convinced them otherwise and this propaganda used history as one of the methods of proof. In several speeches England's past cruelty is highlighted—the opium trade in China, the slave traffic from Africa, the Boer war crimes where Britain instigated the first concentration camps for Boer women and children, and the atrocities in Palestine: "During an attack on the Arab village of Attil five people were deliberately chosen and tortured. They were beaten over the head. *Then their eyes were put out.* After they had been mutilated in this ghastly way they were finally given the *coup de grace*."[9] Nevertheless, the articles proclaimed, England wanted to be the governess of the world but was not in a position to criticize or interfere. England of the 1930s was comprised of arrogant men and shallow women. Class consciousness and loose morals abounded. Yet it ignored its poor—a report of the Ministry of Education on the health of schoolchildren demonstrated that, generally, "every fifth child is suffering from undernourishment."[10]

The Archbishop of Canterbury, then Dr. Lang, also came in for judgment for his prayers of support for the Jewish people. John 8:44 is quoted as proof that Jesus called the Jews liars and murderers; children of the devil. Just as men and women today are still using Bible quotations to suit their own agendas, Hitler was taking the words of Christ completely out of context and failing to recognize that Jesus himself was a Jew. Jesus is talking specifically to those Jews who did not recognize him as the Son of God for they were spiritually blind. The Jews who believed were the sheep of his fold whom he loved and protected (John 10:14–15 NRSV). Only then does Jesus say that believing Gentiles will also be part of his flock (John 10:16 NRSV).

8. Knop, *Beware of the English!*, 52.
9. Knop, *Beware of the English!*, 68.
10. Knop, *Beware of the English!*, 73.

An impressive book, *Inhumanities*, "is an unprecedented account of the ways Nazi Germany manipulated and mobilized European literature, philosophy, painting, sculpture, and music in support of its ideological ends."[11] The content of the German press also included contorted biographical details of persons of history and culture. German backgrounds were emphasized or fatuous links made with Germanic or Nordic origins, for example, Franz Liszt was born and reared in Hungary so there was an emphasis that he came from an "almost purely German area of Hungary"[12] and that Liszt "hardly understood a word of Hungarian: he heard only German in his parents' home and at school."[13] George Frideric Handel, although he lived most of his life in England, remained a true German because he never mastered the English language and retained two German servants in London. German bloodlines were found (or invented where necessary) for cultural giants of history. Where there were Jewish persons of note it was stressed that their only claim to fame was in works that owed their strength and beauty to an abundance of adopted Germanic attributes. There were no specific Jewish cultural achievements that could stand alone. Closely aligned with the Jewish cultural perversion was the Bolshevik threat—Communism was beginning to take hold in Germany and needed to be crushed. By convincing the masses that Bolshevism would create a paradise on earth, Stalin and his Russian cohorts had produced millions of feebleminded and fainthearted workers who were submissive to the political and warlike desires of their leaders. From all this discord Hitler resolved to build a new and narrow view of German culture for the "Volk"—it would be a Nazi Renaissance.

Nevertheless, how could a country who had produced such a plethora of scientists, philosophers, historians, artists, musicians, and writers over hundreds of years—for example, Johann Wolfgang von Goethe, Immanuel Kant, Adolf von Harnack and Ludwig van Beethoven—come under the influence of a narrow, stifling dictatorship where the human spirit was imprisoned within a doctrine of the "Volk" and where community encompassed all and designated any individuality as evil and selfish. From the Reformation of Martin Luther to the theologians of the nineteenth century who claimed to have recovered the real spirit of Christianity from the strictures of the church, Germany had given

---

11. Dennis, *Inhumanities*, front jacket.
12. Dennis, *Inhumanities*, 33.
13. Dennis, *Inhumanities*, 34.

birth in two momentous periods to a vitalized Christianity. In the sixteenth century, Martin Luther had certainly reformed Christianity, taking it back to its true source, Christ alone and his Word, rejecting the superfluous teachings of the Roman Catholic Church with its worship of Mary and the Saints, the diverse religious powers invested in a corrupt priesthood, and the excessive list of sacraments. In the nineteenth century, German theologians were the leaders in theological liberalism. They emphasized the uniqueness of the individual and the individual's experience as a source of meaning; a concept that Hitler rejected as self-serving. Yet liberal thinkers were more open to applying religious thought to the trends of everyday culture. Thus, in some ways, these same liberal thinkers could take on Hitler's emphasis on the community as a social commitment even though it might mean they would be sacrificing their individual worth. Liberal theology was man-centered rather than Christ-centered and Nazism presented a purpose for German mankind solely instituted and controlled by man. In the theological faculties of German universities of the time, professors and lecturers adhered to the historical–critical method pioneered by Friedrich Schleiermacher, and advocated by the great church historian Adolf von Harnack. Theological liberals like Harnack felt it was "unscientific" to speculate on who God was; the theologian must simply study what is there, which is to say the texts and the history of those texts. Karl Barth, who was exiled from Germany in 1934 for his theological approach, became a formidable opponent of the establishment with the publication of his commentary on Romans in 1922. Those theologians who agreed with Barth, the Barthians, disagreed emphatically with the liberals. The words and genre of the texts was not merely an exercise in historical study. God revealed himself through the texts. The whole reason for the presence of these texts was to know God. In many ways it can be understood that, in the beginning, the liberal-minded theologians were willing to approach Nazism with somewhat open minds—you could almost say that they were not even sure of the existence of God.

This is the strange perspective of Hitler's enormous influence—the fact that so many academics and intellectuals were swept along on the tide of change. There were a few extremely influential leaders in various erudite fields whose support of Hitler and his Nazi regime certainly swayed others to follow. Martin Heidegger, a leading philosopher, and Carl Schmitt, a noted political theorist, were two who were carried along with the intoxication of the new movement. But perhaps the most surprising of all was the unbridled enthusiasm of Gerhard Kittel, a Protestant theologian and brilliant lexicographer of biblical languages. He embraced the antisemitism of the Nazis even though his father had been an Old Testament scholar and he himself had taken numerous courses in rabbinic theology. He had always encouraged Jewish–Christian theology, acknowledging that Christianity had its roots in Judaism. However, his views, under the influence of the Volk doctrine of Hitler and his cohorts, began to emphasize the superiority of Christians over Jews—as it can be interpreted that Paul stated men and women were equal in salvation but had differing roles and status, so Kittel saw the Jews as lesser human beings in practice, with even a Jewish convert to Christianity not having the same human value as an Aryan Christian. Even using Paul's teachings when it suited, Kittel believed that the Jewish Paul had perverted the gospel of Christ. His antisemitism developed to the point where he was advocating in lectures the stripping of citizenship and its privileges from the Jews some two years before the Nuremberg Race Laws of 1935. Many theologians feel that the influence that Kittel exerted during the Nazi era was indirectly responsible for the death of millions of Jewish outcasts. The irony of all this is that the German word "Kittel," also spelled "Kitl," means a white robe that served as a burial shroud for Jews.

Even the established churches also became a strange ally to Hitler's policies. Although Hitler quoted Christian teachings in his early years, his ultimate objective was to crush the church. His first step was to bring the various denominations under one umbrella of a German Christian Church. This of course greatly strengthened the state's control of the church—a situation that still exists today. A large percentage of the clergy accepted this move, probably reasoning that as one larger body they might have more influence with the people and perhaps even with the state.

Interestingly, the opponent of theological giants of the time, Karl Barth, was himself originally a supporter of liberal theology, but he grew in his studies to reject its teachings, eventually becoming a formidable advocate of evangelicalism. He openly rebelled against Hitler's takeover of the German Church. He, together with Hans Asmussen, drafted the Barmen Declaration of 1934, which proclaimed that the church could not be run by Hitler because it was the sole dominion of God alone and Christians could only submit to God and his Word. Barth had quite early realized he could not follow the liberal teachings of his former university lecturers when they supported the Kaiser and his policies at the outset of World War I. Thus, his Christ-centered faith made it also impossible for him to support a "Nazi" church, and he was barred from continuing his academic profession. Barth was forced to return to his native Switzerland where he took up a professorship at the University of Basel.

Following Hitler's rise to power it became obvious that one of the major objectives of the new Germany was to eliminate the Jewish people from German lands, originally by transportation to far away countries such as Madagascar—a policy that proved impossible to implement—and finally to extermination, either by working and starving Jews to death, or by execution. Until the 1930s, antisemitism had not been a major problem in Germany. There were many Jews of note in the professions, public and diplomatic services, and the army to name just a few. In the community "More Jewish young people married Christians than married Jews, and until 1933 the term 'mixed marriage' referred to Protestant-Catholic and African- or Asian-German unions, not to Jewish-Christian couples."[14] However Nazi doctrine was founded on racial and ethnic purity. "Germans did not become Nazis because they were anti-Semites; they became anti-Semites because they were Nazis."[15] In pursuit of his ethnic community, Hitler set about persuading those in positions of authority to be perpetrators of racial extermination and these zealots succeeded in exceeding all the required objectives. Any undesirables who would taint the Germanic ideal were included—Jews, Bolsheviks, gypsies, political activists, homosexuals, prostitutes, pederasts, and the physically and mentally disabled. Jews, in particular, were demonized as greedy, lecherous, and even murderous, and as having undue influence in politics and the financial and legal sectors.

In regard to the "Jewish Question" and its proposed solution, the number of people having the courage to stand up to the Nazis was unfortunately too few to stem the tide. As already noted, icons of intellectual society such as Gerhard Kittel made a great deal of impact in learned communities. Another whose writings the Nazis used in their justification for antisemitism was Martin Luther. Because Luther had exemplified what it was to be a true German Christian, with Christ alone as his Savior, his words still held authority in the Germany of the times. But Luther in his last years was plagued with an incredible number of debilitating physical ailments in addition to ongoing depression—he became moody, angry, and absorbed in scatology. He had spoken and written vile things

14. Koonz, *The Nazi Conscience*, 9.
15. Koonz, *The Nazi Conscience*, 10.

about the Jews, and these specific words were used by the Nazis to promote their cause. However, as is often the case, the final words he used were taken out of context. Luther could not be accused of having racial views; rather, he was frustrated because his efforts to convert many of the Jewish people had fallen on stony ground.

Among the general public most Germans embraced whatever appeared to be the lesser evil but there were only degrees of evil prevalent in the Volk. It was easier to believe that the Jews were being transported to attractive work camps than to death camps; it was easier to believe that transportation was better than the beating of Jews and the destruction of their businesses in the streets of their cities; it was safer to keep silent when friends, neighbors, and even children were keen to report any examples of opposition to official policies. Racial "purification," which involved primarily the elimination of the Jewish race, grew slowly and insidiously after the initial brutal actions of the SA (Sturmabteilung, meaning "Storm Battalion") under Ernst Röhm, progressing to a massive program under the auspices of Heinrich Himmler, Reinhard Heydrich, Adolf Eichmann and the SS (Schutzstaffel). In January 1942 at the Wannsee Conference in Berlin, Heydrich, remembered in history as the "Butcher of Prague," announced that the official policy of the government was to be the total annihilation of the Jewish people. If this program was part of Hitler's plan, most people—especially in the beginning—ignored the consequences. Hitler, not God, was to be their salvation.

Besides the work of the SA and the SS to rid Germany of the Jewish threat, one of the greatest proponents of antisemitism was the propaganda icon of Nazism—Dr. Joseph Goebbels. A failed journalist and writer, wooden and puppet-like in his early speeches, Goebbels used various methods to promote his message. He published a vitriolic weekly newspaper attacking the Jews. This well presented, illustrated paper was prevalent with lies but eventually most people began to believe its contents. Legitimate journalists were given interviews and seemed to be unaware of how Goebbels manipulated them with his cordial reception and smarmy words. He also embraced the new medium of color film and used cutting-edge directors to publicize the enormous Nazi rallies. In addition he painted a frightening picture of what the German people faced if they lost the war—slavery or extermination! Always moving with innovative methods of spreading the message, Goebbels stated: "This is the secret of propaganda—the saturation of a group of people with propagandist ideas without their even noticing it. Of course propaganda has a goal but the goal must be so clever and so brilliantly concealed that the people who are influenced by it don't notice anything."[16] Like Hitler, Goebbels knew he had to keep his message simple, but to repeat it again and again to enforce its effect—even a lie constantly repeated is eventually taken as truth.

A study on the SS by Adrian Weale demonstrates that the majority of the vicious barbarity of Nazism, especially against the Jews, was carried out by the SS and the Gestapo (the Secret State Police). The SS was originally set up as a small local protection squad for Hitler and his National Socialist German Workers' Party (Nationalsozialistische Deutsche Arbeiterpartei, or NSDAP) in 1925. The party did have a paramilitary force—the SA, referred to earlier—but its members were mainly street thugs and its practices and brutality soon became harmful to Hitler's cause. By the 1930s the SA had been eliminated, with its leader Ernest Röhm and his cohorts summarily murdered on charges of homosexuality. In contrast the members of the SS were to be the elite—perfect Nordic specimens. When Himmler took the helm in 1929 he strove to develop in the SS, "an image of respectability, exclusivity and discipline"[17] in addition to the requirements of racial purity and physical health, "aloof from the violence and corruption of the SA rabble."[18] Striving for aristocratic recruits he even managed to secure the services, as his adjutant, of Josias Erbprinz zu Waldeck und Pyrmont, a nephew of the Dutch Queen. Himmler was so obsessed with having a higher class of German in his SS that he spent an inordinate amount of time and money trying to obtain the only known copy of *Der Codex Aesinas* from an Italian nobleman. This document traced the history of the Germanic race from earliest times. Eventually Himmler was able to obtain a photocopy of the work. He then selected the passages that described the idealized German to use for propaganda purposes. Sections that chronicled drunken behavior and debauchery were ignored.

From being originally a purely political body, the SS soon took over the role of dealing with the problem of Jews, Communists, and any other nominated enemies of the NSDAP. It was active in the nation's courts, in political indoctrination, and in intelligence and security work. Members were also overseers of the first concentration camps, initially established

---

16. Knopp and Hartl, *Joseph Goebbels*, 1996.
17. Weale, *Army of Evil*, 53.
18. Weale, *Army of Evil*, 53.

to house political prisoners, social misfits, and criminals. The daily duties were designated to prison "trustees," generally the criminals whose methods were barbaric. Also, under the auspices of the SS in pursuit of the Volk, the pure Aryan society, a program of euthanasia and sterilization was instituted. The victims were initially the physically and mentally disabled but the agenda was extended to include alcoholics, those feebleminded in appearance or behavior, and social deviants. Parents were forcibly persuaded to send disabled children to hospitals to be cured but were later informed of their deaths due to natural causes or epidemics. Some doctors and nurses almost felt privileged to partake in a program of purifying the race, bolstered by examples of the ancient Spartans and of reported instances of euthanasia condoned in current-day America.

Unfortunately, this was true. In the 1930s America was fascinated with genetics. Pseudoscientists instigated procedures that they felt would strengthen the human race. The primary objective was to cull all persons deemed unfit. Listed were the mentally slow, physically disabled, epileptics, people suffering from any kind of nervous affliction, the certified insane, alcoholics, drug addicts, criminals, and all women who had sex out of wedlock. Even deaf, dumb, and blind people, and children who were orphans were included. Those deemed the worst offenders became patients in hospitals where they were injected or orally dosed with infected substances to bring about fatal illnesses; others were sterilized. In total, some 20,000 persons in California were officially sterilized.

In Nazi Germany scientific experiments on the corpses that resulted from the practice of euthanasia led many to believe that such research would be invaluable for future generations. This was the beginning of mass murder in Germany. The doctors and nurses who took part in these monstrous procedures often felt they were carrying out a laudable act. Many Germans, in the years since World War I, had become somewhat immune to death.

> Karl Bonhoeffer, the chairman of the German Psychiatric Association and father of Dietrich Bonhoeffer, . . . said in 1920: It could seem as if we have witnessed a change in the concept of humanity. I simply mean that we were forced by the terrible exigencies of war to ascribe a different value to the life of the individual than was the case before, and that in the years of starvation during the war we had to get used to watching our patients die of malnutrition in vast numbers, almost approving of this, in the knowledge that perhaps the healthy could be kept

alive through these sacrifices. But in emphasising the right of the healthy to stay alive, which is the inevitable result of periods of necessity, there is a danger that the self-sacrificing subordination of the strong to the needs of the helpless and ill, which lies at the heart of any true concern for the sick, will give ground to the demand of the healthy to live.[19]

In a further attempt to achieve racial purity and rid Germany of the Jews, gypsies, Communists, homosexuals, alcoholics, drug addicts, and other undesirables, hundreds of camps were constructed, called "work camps" but, in reality, camps where inmates labored for the Reich with little food and brutal treatment, eventually succumbing to death by starvation, brutal beatings, or being torn apart by guard dogs. One of the first was Dachau, established in the suburbs of Munich, initially for political prisoners; one of the most disparate was Ravensbrück, which was designed specifically for women. Very little was known about Ravensbrück and it was one of the last of the camps to be liberated. No records have survived but it is estimated that between 30,000 and 90,000 died there over a period of six years. One small testimony of a survivor is enough to demonstrate the heinous treatment of women there, many just young girls: "I remember a little French girl called Raymonde Sauvage, who had no strength left. So I said hold on to my belt and I'll pull you, and she did, but it was extraordinary because I felt nothing at all. She had the weight of a soul."[20]

In these camps, particularly the Jewish camps, SS doctors once more grasped the opportunity to conduct medical research, but this time on living bodies, conducting the most obscene and unimaginable operations generally without the use of anesthesia. The most active of the medical staff, Joseph Mengele, besides his work with adults where he transplanted limbs from one patient to another and injected the wombs of women with acid, had a fascination with twins. Any children who were twins were immediately transferred to the camp hospital for his experimentation. Some were sewn together whilst others were used as a placebo whilst his or her twin was the source of experimentation. Moshe Offer related:

> One day, my twin brother, Tibi, was taken away for some special experiments. Dr Mengele had always been more interested in Tibi. I am not sure why—perhaps because he was the older twin.

---

19. Weale, *Army of Evil*, 173.
20. Helm, *If This Is a Woman*, 394.

> Mengele made several operations on Tibi. One surgery on his spine left my brother paralyzed. He could not walk anymore. Then they took out his sexual organs. After the fourth operation, I did not see Tibi anymore. I cannot tell you how I felt. It is impossible to put into words how I felt. They had taken away my father, my mother, my two older brothers—and now, my twin.[21]

Other doctors at Auschwitz carried out experiments on young girls:

> The subjects were placed in an ultra-short-wave field. One electrode was placed on the abdomen and another on the vulva. The rays were focused on the ovaries. The ovaries were consequently burnt up. Owing to faulty doses several had serious burns of the abdomen and the vulva. One died as a result of these burns alone ... Sagittal and transverse sections of the ovaries were made. The girls altered entirely owing to hormonal changes. They just looked like old women ... Several died as a result of sepsis.[22]

When it was decided to systematically exterminate the Jews, initial methods proved expensive and too slow. Jews were made to dig ditches and then to undress. Standing on the edge of this ditch they were individually shot in the back of the head. This of course involved a lot of time and use a great deal of ammunition, so often the victims were just pushed in and buried alive. With the invention of gas trucks, in which Jews and other undesirables were crowded in and gas from the motor siphoned into the interior, the elimination moved slightly more quickly. After the banging and screamed ceased, work gangs of Jewish prisoners were assigned to pulling out the bodies and throwing them into a huge trench. The Jews who piled the corpses were often shot at the end of each working day. Some of the men either descended into madness or committed suicide when confronted with the bodies of their families. One of these men, Yakov Grojanowski, who later escaped, recorded his experiences in detail. He also told of discussions the men had in their cell during the night. Two men "lost their belief in God because he didn't concern himself with injustice and suffering. In contrast others, myself included, remained firm in our belief and said, like Mosche Asch, that the time of the Messiah was at hand."[23]

---

21. Lagnado and Dekel, *Children of the Flames*, 71.
22. Gilbert, *The Holocaust*, 374.
23. Gilbert, *The Holocaust*, 262–63.

Then to achieve their aim of extermination more efficiently, Himmler instituted the erection of "death" camps. Here huge gas chambers were built. When the victims arrived, they were told to undress in preparation for a bath. Women, and men not fit enough for work, were pushed into the gas chamber, doors closed, and gas forced in from above. One of the forced laborers recorded: ". . . forty minutes later we went in and carried the bodies out to a special ramp. We shaved the hair of the bodies, which were afterwards packed into sacks and taken away by the Germans. The children were thrown into the chamber simply on the women's heads. In one of the 'transports' taken out of the gas chamber, I found the body of my wife and I had to shave her hair."[24] This man, Chaim Hirszman, also told of other incidents: ". . . a transport with children up to three years old arrived. The workers were told to dig one big hole into which the children were thrown and buried alive."[25] He could not forget how the earth kept rising and falling until the children suffocated. All the adult bodies were examined for valuables: in the anus, the vagina, the mouth, the ears, etc. Gold teeth were extracted. The bodies were then burnt in the crematorium.

Those Jews who, by chance, evaded selection for the crematorium, faced a horrendous battle for survival. It was not the physically fit who necessarily survived but the mentally fit—those who avoided becoming self-absorbed in their situation. Inmates had to find some meaning or purpose to their existence and some future goal for their life. This became excruciatingly difficult when there was no fixed term of imprisonment and no encouraging signs to an end to their torments. "In the Nazi concentration camps, one could have witnessed (and this was later confirmed by American psychiatrists both in Japan and Korea) that those who knew there was a task waiting for them to fulfil were most apt to survive."[26] Ten years after liberation, Viktor Frankl wrote: "Our generation is realistic for we have come to know man as he really is. After all, man is that being who has invented the gas chambers of Auschwitz; however, he is also that being who has entered those gas chambers upright, with the Lord's Prayer or the Shema Yisrael on his lips."[27]

---

24. Gilbert, *The Holocaust*, 304.
25. Gilbert, *The Holocaust*, 305.
26. Frankl, *Man's Search for Meaning*, 104.
27. Frankl, *Man's Search for Meaning*, 134.

Many people did not even reach these camps—either dying at the point of arrest or in transit to the camps on freezing, crowded trains where no one had food or water and there was no room to sit or lie down for days at a time. As mothers boarded the trains with their babies, the babies were often torn from them and flung onto the tracks. The Germans were sadistic with regard to tiny children—they threw them into burning houses, stomped on them, and beat them with rifle butts. One mother who did reach the camp with her child, suffered the depths of horror: "A German guard took the baby by its legs and smashed it against the wall of the barracks until only a bloody mass remained in his hands. The unfortunate mother had to take this mass with her to the 'bath.'"[28] This systematic slaughter of European Jews, now known as the Holocaust, began in June 1941. "By the time Nazi Germany had been defeated, as many as six million of Europe's eight million Jews had been slaughtered."[29]

It seems logical that, in the depths of despair and with no hope, many Jews would lose their belief in their God—after all God had turned away from his chosen people and allowed them to become persecuted to the point of an horrendous death. A spokesman for the "Jews for Jesus" movement was once asked whether the faithful godly Jews from the Holocaust who nevertheless denied the messiahship of Jesus would be received into the heavenly kingdom. He was not prepared to discuss this dilemma. Paula Fredriksen, in her work *Augustine and the Jews*, looks at Paul's words to the Romans in relationship to the Jews. She establishes that Paul has a much broader vision of redemption:

> It is true, he says, that in spurning the gospel, Israel has proven to be disobedient and contrary (Romans 10:4, 18, 21 N). Does Israel's rejection of God's plan mean that God in turn has rejected Israel (11:1)? 'By no means!' Paul answers. The current situation, he urges, is both providential and temporary, for Israel's response to God's initiative is itself determined by God. For the present, God has chosen 'by grace' only a remnant of Israel ... So too he has currently 'hardened' the greater part of Israel (11:12). True, the Gentiles have taken precedent with respect to the gospel, but this, Paul warns them, was not due to any merit whatsoever on their part, but solely to God's surprising plan.[30]

---

28. Gilbert, *The Holocaust*, 457.
29. Gilbert, *The Holocaust*, 18.
30. Fredriksen, *Augustine and the Jews*, 62.

There is then a strong caution from Paul to the Gentiles to guard against being arrogant concerning their election.

> So that you may not claim to be wiser than you are, brothers and sisters, I want you to understand this mystery: a hardening has come upon part of Israel, until the full number of the Gentiles has come in. And so all Israel will be saved; as it is written, 'Out of Zion will come the Deliverer; he will banish ungodliness from Jacob.' 'And this is my covenant with them, when I take away their sins.' As regards the gospel they are enemies of God for your sake; but as regards election they are beloved, for the sake of their ancestors; for the gifts and the calling of God are irrevocable. Just as you were once disobedient to God but have now received mercy because of their disobedience, so they have now been disobedient in order that, by the mercy shown to you, they too may now receive mercy. For God has imprisoned all in disobedience so that he may be merciful to all. (Rom 11:25–32 NRSV)

Nevertheless, from the first century on, discrimination against Jews grew. This came firstly from the fact that Jews had killed Jesus—an actuality that Jesus himself and later Peter claimed. But Jesus was a Jew; he had been brought to the Temple on the eighth day to be circumcised, he observed the Law, he lived on earth as a pious Jew. The writers of the gospels and Paul "all considered themselves and looked on each other as Jews."[31] In Paul's letter to the Corinthian congregation, he rails against the boasting of so-called Christians whom he terms "false prophets": "Are they Hebrews? So am I. Are they Israelites? So am I. Are they descendants of Abraham? So am I. Are they ministers of Christ? I am talking like a madman—I am a better one." (2 Cor 11:22–23a NRSV) Paul continues relating his tribulations, including floggings at the hands of both Gentiles and Jews. Secondly, becoming a Jewish Christian brought dire problems. In those ancient times Jews had lived amongst pagans who had many gods. Judaism has been accepted and even respected as just another religion. Jews had even held public office and wealthy patrons had financed building of synagogues. However, with the seed of Christianity planted, converts became missionaries and threatened the status quo that had existed for centuries. The new Christians did not live well in a pluralistic society and refused to acknowledge the gods of pagan religions, thus threatening the perceived peace of the civic community. The major problem illustrated in the gospels and in Paul's letters was the continual

---

31. Fredricksen, *Augustine and the Jews*, 80.

debate about the correct way to be the gospel people of God and still retain their Jewishness. Eventually, ". . . like the Bible itself, the gospels, once they drifted out of their communities of origin into a wider Gentile world, were read as a standing indictment and perpetual condemnation of Jews and Judaism as such, rather than as a narrative exhortation to change from the wrong kind of Judaism to the right kind of Judaism . . . Jewish sectarian rhetoric, shorn of its native context, eventually became anti-Jewish rhetoric."[32]

An additional reason for the rise of anti-Judaism was the writings of prominent early Christian thinkers who were, as all erudite ancients, trained in Platonic philosophical thought and the exercise of the rhetoric. In various ways they rejected the Septuagint and its god. Marcion of Sinope, for example, believed that a true high god could not have created or subsequently been involved in a physical world where evil people fought wars, sacrificed in blood, and were sexually immoral. It was the antithesis between good and evil, flesh and spirit, law and gospel, works and grace, which led them to an inability to accept the Septuagint as a true precursor of the new Christian writings. So therefore, by demeaning the Jewish Bible, they demeaned the Jewish people. Finally, the consequences of the Jewish war with Rome from 66 to 73 AD resulting in the destruction of the Temple, and the Judean revolt against Rome from 132 to 135 AD crushed by Hadrian who then "eradicated Jewish Jerusalem, erecting upon its ruins a new pagan city, Aelia Capitolina,"[33] were events that further stirred up anti-Jewish polemic. "What else could such disaster measure, if not the depths of God's wrath? In short, by interpreting the whole sweep of biblical history from Cain to Caiaphas and beyond as the record of God's anger against the Jews, Christian theologians combined episodes in the Jewish Bible with these more recent disasters of the first and second century to produce a mass of mutually reinforcing arguments *adversus Judaeos*."[34] And in those ancient times, as today, Jews were different. Their stubborn adherence to an insular lifestyle alienated those amongst whom they lived.

The primary twentieth-century persecutor of the Jewish people, the SS, quickly grew in strength and influence from its small beginnings, dedicated to the elimination of these inhuman and morally corrupt Jews

---

32. Fredriksen, *Augustine and the Jews*, 81–82.
33. Fredriksen, *Augustine and the Jews*, 84.
34. Fredriksen, *Augustine and the Jews*, 85.

in the Nazi state. At the same time, the SS earned the disdain of the German army. The Waffen-SS, an armed military unit of the SS, was created to fight with the armed forces on the battlefield. They were to be the elite of the military but they instead became the force that followed after the main body of soldiers carrying out tasks that the army would refuse to condone. Armed with lists of leaders and influential people (both Gentiles and Jews) in the conquered country, they executed thousands, and sent many other Jews to the camps. As the war progressed it was not long before the Waffen-SS needed to recruit more and more soldiers. The original criteria for membership was consequently relaxed and foreign volunteers began to be accepted. In addition to Austrians, there were some Swiss recruits, and German citizens from Sudetenland, Bohemia, Moravia, and the Baltic states, and even ethnic Germans who had lived in Scandinavian countries for generations. Eventually the door was opened to non-German foreigners, including many men of dubious backgrounds. In fact, a concerted effort was made to form a Special Unit with hunters, poachers, and even hardened criminals being granted amnesty to be sharpshooters in the SS military corps. This particular unit was to be led by Oskar Dirlewanger, a sexually perverse alcoholic who had a murderous past.

Dirlewanger's men were responsible for the deaths of some two million people in Soviet Byelorussia—"by shooting, gassing, hanging, burning, drowning. A further 2 million were deported to the Reich as forced labour."[35] The Ukranian Archbishop, Count Andrij Scheptycky, wrote to Pope Pius XII: "When the German army first appeared to liberate us from the Bolshevik yoke, we experienced at first a feeling of some relief. But that lasted no more than one or two months. Step by step, the Germans introduced their regime of terrible cruelty and corruption . . . It simply appears that a band of madmen, or of rabid dogs, have descended upon the poor population."[36] One of the reasons Dirlewanger had such success was due to his brutality to his own men. This brutality bred further brutality and in Byerlorussia the country descended into a hell on earth. Bandits, in retaliation to the German invaders, in some cases sank to the same level of depravity: "Men found their comrades stripped naked,

---

35. Richie, *Warsaw 1944*, 27.
36. Richie, *Warsaw 1944*, 29.

having been beaten to death or dismembered. One came across a group of dead soldiers whose tongues had been nailed to a table."[37]

Hitler and his cohorts believed that the best way to rule over conquered territories was with cruel and savage oppression. Not only partisans, or as Himmler called them, "bandits," were to be executed, but innocent civilians also, as a punishment for activities of these bandits. Hitler greatly admired the actions of Generalfeldmarschall Freiherr von der Goltz, the military governor of Belgium during World War I, who declared: "It is the stern necessity of war that the punishment for hostile acts falls not only on the guilty, but on the innocent as well ... In the future, villages in the vicinity of places where railway and telegraph lines are destroyed, will be punished without pity (whether they are guilty of the acts in question or not). With this in view hostages have been taken in all villages near the railway lines which are threatened by such attacks. Upon the first attempt to destroy lines of railway, telegraph or telephone, they will immediately be shot."[38] Distressingly this policy of the Old Reich became an established model for the Third Reich.

The barbaric massacres in Byelorussia set the stage for the Pabst Plan in Poland. Hitler loathed Warsaw and set out to destroy the city and its inhabitants with a plan to erect a glorious German city in its place. In 1944, when the tide of war was turning rapidly against the Germans, Hitler, in his madness, deployed vital troops from the front to annihilate this historic center of culture and diversity. Dirlewanger and his criminal contingent were directed to this task. He boasted that Warsaw had no hope when he and his men had had a dress rehearsal in Byelorussia. One witness reported that when he saw the body of a tortured resistance fighter, "the lower part of her body was in shreds."[39] In addition to murder, rape, and torture, Dirlewanger was particularly cruel to the children: "A lot of children were standing on the stairs with raised hands. Lots of children. All with their little hands in the air. We looked at them for a while until Dirlewanger appeared. He ordered that they all be killed. They killed them and then stepped on the children's bodies, smashing their little heads with the butts of their guns. The stairs were covered in blood."[40] There were 350 children massacred.

37. Richie, *Warsaw 1944*, 60.
38. Bilton, *The Germans in Flanders, 1914*, 131.
39. Richie, *Warsaw 1944*, 154.
40. Richie, *Warsaw 1944*, 284.

The Scourge of Nazism

Whilst the human bloodbath, the bombing, and the continuous shelling continued, the Russians stood on the other side of the Vistula River ignoring the desperate cries of the Poles. The Allies also did nothing as both Churchill and Roosevelt were of the one mindset that it would not be diplomatic to upset their ally Stalin by interfering. "Ninety-eight per cent of the Jewish population of Warsaw perished in the Second World War, together with one-quarter of the Polish population: in all, some 720,000 souls . . . undoubtedly the greatest slaughter penetrated in a single city in human history."[41] More than 87 percent of buildings were destroyed—historical universities, churches, synagogues, museums, archives, and libraries, most housing untold treasures that were either looted or burnt.

When the German army retreated in Italy in 1944, it continued its policy of eradicating populations, destroying homes, and burning crops as it withdrew. In just three days the army, reinforced by SS combatants, butchered 1,800 Italian civilians—men, women, and children—plus a number of partisans at Monte Sole (Mountain of the Sun). The actions of these soldiers were deliberately nonchalant and totally reprehensible, yet their commander, Field Marshal Albert Kesselring, called it a normal war operation. As the Germans began shooting anyone in sight:

> Gilberto [a boy of 12] ran up the incline of bodies and jumped six feet through the air to the ground. Just in front of him the Germans were wrestling with a woman, and a baby lay alongside, screaming. Gilberto heard shots, but he kept running across the yard until he reached the edge of the vines. Two others were running with him, and as Gilberto jumped into the leaves, he heard the German clank by in pursuit of the others. Gilberto burrowed his bleeding body deeper into the vines, and he saw that a young girl was doing the same a few feet away. As he lay concealed by the leaves, he saw the Germans rope the young mother to the tree, place the baby in her arms, and lob grenades at them till both were only bits of shattered flesh. An elderly woman in a black dress ran across the fields that widened toward the brush a few hundred yards away, and she gasped for breath and stumbled as she ran. A Nazi followed a few yards behind, laughing and waving his pistol at the old lady, as though to encourage her flight. As Gilberto watched, the woman moved slower and slower, and finally fell to the mud of the field, her hand grasping her throat. The German grabbed her by her white

41. Richie, *Warsaw 1944*, 20.

hair with his free hand, turned her head slowly toward him, and shot her twice in the face.[42]

Retreating Germans destroyed everything in their path. They could not be reconciled to the undeniable demise of the Third Reich. The early easy successes built false hopes: the continual "expectation of a quick victory was one more demonstration of the inability of the Nazis to look at the world as it really was. Germany was ultimately defeated because its leaders lived in a world that they only imagined. Except for its moral depravity, the most striking feature of Nazism was its utter irrationality."[43]

The engagement of the unremitting heinous crimes cannot be laid completely in the domain of the SS. Transcripts of recordings made by the British (MI19) in German prisoner of war camps during and after the war years confirm that many ordinary soldiers took part in regular killing of the Jewish population. Some were encouraged by SS combatants but many others did so of their own volition. Himmler's propaganda had convinced the ordinary serving man that Jews were to be equated with sewer rats and those who were prepared to descend into the sewers to destroy the vermin were committing a noble act for the German people. It was abhorrent but necessary. In this surreal life of the German soldier was a vital component—one that is rarely known—the use of drugs by the German military. Whilst it is often documented that many of the high-ranking Nazis were addicted to various drugs, at the time this was a well-kept secret as the policy to the public was the extermination of undesirables such as drug addicts. Incredibly drugs were easily attainable.

After the cessation of the hostilities of World War I, both France and Great Britain still maintained their colonial outposts, thus they were always able to acquire natural stimulants such as coffee, tea, vanilla, pepper, and other natural medicines. Germany, however, having lost its colonial possessions under the terms of the Treaty of Versailles, had to find other ways— the solution was to produce synthetic stimulants. In fact, Germany had a far greater need of artificial assistance: "the war had inflicted deep wounds and caused the nation both physical and physic pain. In the 1920s drugs became more and more important for the despondent population between the Baltic Sea and the Alps."[44] Germany eventually became a global dealer in drugs. German chemical companies became prosperous manufacturing

---

42. Olsen, *Silence on Monte Sole*, 209–10.
43. Kenez, *The Coming of the Holocaust*, 152.
44. Ohler, *Blitzed*, 10.

morphine, heroin, and numerous other opiates. "Between 1925 and 1930, 91 tonnes of morphine were produced, 40 per cent of global production ... Peru sold its entire annual production of raw cocaine, over five tonnes, almost exclusively to Germany for further processing."[45]

During this same time, nightlife in Berlin became another antidote to depressing days. Immorality and all forms of perversity abounded. When the German currency collapsed in 1923, "Everything whirled apart in a toxicological frenzy."[46] "In 1928 in Berlin alone 73 kilos of morphine and heroin were sold quite legally on prescription over the chemist's counter."[47] But the Nazis condemned the practice. When Hitler came to power he was depicted as a teetotaller, nonsmoker, and an abstainer from coffee and other stimulants. He nevertheless knew "his situation required constant mental alertness, physical vitality and hands-on decisiveness."[48] To combat his ongoing neuroses and stomach problems he turned to what were loosely called vitamin supplements. The physician who became his personal doctor, always on call, was a great believer in injections as a substitute for thorough examination and tests, a situation which Hitler approved as he detested being touched unnecessarily. Dr. Morrell was also a prolific dabbler in opiates and his vitamin supplements invariably contained chemical components in an attempt to achieve success.

Other medical men were also working in this field. At the Berlin Olympics of 1936, Dr. Fritz Hauschild noticed the effect of Benzidine, then a legal doping product, on athletes from the United States. With intensive research and experimentation he developed in 1937 an even more effective Methylamphetamine, which was patented as Pervitin. On taking this drug people felt awake and alert, there were vast increases in energy, and all the senses became very acute. The brain seemed to be working almost overtime with thought processes clear and vital. Such was its attractiveness that the producers of this new wonder drug used innumerable innovative methods of marketing it to doctors, chemists, and the public. It came to be regarded as kind of panacea. Even methamphetamine chocolates were sold and women were encouraged to pop these little pills to ease the symptoms of menopause. Eventually 833,000 of these little pills could be pressed in one day. The Wehrmacht ordered a

45. Ohler, *Blitzed*, 11.
46. Ohler, *Blitzed*, 13.
47. Ohler, *Blitzed*, 15.
48. Ohler, *Blitzed*, 32.

supply of thirty-five million for the army and the Luftwaffe and, interestingly, they were later supplied to Japan for use by Kamikaze pilots.

Consumption by the army during the invasion of Poland in 1939 proved that Pervitin was an invaluable asset:

> War was seen as a task that needed to be worked through, and the drug seemed to have helped the tank units not to worry too much about what they were doing in this foreign country, and instead let them get on with their job—even if the job meant killing: 'Everyone fresh and cheerful, excellent discipline. Slight euphoria and increased thirst for action. Mental encouragement, very stimulated. No accidents. Long-lasting effect. After taking four tablets, double vision and seeing colours.' Even slight hallucinations, clearly perceived as pleasant, enchanted the men, soon to be heady with victory. 'The feeling of hunger subsides. One particularly beneficial aspect is the appearance of a vigorous urge to work.'[49]

What was not generally advertised was that these pills invested the user with an enormous arrogance, leading to unbelievable violent and brutal actions against enemy soldiers and innocent civilians alike.

The army was thrilled with the initial results: "An increase in performance is quite evident among tank drivers and gun operators in the long-lasting battles from 1 to 4 September 1939 and the reconnaissance division, which has used this substance with great success on tough long journeys at night, as well as to maintain and heighten attentiveness on scouting patrol operations."[50] Men could march, motorcycle long distances under dangerous conditions, drive tanks, scout territory, and function day after day without sleep. During the Blitzkrieg, one unit fought for seventeen days without rest. In the Soviet Union, when the Germans were attempting to retreat from the fishing village of Vzvad, where their accommodation had been destroyed and their rations greatly depleted, they faced a fourteen-hour march through heavy snow: "Soon many men were, as the official Wehrmacht report has it, in 'a state of extreme exhaustion . . . Enervated soldiers wanted to lie down in the snow; in spite of the energetic pep talks their will-power could not be revived. Such men were each given 2 Pervitin tablets."[51] With the soldiers after a

---

49. Ohler, *Blitzed*, 63–64.
50. Ohler, *Blitzed*, 65.
51. Ohler, *Blitzed*, 145–46.

short period able to march forward in line, Pervitin proved its value in endurance and survival in addition to the capacity for fearless fighting.

Eventually many harmful side effects surfaced but were largely ignored. Over time men developed a desperate dependency, had high blood pressure, suffered cardiac arrests, experienced psychoses, constant nervous excitement, intense itchiness, pain, depression, and nausea. At one stage the Luftwaffe banned its use because it jeopardized the lives of its pilots. The use of Pervitin continued throughout the war and in the closing years approximately two-thirds of users were suffering from psychoses. As the army marched onward on a diet of uppers, Dr. Morrell was daily injecting his patient, Hitler, with an unknown combination of chemicals, including large amounts of cocaine. When Hitler met with Mussolini he was able to talk uninterrupted for three hours. His long, boring monologues to his inner circle of henchmen were conducted almost every night when at his mountain retreat. All had to feign attention for the whole period. But, by 1943 it was obvious to this audience that Hitler was an ill, prematurely old man.

While the German warriors succumbed to the constant problems of Pervitin, the search for another wonder drug consumed the medical world but failure with dire effects was the result. The Führer's health continued to deteriorate and, by the final months of 1944, his appearance even aroused feelings of repugnance. He now was plagued by insomnia, wheezing, anxiety, loss of weight, dull eyes, and high temperatures and was ceaselessly fumbling and shaking and picking at his yellowing skin.

It has always been known that Göring and others were inveterate drug users—it was difficult to keep Göring's habit a secret. And yet to the public, Hitler espoused the great benefits of living a healthy and drug-free life. Behind this façade Germany was riddled with drugs. The Allies were amazed at the resilience and fighting strength of the enemy. How much shorter would this war have been, how many less atrocities would have occurred, how many lives would have been saved from death and destruction of health, if the government, which exterminated drug users, were prepared to practice what they preached. The acceptance of the use of opiates in the years after World War I opened the door to the acceptance of drugs for evil purposes in World War II.

With the publication of copious numbers of war veterans' diaries and memoirs in recent years, we are able to develop a realistic panorama of the bestiality and inhumanity of war. Even amongst this, many soldiers wrote some enduring prose and poetry, most of it penned in lulls between battles. World War I produced a plethora of soldiers' poetry—some idealistic works written in the early days of conflict and later poems depicting the real horror of war. During World War II, numerous fighting men again took up the pen. John Gillespie Magee Jr. had enlisted in the Royal Canadian Air Force and, just as one he greatly admired, Rupert Brooke, he was killed before he saw conflict. Magee collided with another fighter plane in a training flight and was unable to escape from the cockpit in time. The most well-known of his poems has been repeatedly cited in part in following years, most notably by President Ronald Reagan after the *Challenger* disaster of 1986.

> Oh, I have slipped the surly bonds of earth,
> And danced the skies on laughter-silvered wings;
> Sunward I've climbed, and joined the tumbling mirth
> Of sun-split clouds,—and done a hundred things
> You have not dreamed of—Wheeled and soared and swung
> High in the sunlit silence. Hov'ring there
> I've chased the shouting wind along, and flung
> My eager craft through footless halls of air . . .
> Up, up the long, delirious, burning blue
> I've topped the wind-swept heights with easy grace
> Where never lark or even eagle flew—
> And, while with silent lifting mind I've trod
> The high untrespassed sanctity of space,
> Put out my hand, and touched the face of God.[52]

John Magee Jr., by his early death, was absolved from the turmoil and fear that later airmen experienced when they partook in mission after mission to bomb, not only strategic industrial and military targets but, during the last months of the war, hundreds of thousands of innocent men, women, and children in cities such as Dresden and Hamburg. The depth of their guilt wrecked their lives and the lives of those they loved. In addition, because they were able to wreak such havoc, aircrews who crash-landed or bailed out over enemy territory were often set upon by the inhabitants and beaten to death rather than taken as prisoners of war.

---

52. Magee, "High Flight," August 6, 2017.

9

The Collaboration of the Christian Church

THE CHURCH IN NEW Testament times was "presbyterian" in government, i.e., each community of believers elected presbyters/elders who governed the church under the Lordship of Christ. This system was established in Acts and the various letters of Paul as the biblical norm. These elders had the responsibility of leading, teaching, and caring for Christ's flock. In Acts 15 we see where the first great council of the Church at Jerusalem appointed various men to be set aside as pastors so that, as the church grew, leaders from various regions could meet together to settle any doctrinal matters that might arise in the future. Nowhere in Scripture is one person appointed to be the earthly head of the Christ's church: ". . . you are citizens with the saints and also members of the household of God, built upon the foundation of the apostles and prophets, with Christ Jesus himself as the cornerstone. In him the whole structure is joined together and grows into a holy temple in the Lord; in whom you also are built together spiritually into a dwelling place for God" (Eph 2:19b–22 NRSV) and, "But you are a chosen race, a royal priesthood, a holy nation, God's own people, in order that you may proclaim the mighty acts of him who called you out of darkness into his marvellous light. Once you were not a people, but now you are God's people; once you had not received mercy, but now you have received mercy" (1 Pet 2:9–10 NRSV).

Sadly, almost immediately after the demise of the apostles, Christ's church began to become extremely institutionalized and a system of rule by bishops, with a primary bishop being the only person who had inherited the true apostolic wisdom, developed. "The unity of the church was thus based on the unity of the bishops."[1] "For Cyprian the criterion of church membership was submission to the bishop, and outside of such submission there was no salvation."[2] "The Papacy as we know it really began around 590. To Gregory I (c.540–604), the 'father of the medieval papacy', is ascribed the credit for establishing the temporal political power of the papacy within the Roman Empire. The papal resolve to dominate the life of every man in Europe received further support from the forged *'Donation of Constantine'* . . . in which Constantine reputedly ceded to Sylvester I (314–35) primacy over Antioch, Constantinople, Alexandria and Jerusalem, and dominion over all Italy, including Rome and the 'provinces, places, and civitates' of the Western half of the empire."[3] Thus developed the belief that, although in theory Christ was the head of the church, the Pope was his holy vicar and no person could receive salvation nor forgiveness of sins except through the Holy Catholic Church. "John Wycliffe (c.1329–1384), the 'Morning Star of the Reformation', in his *De potestate papae* maintained that the pope's claims were not grounded in Scripture, that his salvation was no more certain than that of any other man, and that the sole criterion of the rightness of his acts was their conformity to Scripture."[4] "But even if we or an angel from heaven should proclaim to you a gospel contrary to what we proclaimed to you, let that one be accursed!" (Gal 1:8 NRSV) Forgiveness of sins by any priest, repentance incorrectly translated as penance, the development of a concept of transubstantiation, the addition of sacraments other than those sanctioned in the New Testament, the infallibility of the church's councils, and even the claim that all popes had succession from Peter falsely declared as the first pope, were unscriptural and led to the church becoming part of the world rather than remaining the body of Christ.

Throughout the centuries the Roman Catholic Church continued to stray from biblical truths when exercising its doctrinal control over priests and people. A striking example is its attitude to the Jewish nation. Just as Judaism ignores the message of Isaiah 53 because it cannot accept the Messiah as a "suffering servant," so the Roman Catholic Church in World War II ignored Paul's teaching on the Jewish people in Romans 11. Since ancient times the church had absorbed the growth

---

1. Berkhof, *Systematic Theology*, 558.
2. Reymond, *A New Systematic Theology of the Christian Faith*, 838.
3. Reymond, *A New Systematic Theology of the Christian Faith*, 846.
4. Reymond, *A New Systematic Theology of the Christian Faith*, 849.

of "Adversus Iudaeos" in pagan and early Christian society as related earlier. But the New Testament writings recorded that Israel's rejection was not final. Again—noted previously—Paul points out that he himself is an Israelite, a descendent of Abraham, and that God has not rejected his people of Israel. There is a remnant of believers who accepted Jesus Christ as Savior. Christ has saved these believers from their sins and not from the Romans as the Jews had hoped. This remnant formed the first Christian community, the "church." God has not turned his back on the Jews who rejected Christ. He uses the analogy of an olive tree: "A shoot shall come out from the stump of Jesse, and a branch shall grow out of his roots" [The Messiah] (Isa 11:1 NRSV). Some of the branches of this Old Testament tree have been broken off (the non-believing Jews) and other wild branches grafted onto the tree (the remnant of believers). There is a warning that the believers should not become proud: "but stand in awe. For if God did not spare the natural branches, perhaps he will not spare you." (Rom 11:20b–21 NRSV) God has the power to graft in the Jews again. "As regards the gospel they are enemies of God for your sake; but as regards election they are beloved, for the sake of their ancestors; for the gifts and the calling of God are irrevocable." (Rom 11:28–29 NRSV)

Through the unbelief of some Jews, salvation came to the remnant and to the Gentiles. The Israelites were God's chosen people and though the followers of Christ are the new chosen people, "even those of Israel, if they do not persist in unbelief, will be grafted in, for God has the power to graft them in again. For if you have been cut from what is by nature a wild olive tree and grafted, contrary to nature, into a cultivated olive tree, how much more will these natural branches be grafted back into their own olive tree." (Rom 11:23–24 NRSV) In some future age the chosen people of the Old Testament will turn to faith in Jesus as the crucified and risen Messiah. This is clear from Romans 11: 26–36 and Isaiah 11:11.

The church could have played a decisive role in the treatment of the Jewish people but successive Popes chose not to. The Roman Catholic Church throughout history had never treated Jews well. In 1555, for example, Pope Paul IV stated that the Jews "had been condemned by God to 'eternal slavery' for their sin of murdering Jesus and refusing his teachings."[5] The Jesuits (Society of Jesus) were particularly antisemitic. "The charge that Jews were the evil force behind a worldwide conspiracy against Christianity and European civilization had long been heard in

---

5. Kertzer, *The Pope and Mussolini*, 12.

the Vatican; the Jesuits of *La Civilta cattolica* were among its most avid proponents."[6] In 1922 an article warned:

> The world's future would be determined by the battle then being waged in Russia. The leaders of the Bolshevik reign of terror were not 'indigenous Russians' but rather 'Jewish intruders' who slyly masked their true identity behind Slavic-sounding pseudonyms. A list of the 545 highest officials of the Bolshevik regime revealed, the author claimed, that true Russians numbered no more than thirty. 'Those of the Jewish race comprise a full 447'; the rest were a hodgepodge of other nationalities. In short, although Jews comprised less than five percent of Russia's population, 'this tiny minority today has invaded all the avenues of power and imposes its dictatorship on the nation.'[7]

Yet Russians themselves also had a paranoid hatred of the Jewish people. The government made sure they always took advantage of this situation. Whenever there was any discontent in the country, mobs of hooligans went on rampages, destroying Jewish property and even killing the people. The ruling committees took advantage of the riots to stifle any general discontent by making the Jews scapegoats. Thus, if the Jewish leaders went to the authorities asking for justice and protection, they were warned to improve their conduct. If the Jewish labor movement grew, for example, the minister for justice would be forced to take further action against all Jews. Thus pogroms grew in frequency and intensity over the following years.

Achille Ratti became Pope Pius XI in February 1922; Benito Mussolini became the Italian prime minister in November 1922. Pope Pius XI was self-important, arrogant in manner, unapproachable, curt, and prone to angry outbursts, yet desperate to increase the power and influence of the Roman Catholic Church. Mussolini was also self-important—"an odd mixture of geniality and vulgarity."[8] Capable of expressing noble sentiments whilst carrying out vendettas against possible enemies, Mussolini had no experience or training in running a government but possessed exceptional energy and an iron will. Neither of these men had any sympathy for parliamentary democracy, neither believed in freedom of speech, or freedom of association. Both saw Bolshevists/Communists, capitalists, Protestants and Masons as direct threats to Italy and

6. Kertzer, *The Pope and Mussolini*, 193.
7. Kertzer, *The Pope and Mussolini*, 193.
8. Kertzer, *The Pope and Mussolini*, 36.

the church. Over the following years Mussolini swiftly entrenched his ascendancy, brutally destroying any who stood in his way and succeeded in gaining popularity with both the common man and the clergy of the Roman Catholic Church.

In 1929 Mussolini manipulated the Pope into an agreement between the Vatican and the government. In granting the Pope his greatest desires for the church, he acquired the church's future support. The Roman Catholic religion became the official and only religion of the state; Vatican City was established as a sovereign territory under papal rule; but the Pope had to relinquish all former claims for its Papal States. In return the government agreed to recognize church marriages, acknowledge feast days, and Roman Catholic education became compulsory in all schools. Mussolini also allowed the political party of the church—the Catholic Action Group—to operate albeit under ever-changing restrictions. Pius XI made the dictatorship of Mussolini possible because where the Pope went, the church establishment went, and therefore, the people went. However, naively, Pius expected that everything he demanded of the government would be granted but the prime minister only agreed to minor requests—banning of specific publications, enforcing more modest dress for women, and so forth—and ignored those of any merit. Unable to stand up to this powerful leader, Pius came to realize the folly of his chosen path and struggled to speak out against the vile actions of his former ally. The Vatican clergy who felt they were more secure with Mussolini in power, took advantage of the Pope's failing health by either editing or completely suppressing the Pope's encyclicals, especially those in which he condemned the antisemitism of the government. Pius XI died in February 1939 lamenting the fact he was not able to make atonement for the persecuted Jews.

The new Pope, Eugenio Pacelli, Pope Pius XII, had previously been the Cardinal Secretary of State and, as such, had carried out some of his most productive yet disastrous work in the years before his papacy on behalf of, firstly, Benedict XV and then, Pius XI. For centuries the Vatican had protracted agreements with secular governments to gain as many rights for the Roman Catholic Church and its members in that country as possible. In Germany this resulted in the Reich Concordat of 1933, negotiations for which began as early as 1920, but came to fruition when Hitler became chancellor. At all times Pacelli completely ignored the German clergy and bishops and the faithful German Roman Catholics. "When Hitler became Pacelli's partner in negotiations, the concordat thus became the supreme act of two authoritarians, while the supposed beneficiaries were correspondingly weakened, undermined, and neutralized."[9] Pacelli was so engrossed in his belief that "the Church could survive and remain united in the modern world only by strengthening papal authority through the application of law"[10] that he failed to see that Hitler was intent on destroying all Roman Catholic (and Christian) influence in Germany. Hitler demanded that, as in Italy, all Catholic political parties must be disbanded and because the papacy had always found it difficult to control Catholic political activity, it was prepared to see them abolished. This immediately greatly weakened Roman Catholicism in Germany, in particular the resolve of many of the bishops to oppose National Socialism. Now led by two pro-Nazi bishops and feeling completely neglected by the papacy the bishops, as a whole, endorsed a pastoral message "announcing the end of the hierarchy's opposition to the Nazi regime, provided that the state respected the rights and freedoms of the Church—notably in relation to Catholic schools and associations"[11] which, of course, the state never did.

When the treaty was formally signed Hitler added his own introduction: "The conclusion of the concordat seems to me to give sufficient guarantee that the Reich members of the Roman Catholic confession will from now on put themselves without reservation at the service of the new National Socialist state."[12] Consequently the Vatican, despite Pacelli's disclaimers, was seen to be giving Roman Catholic moral approval of Hitler and his regime. "A great Church, which might have formed the basis of an opposition, confined itself to the sacristy."[13] He also did a great disservice to the papacy. His "ambition to become a judge of judges, a world mediator, in the world but not of the world, was not so much underpinned by neutrality as by his estimate of the supreme status of the Vicar of Christ the King on earth."[14] His glee knew no bounds when a small boy once asked him if he was God Almighty. A priest stands between God's holiness and his people with love, a minister of God's character and his mercy; an advocate of this people. He is a servant, not God himself.

9. Cornwell, *Hitler's Pope*, 84.
10. Cornwell, *Hitler's Pope*, 85.
11. Cornwell, *Hitler's Pope*, 145–46.
12. Cornwell, *Hitler's Pope*, 152.
13. Cornwell, *Hitler's Pope*, 157.
14. Cornwell, *Hitler's Pope*, 223.

Contrary to his great ambitions, Pacelli's reign as Pope Pius XII, beginning in 1939, was one of constant appeasement to Hitler. He continually ignored the desperate plight of the Jews even though, through the latest communication networks, he was often the first to know what exactly was taking place. The only public comment was in his 1942 Christmas Eve broadcast: "'Humanity owes this vow to those hundreds of thousands who, without any fault of their own, sometimes only by reason of their nationality or race, are marked down for death or gradual extinction.' Here was the fullest extent of his protest and denunciation, after a year of encouragement, pleading, argument, proof upon proof of what had been happening in Poland and all over Europe. It was to remain the fullest extent of his protest and denunciation for the rest of the way."[15] He scaled down millions to hundreds of thousands and did not mention the word Jews nor the term Nazi Germany. "Hitler himself could not have wished for a more convoluted and innocuous reaction from the Vicar of Christ to the greatest crime in human history."[16] Pius XII failed to come to the aid of departing Jews in Rome itself; refused to give any aid to the persecuted churches in Croatia; but bargained with the Reich to spare the bombing of Rome so that the Vatican would be preserved.

During the 1930s and 1940s the Roman Catholic Church, with the Pope as its temporal head, had the unchallenged ability to fight evil worldwide. Pius XI, because of his desire to establish Vatican City and to control the church in Italy, failed to stand up to the dictator Mussolini. Pius XII, because of his desire to be the head and master of a worldwide church, bargained with the devil, Hitler, and sacrificed a phenomenal opportunity to be a loving and saving pastor to the dispossessed, and to have been an effectual influence on the course of the war. "The internal structures and morale of the Catholic Church began to show signs of fragmentation and decay in the final years of Pius XII, leading to a yearning for reassessment and renewal. The Second Vatican Council was called in 1962 by John XXIII, who succeeded Pacelli in 1958, precisely to reject the monolithic, centralized Church model of his predecessors, in preference for a collegial, decentralized, human community on the move."[17] It is pertinent to record that this pope, Angelo Roncalli, was

---

15. Cornwell, *Hitler's Pope*, 292.
16. Cornwell, *Hitler's Pope*, 293.
17. Cornwell, *Hitler's Pope*, 7.

intimately involved in the rescue of thousands of Jewish refugees during the Holocaust—a truly righteous Gentile.

The German Church

Despite the failings of the Roman Catholic Church during these times, its claim as the Church of the Christ had a powerful influence on one eighteen-year-old sojourning in Rome for the first time in 1924. Dietrich Bonhoeffer, from the age of thirteen, had committed himself to study theology, but he rarely attended church services at the Lutheran Church in his home country of Germany. He noted in his diary that, as he experienced communion of the people and the liturgy of the service in Catholicism, he came to realize that he was coming to a true understanding of the meaning of "church." He now saw the church as universal, not bound by national or racial strictures. He witnessed in Rome the link between the church and its classical past and became exposed to traditional Roman Catholic texts, which he found wonderfully clear in their poetic majesty. Before Bonhoeffer left Rome, he managed to gain an audience with Pius XI who, however, made a disappointingly apathetic impression on him.

Almost a decade later, with the establishment of Hitler as chancellor in Germany and the resultant influence of Nazism on all facets of German society, including particularly the church, Bonhoeffer and others became distressed by the path the German Church was pursuing. By following National Socialism, the church became embroiled in the support of the proposed Aryan Paragraph, reasoning that even Jews who had become baptized Christians should be barred from its community perhaps forming their own separate church. The German Church was to expel all members of Jewish descent including ordained ministers. Bonhoeffer believed that the church must question actions of the state: "The church must 'continually ask the state whether its action can be justified as legitimate action of the state i.e., as action which leads to law and order, and not to lawlessness and disorder.' In other words it is the church's role to help the state be the state. If the state is not creating an atmosphere of law and order, as Scripture says it must, then it is the job of the church to draw the state's attention to this failing."[18] He took this reasoning further by stating that the church has a definite obligation to any victims who suffer because of society's decrees and that, as the church, it has to act

---

18. Metaxas, *Bonhoeffer*, 153.

for them, even if they are not part of the Christian body of believers. Bonhoeffer used as directives from Scripture the following: "So then, whenever we have an opportunity, let us work for the good of all, and especially for those of the family of faith" (Gal 6:10 NRSV), "For thus said the LORD of hosts (after his glory sent me) regarding the nations that plundered you: Truly, one who touches you touches the apple of my eye" (Zech 2–8 NRSV), and "They are Israelites, and to them belong the adoption, the glory, the covenants, the giving of the law, the worship, and the promises; to them belong the patriarchs, and from them, according to the flesh comes the Messiah, who is over all, God blessed forever. Amen." (Rom 9:4–5 NRSV).

As the German Church continued to be absorbed into Nazism, Bonhoeffer wrote: "The question is really: Christianity or Germanism? And the sooner the conflict is revealed in the clear light of day the better."[19] Eventually he knew that the battle for a true German Christian Church was lost—it had become unrepentantly heretical. With the publication of Barth's Barmen Declaration in 1934, Bonhoeffer instigated the establishment of the Confessing Church. "It was incendiary, announcing to the world that a group of Christians in Germany had officially and publicly declared their independence from the Nazified Reichskirche."[20] To Bonhoeffer this was the true German Church. Some Lutherans supported the "Nazi" Church; others followed Bonhoeffer's Confessing Church. Bonhoeffer dedicated his time and efforts to the training of men for leadership and traveled to Britain and the United States of America to establish vital links with academics, theologians, and ecumenicists. He became a constant source of aggravation to the Nazis but they failed to curtail his activities.

In the depth of the war and its accompanying atrocities, Bonhoeffer maintained and strengthened close relationships with his Christian brothers and sisters in Britain and the United States of America, and at home with many influential men in all walks of life, particularly in government and the army. Through his contacts he was able to carry out endless humanitarian work as well as continuing to train young men for Christian ministry in the Confessing Church. Eventually he was imprisoned for helping a group of Jews escape to Switzerland. As Hitler continued on his deranged path, Bonhoeffer felt led to be involved in the conspiracy to assassinate him. He deliberated deeply and at great length

---

19. Metaxas, *Bonhoeffer*, 183.
20. Metaxas, *Bonhoeffer*, 226.

with the ethics of such subterfuge, but came to the conclusion that he had to bring God into the human life of obedience and not just communicate on a spiritual level—the Christian in action in the world of evil. His loved and respected friend, Eberhard Bethge, said at the time, "We now realized that mere confession, no matter how courageous, inescapably meant complicity with the murderers."[21] As a result of his heroic stand Bonhoeffer gave his life for Christ (and Germany) on the gallows at Flossenbürg in April 1945 within the sound of the guns of the approaching allies. "'This is the end', he said 'For me the beginning of life.'"[22] As he had predicted to friends, he was falling into a deep, deep valley, but he would be enabled to ascend and cross from the edge of the world to his heavenly home. His faith was invincible: "Naked I came from my mother's womb, and naked shall I return there: the LORD gave, and the LORD has taken away; blessed be the name of the LORD." (Job 1:21 NRSV)

21. Metaxas, *Bonhoeffer*, 358.
22. Metaxas, *Bonhoeffer*, 528.

10

The Personal Cost

It can be somewhat understood how the brainwashing of the people in Germany over many years made most either desensitized or too afraid to rebel against the state. But there were some who, consumed with guilt and distress, had the courage to rebel against the barbaric acts they were forced to perform. A British intelligence officer, Glenn Gray, reported that a German soldier who had been captured had been fighting for the French Resistance. As a German soldier he had been forced to take part in the massacre of women and children in a French village. He could not live with the guilt of his actions nor with the fact that he had lacked the courage to stand up to his commanding officer. His decision to desert and fight against his former countrymen was an attempt to somehow atone for his actions.

It is not known how many similar instances of desertion occurred, obviously not great numbers, and the German hierarchy continued on its immoral course to the very end. All sections of the civilian family were dragged into its murderous schemes. The use of child soldiers and selective breeding to enhance the master race strains any belief that was professed in the "perfect Aryan family." Yet the resultant Hitler Youth movement was an almost unqualified success—in the beginning. Sebastian Haffner describes how youth were drawn to belong: "During the daytime you had no time to think, no opportunity just to be yourself. During the daytime comradeship brought contentment. It is indubitable that a certain kind of happiness thrives in such camps, it is the happiness of comradeship."¹ But with this comradeship Haffner later wrote: "and yet I know for certain that this very comradeship can become the means of the most terrible dehumanisation, and that it has become just that in the hand of the Nazis."² In the last months of the war when Hitler Youth soldiers were sent into a futile battle with archaic rifles and obsolete rockets many "suffered agonising death at the hands of the advancing Russians, from artillery shells and by tanks being deliberately driven over them."³ They died weeping and screaming for their mothers. Of those who survived some were spared. "One of the Soviet Generals, Gareyev, is quoted as saying: 'There were a lot of terrified lads, who were still just children. One could take pity on them. Many of them we didn't even take prisoner, we sent them straight home.'"⁴ It is difficult to see how the Nazis could not see the immorality of sacrificing their children.

Cruelty and civilian slaughter were not the premise of only Germany. On a less personal scale the bombing campaigns of Britain and America caused an unbelievable number of deaths in cities throughout the Reich. Many of those responsible for the bombs found it morally incomprehensible to acknowledge that they had been an integral part of such destruction. The guilt lived with most for the rest of their lives:

> Nuremberg was but one of many Bomber Command successes. Across Germany, ten million civilians were now homeless. More than six hundred thousand had been killed and eight hundred thousand badly injured in the Allies' five-year-old bombing campaign, the ferocity and scale of which even Churchill, its primary architect, had come to regret. The airborne destruction, which had cost the lives of fifty-five thousand Bomber Command crewmen—more than the total of British Army officers lost in the First World War—in fact sickened the increasing tired and dispirited warlord who urged Sir Arthur 'Bomber' Harris, head of RAF Bomber Command, to concentrate on strategic targets rather than German cities: 'Otherwise what will lie between the white snows of Russia and the white cliffs of Dover?'⁵

---

1. Parsons, *War Child*, 121.
2. Parsons, *War Child*, 122.
3. Parsons, *War Child*, 126.
4. Parsons, *War Child*, 127.
5. Kershaw, *The Liberator*, 253.

The Personal Cost

The wholesale destruction of the historic cities of Hamburg and Dresden saw the annihilation of most of the population by the most horrific means. Experience and expertise by the British had established that a combination of high explosive bombs, notably four-thousand-pound bombs and huge numbers of incendiaries would cause the most catastrophic destruction possible. The bombing of Hamburg in late July 1942 brought about the gruesome deaths of 35,000 people and the injury of a further 125,000. The massive bombs blew out windows, doors, and ceilings; shattered water and gas mains; and left mammoth craters and extensive rubble all through the city streets making it impossible for fire trucks and ambulances to reach victims. Hamburg had already experienced a long, hot summer so the incendiaries sucked out all the oxygen and created firestorms, which turned into tornados sweeping people into great surges of flames. The winds were of hurricane force: the air temperature at the center reached 1,472 degrees Fahrenheit. Those who sheltered in cellars died of carbon dioxide poisoning or simply suffocated, even cooked. Those who fled in the streets disappeared in fireballs or were stuck in the melting roads to be reduced to ashes. People who fled to the river were boiled in the water. So much damage was wrought throughout the whole city that any hospitals or first aid centers that were not destroyed were unable to cope with the consequences of the vast inferno from Hell. Pilots who surveyed the damage were transfixed yet repelled. Such memories would never be erased.

> We climbed the highest peaks in the area, crossed many glaciers and found many new friends—all of them Austrians and Germans... We talked for hours together about the Berlin problem. "What a great tragedy," said one of them, "that our two countries should ever have fought each other." Each year I get letters and cards from Germans I have met in the mountains—all of them fine men, self-effacing, honest and sincere. [July 1961][6]

Aftermath

The actions of Stalin both during and after the war illustrate how, in order to defeat Germany, Great Britain and the United States were forced to ally with a heinous tyrant—from the embodiment of evil to an equally evil human being. To achieve the vital collaboration there were "four long

---

6. Griffin, *Heritage of Lakeland*, 55.

years of acrimonious diplomacy. 'Surly, snarly and grasping', Churchill wrote later, 'the Soviet Government had the impression that they were conferring a great favour on us by fighting in their own country for their own lives.'"[7] Stalin always used his allies for his own advantage and often refused to cooperate with their requests, for example, he would not allow the British to use specific airfields to launch attacks against the Germans during the Warsaw Uprising of 1944. In fact, as recorded earlier, the Soviet army remained dormant on the other side of the Vistula River whilst thousands of Poles were slaughtered. Stalin provided poorly trained, inadequately armed, and frail starving "soldiers" to fight the invading Germans, operating on the premise that his superiority in numbers would have the eventual advantage. Ilya Frenklakh, a member of the People's Levy in Leningrad, on duty scouting the enemy lines, studied the ravaged land with its decaying bodies, trying to fathom why the Russian losses were so great: "why are the Germans so well-trained, while all we do is try to overwhelm them with numbers? Why do they use technology and brains, while all we've got is bayonets? Why is it that every time we attack, our blood flows in rivers and our dead pile up in mountains? Where are our tanks? . . . If our generals and colonels had done their jobs properly, we would have won with a quarter of the losses."[8]

Even before World War II Stalin had been responsible for the deaths of many of his faithful. General Francisco Franco had led a successful military rebellion to overthrow Spain's floundering democratic republic. During the Spanish Civil War of 1936 to 1939, men and women, committed to freedom for the Spanish people, traveled from their home countries to fight Franco's armies. Many of these were Communists. After Franco's success and the establishment of his brutal dictatorship, returning Russian combatants were unprepared for the consequences: "one knows that most of the communist leaders of the International Brigades who survived were ruthlessly put to death by Stalin during the years following the Spanish Civil War, accused of having served the interests of foreign powers, of being 'Hitlero-Trotskyists', and more besides."[9]

Leningrad, originally called St. Petersburg, and since the fall of Communism now once again St. Petersburg, was besieged by the Nazis in September 1941, beginning 900 days of terror, starvation, and death

---

7. Reid, *Leningrad*, 313.
8. Reid, *Leningrad*, 329–30.
9. Maspero, *Out of the Shadows*, 66.

to its inhabitants. Of three million, some 500,000 Leningraders were drafted or evacuated and the remainder struggled to exist through bitter winters, the first year being one of the coldest on record. There was a failure to obtain adequate food and fuel before the routes in and out of the city were permanently blocked. Over the months ahead occasional shipments of essentials were organized from Moscow but the extreme circumstances of the siege were never allowed to be broadcast to the rest of Russia. "Internally, euphemisms were coined to disguise the tragedy's stark simplicity: instead of 'hunger' or 'starvation' ... government reports talked of 'exhaustion', 'avitaminosis', 'the cumulative effects of malnourishment', 'death due to difficulties with food supply', or most commonly of 'dystrophy', an invented pseudo-medical term which passed into common parlance and is still current today."[10] But the situation was more than desperately critical and could not be denied to any inhabitant. "In shops and on the streets one often hears a piercing, tearing scream—and you know that someone's cards have been stolen, or that a piece of bread had been ripped from someone's hands. It is unbearably depressing, and what saves you is bestial indifference to human suffering."[11]

By the beginning of World War II the citizens of Leningrad had lived through three major conflicts—World War I; then, following the Revolution, the internal war between the Bolsheviks and the White Russians; and the war with Finland between 1939 and 1940. They had also suffered under two great famines. The first famine occurred during the civil war and the second was the result of Stalin's grandiose plan to seize the farms from the peasants and instigate a system of collective farming. All through these years the people lived in constant terror of one type or another. The class system had collapsed, whole families lost their income and starved, men and women were imprisoned without trial or exiled to Siberia for undisclosed crimes. Now with the siege in Leningrad, came the "hidden" culmination of horror—inhabitants fighting for food whilst Party officials were making sure they had sufficient and more; disease spreading rapidly; starvation and death by the thousands; and, even cannibalism. There were plenty of corpses available—people were too exhausted from lack of food to dispose of bodies so they were left in the snow or piled up in vacant buildings. People admitted they had been inhuman, behaving like animals, committing unbelievable acts to survive.

10. Reid, *Leningrad*, 335–36.
11. Reid, *Leningrad*, 233.

Others wandered the city like robots, devoid of thinking or emotion, just concentrating on somehow surviving "Not long ago Prendel told us that corpse-eating is on the rise. In May [1942] his hospital dealt with fifteen cases, compared with eleven in April . . . He told us about a cannibal couple who first ate the small corpse of their child, then entrapped three more children—killed them and ate them."[12] Families who kept a routine even when there was no food available by washing their hands, dressing daily, and having constructive activities—reading, praying, or walking short distances if fit enough—often managed to survive the worst times. Incredibly, during the same period, people were still being arrested and executed or banished for so-called anti-Soviet speech and actions.

The poet, Olga Berggolts, found it almost impossible to cope with the arrest of her father. He was a distinguished medical doctor who loved his country but, nevertheless, he had been arrested, denigrated, and eventually sentenced to death for an innocuous crime. No matter how hard she tried, or whom she approached, she had been unable to do anything to free him. This had become the norm for all of Russia. Even when Leningrad was once again free from the Germans and the war over, hopes of a freer life with the re-establishment of the intelligentsia, were quickly dashed by Stalin.

During World War II hundreds of thousands of Allied fighting men were held in German prisoner of war camps. "Russian POWs were treated particularly badly and many British POWs are still haunted by memories of the starved and broken bodies they glimpsed through the barbed wire that separated the compounds. Like the Japanese, the Soviet Union had no sympathy for soldiers who had allowed themselves to be taken prisoner and these men (and some women) became non-persons."[13] German forces slaughtered an estimated three and a half million captured Russian troops. In addition, over 50 percent of Russians who were taken prisoner died in German camps compared to less than 5 percent of British and American prisoners. Because of the horrific treatment, some Russians did collaborate with the Germans in exchange for better conditions. On their repatriation to the Soviet Union men were sent to special camps where they were interrogated by the NKVD to establish who might have been guilty of treason. As a result, some were executed but most of them—approximately one-tenth of the returnees—were sent to the gulag.

12. Reid, *Leningrad*, 286.
13. Gillies, *The Barbed-wire University*, 7.

On the death of Stalin in 1953, an amnesty brought any survivors of the gulag's harsh conditions freedom at last. A figure for comparison: "almost four in ten of the 3.2 million Axis soldiers taken prisoner by the Soviets died in captivity."[14]

Stalin had no hesitation in treating his own people as ruthlessly as those against whom his country fought. To increase and consolidate his power he brutally declared specific races and troublesome classes collaborators, traitors, or cowards to justify their deportation to Siberia, the Urals, and the Far East. In December 1943, for example, he designated the Kalmyks as enemies of the state. In 1941 the German army had invaded and taken control of the Kalmyk Autonomous Soviet Socialist Republic. In 1942 the Red Army regained the Republic and set about accusing the Kalmyks of collaborating with the Germans. In a twenty-four-hour period Stalin dissolved the Republic and monstrously deported the entire population. The sons and daughters of Kalmykia who were fighting Nazi Germany alongside their compatriots of more than ninety-five ethnicities comprising the USSR, were removed from the fronts and sent to the Molotov Region (now the Perm Region) for the construction of the Shirokovskaya HPP. Many were murdered in Soviet prison camps. The elderly and the children were carted off in unheated cattle railway wagons. Consequently, many died of cold, hunger, thirst, and suffocation in the overcrowded conditions on the long journeys. Despite the dire conditions on arrival at their destination, conscious of the need to help the Soviet Army Front, a large number continued to work in places of deportation, contributing to the destruction of Nazi forces. Nevertheless, the deportation inflicted irreparable damage on the Kakmyk people and the total losses of the original population amounted to more than half its number.

Yevgenia Lazarevna Klemm, a history teacher from Odessa who lived the Bolshevik dream, had served as a Red Cross nurse in World War I, and was captured by the Germans in World War II when part of the Red Army was fighting in her home town. As a designated leader of Russian women in the concentration camp of Ravensbrück, she knew that Stalin had refused to sign the Geneva Convention but, nevertheless, told the Gestapo chief that he could not force Russian prisoners to work in factories manufacturing armaments. She encouraged the younger prisoners to ensure that they continued to wear their uniforms, even those in tatters, so that they would have some protection as part

---

14. Reid, *Leningrad*, 4.

of an official army. "She told us we mustn't 'break the circle'. That was an expression she always used. Nobody must 'break the circle'. We must stand together and then we'd be all right. And suddenly we had the feeling that maybe we would not all be killed after all."[15] In the camp Klemm became a source of constant encouragement, maintaining a dignity for all, befriending the younger girls, nursing the sick and wounded, reading to the women, teaching them history and languages, all the time telling them to stay together, to "keep the circle." She was the reason so many survived. On her return to Odessa after the war, Klemm found lodgings and resumed her teaching. She was often interrogated and rumors a few years after her return home implied that she had been a collaborator. Her teaching work was cut back and eventually her position terminated. On September 3, 1953, she committed suicide: "In a suicide note she said that she had taken her life because she was not allowed to teach anymore and nobody had bothered to tell her why."[16]

Even today with the purges of Stalin a part of history, Russia continues to exhibit an iron fist in its culture, "Russia's army incubates a vicious behavioural virus known as the rule of the Grandfathers—this involves second year recruits abusing those in their first year with terrifying violence—dozens have been killed; thousands have sustained grievous injuries; hundreds have attempted suicide, many succeed—yet these crimes are routinely hushed up by everyone involved."[17] In 2006, Arkady Babchenko published a book on his experiences during the war with Chechnya. He talks of first-hand experiences of life in the Russian army, describing how his Jewish friend Vic Zelikman is continually terrified of the "gangs" of officers. Every time they waylay him, he sinks into further depression. The Russian senior officers scream, punch, and beat the men in the lower ranks. The cadets, on the bottom rung, suffer the worst. It is an inbred culture and the higher the rank the more power to exercise brutality. Constant beatings, starvation diets, and demands for money force many of the younger Russian soldiers to constantly go AWOL sometimes into the hands of the very enemy they are fighting: in Chechen wars to be crucified, castrated, or strangled with one's own intestines.

---

15. Helm, *If This Is a Woman*, 269.
16. Helm, *If This Is a Woman*, 643.
17. Dimbleby, *Russia*. Film.

Every war has a tyrant who craves power. This tyrant often believes he is invincible—King of all Kings, Emperor of a mighty Empire, Leader of many Nations.

> I met a Traveller from an antique land,
> Who said: Two vast and trunkless legs of stone
> Stand in the desert. Near them, on the sand,
> Half sunk, a shattered visage lies, whose frown,
> And wrinkled lip, and sneer of cold command,
> Tell that its sculptor well those passions read
> Which yet survive, stamped on these lifeless things,
> The hand that mocked them, and the heart that fed:
> And on the pedestal these words appear:
> "My name is OZYMANDIAS, King of kings:
> Look on my works, ye Mighty, and despair!"
> No thing beside remains. Round the decay
> Of that colossal wreck, boundless and bare
> The lone and level sands stretch far away.[18]

---

18. Shelley, *Selected Poems*, 358.

11

A Forerunner of the War in the East

ON SEPTEMBER 18, 1931 the Japanese army, stationed in northern China under unequal treaties, invaded the area known as Manchuria. The Japanese ignored all moves by the League of Nations to cease their systematic advance. A Manchurian Republic divorced from China was established by the Japanese under a puppet governor, Hsuan Tung (Pu Yi), the former Chinese boy emperor. Japan had previously been the victor in the Sino-Japanese War of 1894 to 1895 and the Russo-Japanese War of 1904 to 1905 and visualized itself as a mighty nation in Asia capable of establishing an extensive Japanese empire.

Then on July 26, 1937 Japan, with a well-trained military and the most up-to-date equipment of the day, launched a full-scale war against a fragmented China. Within a few months China had suffered the loss of 30,000 men with a further 200,000 soldiers disbanded to the south. In the subsequent battle for Shanghai, thousands upon thousands were killed and possibly as many as a million peace-loving citizens lost their homes in a series of bombing attacks. A Swedish mining engineer, J. Gunnar Andersson, resident amongst the International Community of that city, wrote: "How many old people, pregnant women and little children were left to be roasted to death among the glowing ruins?"[1] In December, "the Japanese soldiers who entered Nanking attacked the Chinese civilian population in an orgy of destruction . . . more than 200,000, and 90,000 soldiers were killed."[2] There were specific orders on the methods of ex-

---

1. Gilbert, *A History of the Twentieth Century. Volume Two*, 157.
2. Gilbert, *A History of the Twentieth Century. Volume Two*, 162.

ecutions with rewards offered for formidable results. "Japanese officers used their swords to chop off the heads of their prisoners. Soldiers bayoneted prisoners to death, often tying them up in batches first."[3] With regard to the civilians, it was the women who endured the worst. Takokoro Kozo, a Japanese soldier recounted: "No matter how young or old, they all could not escape the fate of being trapped. We sent out coal trucks to the city streets and villages to seize a lot of women. And then each of them was allocated to fifteen to twenty soldiers for sexual intercourse and abuse. After raping we would also kill them. Those women would start to flee once we let them go. Then we would 'bang!' shoot them in the back to finish them up."[4] "No attempts to take prisoners were made. I saw a man who was kneeling to the troops and begging for mercy pinned to the ground with a bayonet while his head was hacked off with a sword . . . An old man on his knees in the street was cut almost in two . . ."[5] The invasion of China was the beginning of World War II in the Pacific region.

However, by 1939, the Japanese progress was somewhat stymied by the growth of Chinese guerrilla activity, mainly led by adherents to Communism. Furthermore, the Nationalist government managed to retain control of Chungking (this city never fell to the Japanese). Civil war erupted between the Nationalists and the Communist forces bringing even more despair and misery to the Chinese people. To add to the constant warring groups the Russians began attacking the Japanese in Manchuria. During all these years of Chinese suffering the League of Nations failed to act to cries for help mainly because the European powers were greatly divided towards these events in Asia—Germany and Italy were in sympathy with the Japanese whilst Britain and France were in support of China. With the worsening situation with Hitler and Mussolini, those who wanted to act feared that any intrusion into the Chinese situation would damage the fragile negotiations on the continent of Europe. It seemed that everywhere in the world the European colonial empires were under threat and political leaders were impotent in choosing which path to take. In 1939, the Nobel Peace Prize winner Sir Norman Angell, wrote: "For seven years Japan has been proclaiming to the world that her military operations against China (which are not a war at all, be it remembered, only an 'incident'), the laying waste of great cities,

---

3. Gilbert, *A History of the Twentieth Century. Volume Two*, 162–63.
4. Gilbert, *A History of the Twentieth Century. Volume Two*, 163.
5. Lewis and Steele, *Hell in the Pacific*, 65.

the slaughter of helpless civilian populations, the bombing and machine gunning of British ambassadors, all these Japan, probably with complete sincerity, is persuaded are but incidents of her defence."[6]

Eventually, with the Japanese in control of half the country, the Nationalist Forces and the Red Army formed an uneasy alliance as the 8th Route Army to defend their people, with many Communist guerrillas still continuing their forays into battle behind the Japanese lines. Finally, finding their plans for a short war of months and for the resultant growth of a Japanese Imperial Empire in China thwarted, the Japanese turned their attention to the Pacific region. By the latter part of the 1930s Japan had control of a great deal of the Pacific area—in particular, the Marshall Islands. One of the great mysteries of 1937 was the disappearance of Amelia Earhart who was on her final leg of a flight around the world with a navigator named Fred Noonan. It has always been claimed that she ran out of fuel and crashed into the ocean. Recent research has established that she, in fact, managed to land on the island of Endtikren in the Mili atoll. Being then captured by the resident Japanese and taken to Saipan, Noonan was beheaded and eventually Earhart died in a prison cell as an American spy. Her Electra plane was towed from Endtikren and destroyed. The United States navy intercepted Japanese radio messages and knew that she had been captured but failed to act as to do so would make known to the Japanese that they had managed to crack their codes. As in countless times during war the "greater good" took priority over individuals.

---

6. Gilbert, *A History of the Twentieth Century. Volume Two*, 238.

12

Japan's Ambitions in the Pacific

"'There are superior and inferior races in the world,' said the Japanese politician Nakajima Chikuhei in 1940, 'and it is the sacred duty of the leading race to lead and enlighten the inferior ones.' The Japanese, he continued, are 'the sole superior race of the world.'"[1] On December 7, 1941 the Japanese, "the sole superior race of the world" expanded their Pacific ambitions and launched a surprise attack on the United States naval base of Pearl Harbor.

The British and the Americans, both of who had extended their empires to the Asian regions, had not believed the Japanese were capable of waging modern successful warfare. "Dick Lee, a motorbike despatch rider with the Royal Artillery, is still livid at the misinformation and colonial propaganda the men were fed: 'They told us, in the early days, the Japanese can't see, they all wear glasses, can't shoot straight, and [have] crap equipment.'"[2] Another misconception widely held was that the Japanese could not fly at night. Consequently, when they attacked the Philippines and Singapore almost simultaneously with the attack on Pearl Harbor, Singapore was ablaze with lights. There had been warnings of the eruption of war in the East but they were disregarded. Individual messages were never put together to gain an overall picture of overwhelming disaster. And, of course, all opinions of the British in Singapore were accentuated by racial prejudice. When General Percival woke up the governor of Singapore, Sir Shelton Thomas, to relay the news that the Japanese had

1. Hillenbrand, *Unbroken*, 43.
2. Lewis and Steele, *Hell in the Pacific*, 29.

invaded Malaysia, the governor's comment was: "I trust you'll chase the little men off."[3]

There were some who knew the real situation but their advice, when given, was arrogantly ignored. According to Colonel G. T. Ward, the British military attache in Tokyo, the Japanese military was a first-class fighting machine. He stressed the fact that all enlisted men maintained excellent physical fitness and they were extremely nationalistic. Ward also expressed an opinion that the men of the high command were extremely intelligent.

Much like the Germans under Nazism the general populace had been brainwashed but over a much longer period of time. When the Meiji Restoration took place in 1868 a cult emerged whereby the emperor became a god-like figure receiving an incredible degree of loyalty from his obedient subjects. Militarism was established as the ideal to be attained and valued. With the striving to become a great soldier came a degree of commitment, which eventually led to a frightening level of brutality. "Oppression gathered momentum as it rolled through the ranks, each tier heaping physical abuse and mental anguish on the men beneath them, until it reached the first-year recruits. These were the lowest of the low: men without rights . . . The peasants who had always made up the bulk of the army were treated to an incessant stream of humiliation and beatings."[4]

Japanese soldiers were rewarded for acts of atrocity—any hesitation to be involved was regarded as cowardice and affected promotion. Furthermore, to surrender or be taken prisoner in the course of battle was to bring unbearable shame on the soldier and his family—not only was the combatant expected to commit suicide but his family was also. Suicide was the honorable alternative. The Japanese race was superior to all other races. And, within the Japanese culture itself, there were degrees of superiority. Women were inferior to men, for example. All other races were inferior to the Japanese race. If enemies surrendered, they were beneath contempt. Consequently, all those who did would have no rights, they were the "lowest of the low" and could be treated as such—with scorn and loathing. The military culture of the Japanese led to the extremes of barbarity and cruelty experienced by their enemies, particularly those who surrendered and became prisoners of war.

---

3. Lewis and Steele, *Hell in the Pacific*, 25.
4. Lewis and Steele, *Hell in the Pacific*, 64.

In battle they were extremely cunning—hanging down from trees and lying in the open as if dead. Any close approach to such a "corpse" resulted in the duped soldier being shot or bayoneted. "A group of some twenty marines went up the coast on a mercy mission to bring in a group of starving and wounded Japanese believed to be willing to surrender. When they reached the beach, the Japanese ambushed them. All but three marines were killed. The last man to escape looked back as he swam away to see the Japanese mutilating the dead, their swords flashing in the sun as they did so."[5] In early 1945, the British 14th Army were advancing through Burma when they came across dead soldiers who had been in an earlier conflict with the Japanese. These men had been beaten, stripped of their boots, and suspended by electric flex upside down from trees.

Downed aircrews came in for particularly barbarous treatment—civilians fell upon them and beat them to death; any who survived were beheaded by Japanese soldiers. In fact, as in Europe, any aircrew who survived a crash landing, seemed to suffer instant reaction. "Japanese moral indignation caused many US aircrew captured in 1944–45 to be treated as 'war criminals.' For instance, eight B-29 crewmen of the 29th Bomb group were killed in 1945 by suffering un-anaesthetised vivisection carried out in front of medical students at a hospital in Fukuoka on Kyushu. Their stomachs, hearts, lungs and brain segments were removed. Half a century later, one doctor present, Dr Toshio Tono, said: 'There was no debate among the doctors about whether to do the operations—that was what made it so strange.'"[6]

In the battle for supremacy at sea, Japanese have been guilty of being merciless with survivors of naval battles. Many survivors had been machined-gunned in the water whilst awaiting rescue. Early in the war in the Atlantic, German submarines had rescued British sailors—some had been taken on board, rubbed down to restore circulation, and given hot drinks; others had had their leaking lifeboats quickly repaired and taken in tow. Admiral Dönitz declared the great displeasure of the Führer with such an action, whilst leaving a group of submarines on the surface in an extremely vulnerable position for attack. The following order was issued forthwith: "No attempt of any kind must be made at rescuing members of ships sunk, and this includes picking up persons in the water and putting them into lifeboats, righting capsized lifeboats and handing over food

5. Lewis and Steele, *Hell in the Pacific*, 113.
6. Hastings, *Nemesis*, 398.

and water. Rescue runs counter to the rudimentary demands of warfare for the destruction of enemy ships and crews."[7] Although the German navy was found from then on to be merciless in its execution of duty on the seas, there was only one case of capital punishment for war crimes of this nature as there was evidence that the machine-gunning of survivors, wallowing in the waves, was committed by both sides.

The Japanese culture probably found it unnecessary to issue similar orders? In March 1944 the Dutch-owned *Tijisalak*, when on her way from Perth to Colombo, was torpedoed by the Japanese submarine I-8. After she sank the submarine surfaced and commanded the lifeboats to come alongside. The captain and several of the crew climbed onto the deck whilst Japanese ratings began to appear armed with rifles, samurai swords, and hammers. After ordering the survivors to remove their life jackets and tying some in groups of two, four, and six, the Japanese sailors brutally shot, sliced, and bludgeoned these men, pushing them back into the ocean in the process. There were many instances of such horrific actions on the high sea, machine-gunning survivors of shipwreck being the norm. Sadly, there were also documented instances of genocide by the United States. Because of the surprise attack on Pearl Harbor before war had been officially declared, "the US Marines adopted the unofficial slogan, 'Remember Pearl Harbor—keep 'em dying' ... At sea US sailors were not averse to sinking hospital ships, firing at survivors in the water and shooting at helpless enemy pilots as they descended by parachutes. In late 1943, one young sailor recorded in his diary, 'A few Japs parachuted when they were hit, but some sailors and Marines on the 20mm opened up on the ones in the 'chutes and when they hit the water they were nothing but a piece of meat cut to ribbons.'"[8] The worst US massacre took place in Wewak Harbor in 1943. The USS *Wahoo* under the command of Dudley W. Morton had successfully sunk a destroyer, two freighters, and a transport. On surfacing to recharge his batteries, Morton found the ocean awash with Japanese. "The water was so thick with bobbing heads sticking up from kapok life-jackets that it was impossible for the submarine to move forward without pushing them aside like driftwood ... dotted among them were the boats and rafts and general flotsam and jetsam ... [Morton] ordered the deck guns to open fire ... The horrific massacre continued for about an hour, at the end of which they had

---

7. Bridgland, *Waves of Hate*, 85.
8. Bridgland, *Waves of Hate*, 115.

destroyed all the boats and most of the men. The sea ran pink and the sharks were closing in."[9] Returning to Pearl Harbor the submarine flew a sheet with the words "Kill the Sunza Bitches." No official criticism was recorded; only praise and adulation. The Americans, smarting from the unheralded 1941 attack, had plummeted to the enemy's depth.

There was strict Japanese order in all things military—from the battlefield to the handling of survivors on sea and on land. The regular execution of captured soldiers reflected this. "On the Bataan Death March . . . 2330 Americans and 7000 Filipino prisoners died of starvation, sickness, torture and execution after General Douglas MacArthur's forces surrendered to the Japanese in the Philippines on 9 April 1942 . . . in Rabaul in 1942 Japanese troops tied 160 Australian prisoners to palm trees and bayoneted them to death, as practice, placing a sign, 'It took them a long time to die', beside the bodies."[10] Also in 1942, when the Indonesian island of Ambon fell to the Japanese, a unit of approximately 1,150 Australian defenders was taken prisoner. Several hundred of these men were mercilessly slaughtered:

> Thirty Japanese troops were sent to dig holes in a coconut plantation . . . Lieutenant Nakagawa divided his men into three groups: the first to move the prisoners out of the house where they were confined, the second to prevent disorder on the way to the execution and the third to bayonet or behead them. The sheer mortal terror that consumed the captured men can only be imagined. They knew what was happening but were spared the sight as one by one they were led to a spot and made to kneel, with their eyes bandaged. A member of the third group of Japanese then appeared with a sword or bayonet and with one deadly stroke or stabbing motion calmly beheaded the POW or thrust his sharpened blade through the prisoner's chest.[11]

The remainder of the men struggled to survive captivity over the following three years; many of them succumbing to death by torture, beatings, starvation, and untreated tropical diseases. As the captured Australian doctor, "Weary" Dunlop recorded in his *War Diaries*: ". . . we were going to be engaged in a new war, a war for physical and moral survival, a war against disease, malnutrition and most probably a protracted process of starvation as well as against disintegration from within

---

9. Bridgland, *Waves of Hate*, 122.
10. Ham, *Hiroshima Nagasaki*, 12.
11. Maynard, *Ambon*, 68–69.

by the apparent helplessness and futility of life in the prisons . . ."[12] Even after men had survived imprisonment and hoped for eventual release the barbarity continued. "In Palawan, in December 1944, the Japanese commander ordered the elimination of 150 American prisoners, who were drenched in petrol, crammed into air shelters, and ignited; those who tried to escape were shot."[13]

All nationalities were subject to the brutality of the Japanese. In fact, "There seemed no limit to Japanese inhumanity. When a cholera epidemic struck Tamil railway workers at Nieke in June 1943, a barracks containing 250 infected men, women and children was simply torched. One of the Japanese who did the burning wrote later of the victims: 'I dared not look into their eyes. I only heard some whispering "*Tolong, tolong*"—"Help, help." It was the most pitiful sight. God forgive me. I was not happy to see them being burnt alive.'"[14] Unlike this soldier most Japanese seemed to be immune to suffering—whether suffering of many or suffering of one alone. "One of many post-war medical reports described the case of Private Barton of the 2nd Loyals, sentenced to five years' solitary confinement for an attempted escape from Changi in July 1942. Barton served three years, during which he received a daily allowance of ½ pint rice pap for breakfast, ½ pint dry rice and ½ pint green soup for tiffin and supper. Developed scrotal dermatitis, burning feet, glossitis, weakness of the legs, deafness and retro-bulbar neuropathy. When examined in October 1945 Barton showed bilateral nerve deafness, posterior column degeneration and severe memory defect."[15] Under these heinous conditions how did some survive and others fade away and die? As in the concentration camps in Europe, it appears that it was not physical fitness or strength that made the difference but a positive mental attitude grasping at anything available to keep the mind active and full of purpose.

Prisoner of war camps were set up all over captured territory. Conditions were brutal and merciless, in the camps themselves and in the jungles, factories, mines, or quarries where the prisoners toiled, because of the attitude of the Japanese to men who surrender. In the beginning, when some British sought to keep up morale by parading and singing, guards were bewildered by their almost arrogant behavior. Historically

---

12. Dunlop, *The War Diaries of Weary Dunlop*, xi.
13. Ham, *Hiroshima Nagasaki*, 12.
14. Hastings, *Nemesis*, 375.
15. Hastings. *Nemesis*, 384.

Japan had always been an isolated nation. The Japanese had never been exposed to other languages and other cultures, so much of the frustration they vented on prisoners was a result of miscommunication and miscomprehension. Guards also entertained themselves by humiliating prisoners, forcing them to dance and sing and then to crawl around the earth to pick up the only pieces of rice that represented their meal. Some men refused to eat unfamiliar food, they mourned their loved ones in the home country, and they often abandoned hope because of their loss of dignity. Not knowing how long their captivity would last and realizing that there was no possibility of a successful escape because they were unable to blend into the local populace compounded their miserable lot. Only those who were adaptable to every changing situation had a chance of survival. Constant bowing to their captors had to be tolerated and punishment had to be accepted without complaint. Those who reacted either to their own beatings or the maltreatment of others were forced to stand on parade grounds for hours on end, left in tin cages in the extreme heat for days usually without water, battered with rifle butts, tied to trees and bayoneted or set on fire, buried alive, or subjected to the infamous water treatment with stomach areas encased in barbed wire. A particularly sadistic punishment was being tied in such a way that the prisoner needed to keep his head stretched upward—if his head dropped with fatigue a sharpened bamboo stick pierced his neck. Prisoners were also lined up and forced to punch each other continuously in the face. All prisoners were starved and neglected and not only was there no real medical aid for injuries or illness, some Japanese doctors experimented on them with injections of unknown solutions.

There were a small number of camps, generally in major towns where the treatment of POWs was slightly better than the norm, but obviously this was greatly dependent on the Japanese officer in charge. Nowell Peach, a medical doctor who had planned to further his studies in surgery was given a second hand copy of *Gray's Anatomy*, which Weary Dunlop purchased for him in Bandung. With this in hand and the experience of working with Dunlop he became a credited surgeon who had little trouble in signing the "no escape" document forced on prisoners by the Japanese. Whereas POWs, at the point of a machine-gun signed with acknowledgment to themselves of duress, Peach felt he could sign because, as a doctor, it was his duty to stay. Working under the most basic conditions he was eventually transferred to a hospital in the backstreets of Batavia. There the patients actually slept in real beds. "The

Dutch doctors were already well-established at St Vincentius and one of them had even managed to produce ether using alcohol and sulphuric acid extracted from lorry batteries by men on working parties."[16] Peach had a small number of medical tools for surgery but in all camps doctors had to be extremely inventive to make vital operations possible. POWs came to the fore with substitute tools and apparatus. In one hospital there were "surgical retractors made from motor vehicle springs."[17] Incredibly the doctors at Batavia "struck up a good relationship with a Japanese doctor who was keen to learn English and who arranged for medicine, food, clothing, books and even a gramophone to be sent to St Vincentius. He also helped them to get an X-ray machine but, like everything else, the barium meal had to be recycled and they reckoned they could recover about 700gm of the original 800gm each time."[18]

Peach wasn't the only prisoner to further his education. As in the German camps, prisoners in the Far East established their own "universities," where academics and teachers or others with an extensive knowledge of specific subjects ran classes, which prisoners embraced primarily to fill the time and monotony of prison life but also to equip them for life after the war. Generally, in Germany, this education proved invaluable to prisoners returning to their home countries from the camps. However, the system was far more difficult to maintain in Japanese camps, as the Japanese often did not allow books or paper in the camps and banned any such classes being held. The most devastating problem was that, eventually, the men became too weak and ill to continue with learning although some managed to retain facts in their memories to keep themselves sane.

Many of the prisoner of war camps automatically became a source of a workforce for the building of roads, bridges, and railways throughout the jungle. The Thai–Burma Railway, conceived to supply Japanese troops in Burma whilst blocking Allied supply, was expected to take eighteen months to construct but was completed in twelve—the set task was thirty-five cubic feet per man per day. The laborers included 200,000 Asians (Burmese, Javanese, Malays, Tamils, and Chinese) and 60,000 Allied prisoners of war—half of the Asians and one-fifth of the Allied prisoners of war died in the process. Men died from starvation, brutal treatment by the guards, and diseases (mainly dysentery but also cholera,

---

16. Gillies, *The Barbed-wire University*, 182.
17. Gillies, *The Barbed-wire University*, 182.
18. Gillies, *The Barbed-wire University*, 183.

beriberi, pellagra, malaria, and tropical ulcers). In the case of leg ulcers, when they reached a stage where the bones and tendons were exposed, treatment was impossible. Legs were often amputated and the work on producing artificial limbs with whatever could be sourced in the jungle or the camps themselves was amazingly quite successful. Daily truckloads of the sick would often be dumped back at base hospitals where, although medical conditions were slightly better, doctors still labored with little or no medicines, using the primitive instruments they had devised from bamboo, buffalo hide, and other scavenged materials. "It is impossible to describe adequately the condition of these men. I remember one man who was so thin that he could be lifted easily on one arm. His hair was growing down his back and was full of maggots. His clothing consisted of a ragged pair of shorts soaked with dysentery excreta; he was lousy and covered with flies all the time, which he was too weak to brush away from his face and his eyes and the sore places on his body."[19]

Those who labored on the line had no wheelbarrows or proper tools to dig and excavate. The Konyu Cutting, which was called Hellfire Pass by the Australians, did have the use of two old diesel-driven jackhammers with blunt drills, which men were forced to use in twelve-hour shifts. The Pass was a solid granite hill up to 165 feet deep in places and approximately 245 feet in length. Not only did men work eighteen-hour days with "hammer and tap," they labored in the monsoon season with little relief in the water-logged tents provided for them after their shifts. At least 700 prisoners died in this section of the line—one-tenth of these were beaten to death by the guards.

Some prisoners were marched long distances through the jungle supposedly to another camp, but often just to be shot when they reached a specific destination. Such was the case with the Sandakan Death Marches from 1942 to 1945. In March 1942, 2,700 British and Australian soldiers were marched through Borneo to build an airstrip. Eventually the entire group of prisoners was executed. Initially the men were callously starved then:

> Terribly weakened men then faced relocation by walking to Ranau, some 300 kilometres away as the Japanese commander at Sandakan feared an Allied invasion. He wanted to keep his prisoners as far away as possible from the prospect of liberation. Those who fell out of the march were shot, yet remarkably only 20 of the 470 prisoners in the first death march died on

---

19. Toosey, "Tamarkan Base Hospital," 32–33.

the track . . . The second march lasted four weeks in all; of the 560 men who set off, 142 Australians and 61 British mustered at Ranau. This attractive hill station then became their killing ground. By 18 July 1945 only 72 of perhaps 650 men were still alive. Ten days later this number had dwindled to 30, the others starved and brutalised to death. These remaining prisoners were executed, most probably on 1 August 1945, cruelly so close to the victory.[20]

POWs were also transported on what were termed "hellships" to Japan itself to work in shipyards, railyards, truck-loading stations, coal mines, and other vital war industries. One of these prisoners who traveled on the *Dainichi Maru* was a British man, Terence Kelly—to him it was a voyage beyond belief. On this rusty, leaking vessel were 1,000 Japanese soldiers and 1,200 prisoners. The hold in which he was confined had a floor of wet iron ore with sloping sides. There were 268 men, plus numerous rats, cockroaches, and flies, and the space allocated for each prisoner meant that if one moved the person beside him was forced to move the same way. One light at the entrance was the only guide to the iron ladder that led to the nine latrines on deck assigned for all the prisoners on board. On the voyage from Singapore to Japan there were no escort vessels and the *Dainichi* was left behind by the convoy when her engines failed. This created an atmosphere of trepidation because, as the Japanese failed to mark their ships as prisoner of war transfers, these hellships were openly defenseless against attacks by submarines and aircraft. Consequently, many men died in the sea as a result of fire from their allies. In such cases other Japanese ships in the area picked up their men but left the prisoners in the sea to drown. In the case of the attack on the *Lisbon Maru* when the vessel began to sink after being torpedoed in the East China Sea, prisoners were battened down: "many who managed to break out of the hold were machine-gunned on the deck and in the sea itself."[21] Fortunately for Kelly and his comrades the *Dainichi* was not attacked as it floundered in gale force winds and relentless rain. But by the time the ship was once again under steam many of the men were desperately ill, so badly that they were unable to climb the ladder to the latrines and the hold was covered with feces, blood, and mucus and the stench was unbearable. So many died that there were no burial services and no

---

20. McKernan, *This War Never Ends*, 63–64.
21. Kelly, *By Hellship to Hiroshima*, 40.

dignity—the corpses were "pitched into the sea like rotten carcasses."[22] A manual of these "hellship" voyages was published in September 1982, stating that approximately 34,000 prisoners were transhipped to Japan between 1942 and 1945. The report was entitled, "Unprepared Regrettable Events."

One of the resultant disastrous conditions for the survivors of these hellships was alleviated by an Australian doctor, Captain Les Poidevin: "In early 1944 he performed the first tendon lengthening operation. His patients were men who had been confined to the holds of ships and had spent so long curled up in a foetal position that their tendons had contracted. The emaciated condition of the patients made it difficult to know how to treat them: it was too painful to try to straighten their legs manually and their skin was too thin and their bodies too light for traction to work. Surgery proved successful in several cases."[23]

For the prisoners moiling in Japan every opportunity was taken to sabotage the war effort. Men at the work sites at Omori:

> ... switched mailing labels, rewrote delivery addresses, and changed the labeling on boxcars, sending tons of goods to the wrong destinations. They threw fistfuls of dirt into gas tanks and broke anything mechanical that passed through their hands. Forced to build engine blocks, American Milton McMullen crafted the exteriors well enough to pass inspection but fashioned the interiors so the engines would never run ... In one celebrated incident, the POWs loading heavy goods onto a barge hurled the material down with such force that they sank the barge, blocking a canal. After a Herculean effort was put into clearing the sunken barge and bringing in a new one, the POWs sank it, too.[24]

Invariably a Japanese officer or guard would take a particular dislike to a specific prisoner and take every opportunity to make that prisoner's life a living hell. Such was the case with the American airman and former Olympic runner, Louis Zamperini. In her book *Unbroken*, Laura Hillenbrand details how a Japanese corporal, Mutsuhiro Watanabe, nicknamed "the Bird" by his prisoners, took an instant dislike to Zamperini when he arrived at the Omori POW Camp on an artificial island in Tokyo Bay. Watanabe was a man of violent and erratic behavior;

22. Kelly, *By Hellship to Hiroshima*, 39.
23. Gillies, *The Barbed-wire University*, 183.
24. Hillebrand, *Unbroken*, 242.

probably he was a psychopath. His brutality even made Japanese soldiers of higher rank avoid him. "Watanabe beat POWs every day, fracturing their windpipes, rupturing their eardrums, shattering their teeth, tearing one man's ear half off, leaving men unconscious . . . When gripped in the ecstasy of an assault, he wailed and howled, drooling and frothing, sometimes sobbing."[25] "He combined beatings with acts meant to batter men's psyches. He forced men to bow at pumpkins or trees for hours. He ordered a clergyman POW to stand all night saluting a flagpole, shouting the Japanese word for "salute," keirei: the experience left the man weeping and out of his mind . . . he brought men to his office to show them letters from home, then burned the unopened letters in front of them."[26]

Each day Watanabe fixated on Zamperini and beat him incessantly, concentrating on battering his face and head. Any resistance was rewarded with more violence. At the end of 1944 American B-29 Fortresses began bombing Tokyo—as the bombing intensified so did the veracity of his attacks on his chosen scapegoat until Zamperini became convinced that only when Watanabe succeeded in killing him would the nightmare be over. When Watanabe was relocated to another camp he engineered the transfer of Zamperini. "Louie would remember the moment when he saw the Bird [again] as the darkest of his life."[27] The slapping, punching, battering with clubs and kendo sticks, and berating began again. At the new camp Louis and his fellow prisoners were nothing more than slaves working harder and longer, shoveling coal onto barges, with fewer rations to sustain them. The men stole food wherever possible and used ingenious methods to obtain vital ingredients for their survival. Even the food they managed to steal or scrounge was found wanting of vital ingredients. The lack of salt left prisoners deficient in sodium so that they were constantly subjected to nausea, vomiting, vertigo, and severe muscle cramps. By devious and laborious methods, men who worked on the salt barges managed to forage raw salt, which was then cunningly converted to an edible salt residue. With Watanabe threatening to drown him and the onset of beriberi, Louis had a tenuous hold on life when war came to an end and the guards disappeared. A handful of letters from his family, written many months earlier, gave him the impetus to hang on and await rescue.

25. Hillebrand, *Unbroken*, 237.
26. Hillebrand, *Unbroken*, 237.
27. Hillebrand, *Unbroken*, 277.

At the end of their incarceration journalists who encountered the survivors of the camps, "wrote of wizened, prematurely old men suffering from malnutrition and tropical diseases . . . men hardly better than skeletons covered with skin. They were listless and motion-less the only movement being their eyes."[28] "Squadron Leader Frederick 'Jock' Birchall, war crimes investigator, spoke with dozens of ex-prisoners of war and former internees from Kuching and Singapore before setting out for Sandakan. In a letter to his nephew Tom he explained: 'Some of the stories of the horror camps are too ghastly to be described. For all the refinements of brutality, sadism and inhuman cruelty the Japanese must be unsurpassed.'"[29]

It is incredibly difficult to believe that POWs could ever recover from such brutality and go on to live productive lives. Eric Lomas, who wrote of his experiences in his book, *The Railway Man*, beaten in the camp until bones were broken and waterboarded each day for an interminable period of time, took nearly fifty years before he was able to face his demons. He physically lived a life with marriage and children but mentally and emotionally he didn't exist. On locating news of the man who was his primary tormentor in the camps, and, with the support of his second wife, he traveled to Thailand to meet Takashi Nagase with the prime purpose of killing him. Under the shadow of a bridge over the River Kwai he found he was able to put all the accumulated hate behind him and forgive Nagase. When Louis Zamperini came home, he "turned to alcoholism to help him deal with the flashbacks and nightmares. It was not until Billy Graham converted him to Christianity in 1949 that he found peace."[30]

Serving women also were not spared from Japanese cruelty. Vivian Bullwinkel, after the war the Matron of the Heidelberg Repatriation Hospital in Melbourne Australia, for many years proudly marched at the head of veterans of the Royal Australian Nursing Corps each Anzac Day. She was a survivor of a group of Australian nurses attempting to escape Singapore aboard the *Vyner Brooke*. After two days at sea the vessel was bombed by Japanese planes and sank quickly. About one hundred survivors managed to reach Rajik Beach and some set off to surrender to the enemy leaving a number of men and twenty-two nurses. When

---

28. McKernan, *This War Never Ends*, 114.
29. Moremon, *Victory in the Pacific, 1945*, 23.
30. Gillies, *The Barbed-wire University*, 230.

the Japanese arrived, they took the men around the bluff to an adjacent beach—some time later they returned, wiping blood off their bayonets. The nurses were ordered to walk into the sea until the water was at waist height. The Japanese then machine-gunned them from behind. Vivian knew she had been hit but, to her amazement, she discovered she was still alive. She became quite terrified as she sensed the soldiers walking through the shallows checking their victims. She had swallowed a lot of salt water therefore was being horribly seasick and felt sure they would see her shoulders heaving so she struggled to remain still. She lay there as long as she could as she was too frightened to sit up. Gradually the waves brought her back to the beach. Finally, she plucked up enough courage to sit up and look around. There was no sign of the other nurses and the Japanese party had gone. With a bullet wound in her side she crawled into the jungle and came across an Australian soldier who had survived the massacre around the bluff and crawled into the shelter of the trees. Together they hid for a few days and then gave themselves up to another Japanese unit. Once in captivity, Vivian kept the massacre secret to protect herself and other prisoners, some of whom had been in the group who had left the Rajik beach before the massacre to find help. In 1947 she flew to Tokyo to give evidence at the War Crimes Tribunal.

Civilian women and their children were sometimes held in prison camps but there were a number of groups, specifically the Dutch in Sumatra, who were continually walking through the jungle and never gaining access to any camp. On the whole, women were accommodated in empty houses or in primitive wooden huts with no windows and with palm thatch roofs, which leaked consistently in the monsoonal weather. Floors became thick with mud where rats scurried and mosquitoes bred. Pallets, when provided, were thick with bugs and fleas. Being often housed with a number of different nationalities became an added challenge. However, most women, though used for manual labor—carrying water for Japanese baths (with only a cupful of water a day for their own use), shifting furniture into Japanese residences, cleaning cesspools in the camp, and such like—whilst deprived of an adequate diet, still strove to retain their dignity and their femininity. Caring for children provided a real purpose for many, although it became overwhelmingly distressing when the children were starving or became ill. Also, boys, once they turned ten years of age, were generally forcibly removed to the men's camps. Rape by the guards was not uncommon. Truus de Vos remembers: "We knew there was torture going on in the church because we could often hear the screams. If they took you to the church you knew you were in for trouble. Women were tortured for stealing sugar. Mother had to clean up the torture rooms the next day. The poor women had let everything go, urine, faeces and vomit. It was horrible. They used electric needles under your fingernails and also cigarette burns. They did that to me when I ate the carrots."[31] Truus was then fourteen years old.

No matter how horrific the war had been to this stage, in August 1945 the ultimate terrifying and inconceivably surreal climax was experienced by the people of Hiroshima and Nagasaki with the dropping of atomic bombs by the Americans. In Hiroshima "Tens of thousands of people within a 2-kilometres radius [of the detonation] were burned, decapitated, disembowelled, crushed and irradiated. The sudden drop in air pressure blew their eyes from the sockets and ruptured their eardrums; the shock wave cleaved their bodies apart . . . The ground temperature ranged briefly from 3000 to 4000 degrees Celsius."[32] People further out were scorched so badly only their visible teeth distinguished the front of their bodies from the back. Men, women, and children died where they stood or sat, in factories, at school desks, on trams and buses, or melted onto their bicycle frames. The intense heat instantly dehydrated their bodies and no amount of water could replace the electrolytes and proteins before death overtook them. When rescuers tried to pull people out of the debris their skin peeled off like gloves. One child survivor said that the flash "felt like the sun had fallen out of the sky and landed right in front of us."[33] When she recovered from the initial shock and examined herself she found that "her skin rolled off her legs like stockings."[34] The worst were the mothers who "clung fast to the inert bundles as if the very possession would somehow resurrect the child's life."[35] Some victims silently crawled to the side of the road and died; others slid into the river and drowned themselves. For those who were still alive by the end of the year, in front of them lay a life of debilitating illness, continual exhaustion, and unrequited sorrow.

The deliberate annihilation of civilians was not a new form of war. From the onset of the London Blitz through to the saturated bombing of

31. Huie, *The Forgotten Ones*, 136.
32. Ham, *Hiroshima Nagasaki*, 317.
33. Ham, *Hiroshima, Nagasaki*, 322.
34. Ham, *Hiroshima, Nagasaki*, 322.
35. Ham, *Hiroshima, Nagasaki*, 329.

Dresden and Hamburg, civilians had been targeted in addition to military installations. "Father Siemes, [a German Jesuit priest in Hiroshima] wrote in a report to the Holy See in Rome: '... The crux of the matter is whether total war in its present form is justifiable, even when it serves a just purpose.'"[36]

---

36. Hersey, *Hiroshima*, 117–18.

13

War and Racism

How big a part does racism play in the origins of war? Even when we look at World War II in the European sector and then in the Pacific region we find historians treating the areas differently. There is a constant plethora of information about all the major participants in Europe—Hitler and all his cohorts, Churchill and his War Cabinet, Roosevelt and his isolationist opponents, and so on. How many works are published on the life and times of Hideki Tojo, for example—how many people today know who he was? Is it because writers want to explore each "white" person, delving into their life and character to try to find out why they did the things they did? Is it harder to fathom why they should wage war and commit atrocities than so-called lesser races? Approaching the Asian leaders, it seems that these people are studied en masse as if their lives and actions could be a direct responsibility of the bodily appearance, color of their skin, and inherited characteristics of their particular race. There is no intelligent reason to suppose that "white" people are superior to "black" people. All are created "Imago Dei": "So God created humankind in his image, in the image of God he created them; male and female he created them." (Gen 1:27 NRSV) Only those who do not believe in a Creator God can attempt to establish some obscure reason why "colored people" are lesser mortals. Christians who cannot accept a Genesis creation still must face the fact that Jesus was from the Middle East and therefore was not an acceptable image for a "white" racist.

Are not the barbaric practices of some races the result of their culture and not their color? Certainly, the Anglo-Saxon warrior can be guilty of "uncivilized" actions. When Major General Kitchener sought to recapture Khartoum in 1898 and avenge the death of General Gordon some thirteen years previously, he, "ordered the dome, cupola, plinth and every trace of the Mahdi's tomb to be razed to the ground, and his bones cast into the Nile. (The skull was recovered, it was claimed, for the Sirdar to use as an inkstand. But the Queen, was shocked to hear of this; the skull was decently buried at Wadi Halfa.)"[1]

In 1900 Edmond Morel, a freelance journalist, was investigating rumors of atrocities in the Belgian Congo. It had always been assumed that, if outrages had occurred, it would have been the work of African soldiers as, after all, "he had eaten and drunk with these cheery Belgians on the quays of Antwerp, and found it hard to imagine them having a hand in atrocities."[2] But, "while labouring over the desiccated statistics of the Free State, he suddenly stumbled on an amazing discovery . . . the King had had the trade figures doctored . . . Thousands of tons of tropical products, mainly rubber, were reaching Europe without any corresponding trade in exchange."[3] It was eventually revealed that natives were forced to farm rubber without any payment. In the jungle they were underfed whilst they worked and many died from exposure, starvation, or attacks by leopards. Soldiers killed thousands who either refused to work or failed to bring in the required quota. Notable gruesome acts included the severing of ears and hands, enslavement of men, and the hacking to death of women and children. This was Leopold's private war with the objective of enriching his coffers and with scant regard for black humanity.

It was Theodore Roosevelt, then the Assistant Secretary of the Navy, and other men of a similar disposition, who saw in 1898 the opportunity for the United States of America to procure a Pacific Empire—firstly Hawaii and then the jewel of the Pacific, the Philippines. For hundreds of years the Philippines had suffered under the cruel misrule of the Spanish. Now the true inhabitants of this archipelago were fueling their desire for independence. America prepared to wage war with Spain and become the new rulers of the Philippines. In an address at the Naval War College in 1897, Roosevelt stated: "No triumph of peace is quite so great as the supreme triumphs of war."[4]

---

1. Pakenham, *The Scramble for Africa*, 546.
2. Pakenham, *The Scramble for Africa*, 591.
3. Pakenham, *The Scramble for Africa*, 591.
4. Jones, *Honor in the Dust*, 26.

War and Racism

The war with the Spanish over the Philippines had developed simultaneously with the invasion of Cuba by the United States. With Cuba being on its virtual doorstep the United States had always had more than a passing interest in this country's affairs and had witnessed the Cubans' attempts to break away from Spain's brutal and callous rule in their homeland. On the ground, and in the harbor at Havana Bay, the United States concluded a successful campaign in the July of 1898. By blaming the Spanish for the mysterious explosion and sinking of the warship USS *Maine*, America justified its invasion of the country. In this same month American troops, with the aid of the previously exiled independence leader, Emilio Aguinaldo, again waged war against Spain but this time in the Philippines. Aguinaldo was of course duped by the larger power who reneged on an earlier promise of support for an independent Philippine republic. Albert Jeremiah Beveridge, a leading Republican celebrity stated, "America could not in good conscience return the islands 'to the savage, bloody rule of pillage and extortion from which we have rescued them,' he said . . . As for granting self-rule to the little brown-skinned Filipinos, he proclaimed, 'It would be like giving a razor to a babe and telling it to shave itself.'"[5]

Now, with Cuba, Hawaii, and the Philippines acquired over a short period of time the United States of America was entering the twentieth century with an imperial empire like the Europeans. Roosevelt firmly believed that the Old World should not have a foothold in Asia: the New World was entitled to growing an empire in the Pacific. In the Philippines the United States had rescued the "little browned-skinned" people from a harsh, inhuman rule where the extremes of torture were used to subdue dissent. Amazingly, the righteous Americans continued with the same agendum as the "cruel" Spanish. Water torture was prevalent, whereby the victim was held down, his or her mouth prized open with bamboo and dirty salty water poured down the throat until the stomach was full and distended. The body was then pounded with fists until water mixed with gastric fluid was regurgitated and the procedure repeated again and again until the victim cooperated. This Spanish torture from medieval times, was now used extensively by the Americans and there is much evidence that it is still used today. The new governors were advised to rule with wisdom and justice. Unfortunately, there was little chance of this happening. The US army crushed any sign of rebellion. There was

---

5. Jones, *Honor in the Dust*, 95.

desperate fighting between the army and Filipino guerrillas: termed as terrorists or freedom fighters dependent on which side you supported. The fighting was ferocious, violent, and bloodied. Villages were burnt to the ground, crops destroyed, people were executed, or became refugees in their own land. Reports of the massacres by both sides were watered down or withdrawn from American public scrutiny. Justification for inhuman actions by the army was blamed on the inherency of lesser races: "In a fight with savages, where the savages themselves perform deeds of hideous cruelty, a certain proportion of whites are sure to do the same thing. This happened in the warfare with the Indians, with the Kaffirs of the Cape [in South Africa] and with the aborigines of Australia. In each individual instance where the act is it should be punished with merciless severity; but to withdraw from the contest for civilization because of the fact that there are attendant cruelties, is, in my opinion, utterly unworthy of a great people."[6] Nothing would deter Theodore Roosevelt from his grandiose ambitions. Roosevelt divided the world into two parts—the mainly white, civilized, industrial, and manufacturing nations and the mainly colored, uncivilized nations, which supplied the raw materials and were incapable of self-government.

In World War II America needed every man of military age to respond to the call: "Uncle Sam needs you!" The army needed black as well as white men—black men to dig ditches, build shelters, and to load and unload transports and ships—to do all the menial tasks to free the white man up to fight. It was not thought advisable to arm "negroes" and train them to fight. "Blacks given combat training would be better prepared for an armed struggle against whites. They would also learn how to be organized, how to give orders as well as take them. Dangerous stuff. But there was another worry, which went to the heart of the country's obligations to its fighting men: that black men willing to fight and die for America would demand equality on their return. If this was not freely granted, then their experience in the front lines might encourage them to fight for their rights. By then, fighting was something they would be rather good at."[7] And adversely, here was a country with a frightening legal provision for all its people—the right to bear arms even in times of peace. It was also ironic that blacks were being used to fight a system of white Aryan supremacy in Germany whilst existing in a segregated America.

6. Jones, *Honor in the Dust*, 275.
7. Lewis and Steele, *Hell in the Pacific*, 96.

Many politicians were disturbed by this paradox. But, "America could not afford to have large numbers of whites die in combat, leaving vast numbers of young blacks back home, alive and kicking."[8]

Ultimately the government rethought its policies regarding blacks (and Americans of Japanese descent) and these soldiers fought alongside white soldiers with equal bravery and distinction. In Vietnam, African American soldiers often claim that they were still being used as "cannon fodder" and it is often a common but unsubstantiated assumption that there were more colored people than whites sent into battle. The latter claim belies the actual situation. There were 7,243 African Americans in comparison to 49,830 whites. However much of the discrimination then apparent in the United States was obviously existent in the battle areas of the Vietnamese jungles for the African Americans to feel that way. In fact, an Australian serving in Vietnam, noticed that groups of Native Americans, Asian Americans, African Americans, Hispanics, and Americans from Hawaii and other Pacific Islands—basically any American of color—used to meet together regularly in the mess hall. It appears that they were giving each other encouragement to develop the ability to persevere, not only in fighting a war, but in coping with the derogative comments and unjust treatment they continually endured from their fellow Americans.

The Indigenous peoples of Australia fought valiantly in both world wars for their country and the British Empire. As experienced stockmen, many were absorbed into the Light Horse Brigades of World War I. Sadly, it is only recently that their contribution has been recognized. Certainly, they were not always party to many of the benefits extended to other returned soldiers of both wars. Reginald Saunders came from a military family—his father was a machine-gunner in World War I; an uncle served in the 29th Battalion. Another ancestor was in the Commonwealth Horse in the Boer War and the Victoria Rifles in World War I. Reg was the first Aboriginal Australian to be commissioned as an officer in the Australian army. He served in World War II and the Korean War. In 1953 the Returned and Services League (RSL) recommended Saunders to be included in the contingent being sent to Britain for the coronation of Elizabeth II. The Federal government refused the request. At the conclusion of his war service, Reg immersed himself in community affairs and was responsible for legislation and funding that benefited the Aboriginal

---

8. Lewis and Steele, *Hell in the Pacific*, 97.

people. In 1971 he was appointed a Member of the British Empire for his work. Incredibly, in later years, one of the leaders of the RSL suggested to him that all Aborigines should be blood-tested to determine if they were eligible for government benefits.

Part Three

The Wars Continue

One has to always remember that peacebuilding is very hard work because we swim upstream in deep and unclear waters.

SPEECH BY VISAKA DHARMADASA AT BUCKINGHAM PALACE, LONDON, INTERNATIONAL WOMEN'S DAY 2019

14

Korea: The Forgotten War

How many years and how much bloodshed and misery does it take for wars to cease.

Throughout history the desire for power and territory motivated rulers and dictators to wage wars. Today that is still the case in some instances but many of the wars waged presently are motivated by a desire to control the wealth of the world. The Cold War, which followed the cessation of World War II hostilities, came about through Stalin and his grab for territories as one of the Allied victors. Communism spread through Europe and Asia threatening the peace of the "Free World" and nations seemed to be on the brink of another war whenever one or another of the political leaders tried to flaunt his might. Just five short years after Hiroshima and Nagasaki, soldiers of North Korea marched into South Korea in an attempt to impose Communism on their southern neighbors. China came to the aid of North Korea and the Soviets actively lent assistance. The South Koreans were supported by the United States, with armies also from Great Britain, Australia and New Zealand, and some smaller nations. Again, there ensued the senseless slaughter of human beings—this time the death toll was two-and-a-half million.

In the late summer of 1950, the UN troops led British and Australian regiments north to force the invading North Korean forces to retreat. However, the armies were astounded at the ferocity and cunning tactics of the North Koreans. In addition, an unexpected enemy materialized—the North Korean army was boosted by countless thousands of legions from Mao's China armed with Soviet materiel. Unexpected problems also occurred when US and UK troops mistook North Koreans for South Koreans and North Koreans mistook Allied forces for Russians, usually with devastating results. The Allies were also disturbed at the military procedures of the South Koreans who had similar methods of interrogation to those from the North. Korea had previously been a Japanese colony and a source of many of the guards in the prisoner of war camps where they exhibited as much cruelty as their masters. "'Suffering thirty years of Japanese domination had taught the Koreans some really bad habits,' said [John] Slim. Watching a group of South Korean policemen conducting an 'interrogation'—a mass beating of a suspect with batons and clubs—[Julian] Tunstall wondered if his allies were worth fighting for . . . 'We noticed these trucks going up into the hills crowded with people and coming back empty,' [Stanley] Boydell said, 'We thought they were just being transported.'"[1] Sometime later, when hearing of atrocities, Boydell realized what the fate of these people in the trucks was—execution. Although enemies ideologically, they were their own countrymen and women. After a successful action at the Chongchon River, Reg Bandy, an Australian company sergeant major, says: "When they reached the other side they were surprised to see North Koreans surrendering as they neared the Australians. But then from a nearby hill the enemy opened up with heavy but inaccurate fire on both the Australians and the prisoners."[2]

As the UN advance proceeded into the hills, massive ambushes, guerrilla tactics, slit trenches ingenuously concealed, and innumerable booby traps abounded, thrusting the soldiers into a far different war than they had previously experienced. There were instances where whole villages were wired for explosion. In some of these hamlets soldiers viewed the remains of tattered banners reading, "Welcome UN Army," fluttering amidst the blackened ruins of peasants' homes. Civilians, carrying their fearfully wounded family members, were returning to seek medical aid as the soldiers marched through. "Such scenes spurred reflection. 'It made you think quite deeply whether it was morally right to go in and decimate the country of a simple people who probably did not give a damn if they were communist or what, their main concern was just to get enough food,' said Boydell, who began to question the frequent use of the

---

1. Salmon, *Scorched Earth, Black Snow*, 87.
2. Thompson and Macklin, *Keep off the Skyline*, 33.

word 'liberated'. 'It crossed my mind that this is a funny sort of liberation because these people would perhaps have been better off without us.'"³

The UN forces primarily used roads; the enemy accustomed for generations to jungle warfare, did not. The UN had all the vehicles and equipment necessary to fight a war; the Chinese carried and dragged their second-rate equipment through the jungles. These men were poorly armed, sometimes with archaic weapons and badly dressed:

> ... hundreds of Chinese soldiers clad in cotton khaki suits; plain, cheap, cotton caps; rubber-soled canvas shoes upon their feet; their shoulders, chests, and backs criss-crossed with cotton bandoliers of ammunition: upon their hips, grenades—rough stick grenades so like the Boche 'potato-masher,' but inferior ... Those in the forefront of the battle wear steel helmets that are reminiscent of the Japanese. Their weapons—rifles, carbines, 'burp' guns, and Tommy guns that we supplied to Chiang Kai-Shek—are ready in their hands. Behind, on mule or pony limbers, are drawn their guns and ammunition. Between the two lines, on sweating backs, or slung between two men upon stout bamboo poles, their mortars and machine-guns travel forward.⁴

But, in the intensity of combat, the Chinese were fanatical and came in continual waves of apocalyptic numbers until they either destroyed or were destroyed. This was the primary advantage of the enemy—the thousands of men they had at their disposal. These men seemed oblivious to their comrades as they fell. "For every casualty suffered by the enemy, two, three, four more Chinese will appear to take his place."⁵ "This is not a battle in which courage, tactical and technical superiority will be the means to victory: it is a battle of attrition. Irrespective of the number of casualties they inflict, there is an unending flow of replacements for each man. Moreover, in spite of their tremendous losses, the numerical strength of the enemy is not merely constant but increasing."⁶ In addition to numbers the enemy had the all-important advantage of speed and surprise. Small "suicide" parties were sent out to establish the position and extent of the front. "The seven moonlight figures still come on ... The light machine-guns fire! The silence dies abruptly as the guns' fierce echoes sound east and west along the river between the cliffs ... The seven men are gone, swept away, lifeless,

3. Salmon, *Scorched Earth, Black Snow*, 139.
4. Farrar-Hockley, *The Edge of the Sword*, 23–24.
5. Farrar-Hockley, *The Edge of the Sword*, 27.
6. Farrar-Hockley, *The Edge of the Sword*, 44.

by the fast flowing water ... But there are more coming, many screaming, as they run into the water, firing their weapons, splashing; careless of noise now that they see from whence the crossing is opposed. Seven, seventeen, twenty-seven, thirty, more than thirty..."[7]

The only members of the UN forces that could be compared with the fighting methods of the Chinese were the Turks. Peter Baldwin reported that a group of bedraggled Turks had arrived at Brigade HQ, attempting to converse with [Basil] Coad in French. These soldiers had a reputation as fierce fighters and they proved this in their first engagement when they fought with bayonets. However, the battle had taken its toll: they had suffered more than 1,000 casualties.

Eventually, in the depths of a Korean winter, the UN troops were in the height of the Korean mountains. They were camped at Chosin Reservoir in the Korean province that bordered Siberia. Here the men fought in a "white hell." After one of the few successful commando assaults, SBS Corporal Harry Langton sat down on a boulder: "It turned out to be a Chinese who had been hit by napalm—he had rolled himself into a ball, he was just a gooey mess, unidentifiable as a human,' said Langton. 'Napalm was effective but very, very bad.'"[8] However impressive such commando raids were, they were greatly limited in their overall outcome. The Chinese were relentless and cunning, slowly but steadily (and stealthily) moving down to the reservoir. Fighting to survive, battling the enemy and the blizzard-like conditions the men struggled on, "The effect of the temperature on the badly wounded was just one horror Chosin Reservoir had in store. In the cold, blood froze more quickly than it could coagulate, with the result that hideous wounds, which would normally prove fatal did not kill outright. Men with limbs blown off might survive until they reached warmth. Then, once blood started flowing, they had little chance."[9]

Finally, at the end of 1950, with the precision bombing of the Chinese by close air support, the UN-led troops retreated from Chosin Reservoir to the safety of the South. North Korea was now lost to the UN and its allies. The Chinese kept up their relentless attacks as the men struggled to safety. The Chinese thought they would be able to completely annihilate the marines but the UN held fast in their retreat and, with self-control, determination, tactical skill, and firepower, reversed the odds and the

7. Farrar-Hockley, *The Edge of the Sword*, 19.
8. Salmon, *Scorched Earth, Black Snow*, 335.
9. Salmon, *Scorched Earth, Black Snow*, 339.

Chinese themselves were annihilated. A short time later a cable to Mao, Peng [Te-huai] was detected appealing for 60,000 replacements for the 9th Army. Such a request illustrates the enormous resources in human fighters that were available to the North Koreans

Peace between the two Koreas was not achieved until 1953 when the UN brokered a solution to both parties. The Korean War is often known as The Forgotten War. Korean veterans often express surprise at the newspaper coverage that focusses on present-day US troops fighting a war in Afghanistan, which appears to them to be significantly less perilous than that in Korea. Almost every casualty is given huge media coverage back home. In Korea the casualties weren't reported individually. Entire units were wiped out at any one time in Korea. "For the US Army, the decimation of two regiments at Kuni-ri, and the destruction of another at Chosin, were disasters unequalled even in the heaviest combat in Vietnam."[10]

> Overshadowed by the sheer magnitude of its predecessor, World War II, and the domestic trauma of its successor, Vietnam, the Korean War has been almost as unpopular with historians as it was with contemporaries. When it is remembered, moreover, people generally focus on the dramatic events of the war's first year: the North Korean invasion; the defense of the Pusan Perimeter; Inchon; the Chinese entry; the Truman-MacArthur controversy. Almost half of all U.N. casualties occurred after the start of peace negotiations in July 1951, but the final two years represent the forgotten part of the forgotten war. In particular, few have asked what would seem to be an obvious question: why did the belligerents wait so long, and fight so hard, before accepting in July 1953 a settlement that was practically identical to their positions two years earlier?[11]

General Douglas MacArthur did not help matters. Having been given "carte blanche" by the US government, MacArthur acted belligerently to the earlier peace negotiations and attempted to sabotage any efforts by the UN to work towards achieving an end to the war. President Truman dismissed MacArthur and brought him home so that armistice talks could proceed. Truman was no longer in office and Eisenhower was in the White House when the the Korean Armistice Agreement was eventually signed.

10. Salmon, *Scorched Earth, Black Snow*, 5.
11. Rose, *How Wars End*, 125.

15

Vietnam: The Lonely War

VIETNAM IS OFTEN REFERRED to as "The Long War." In the dedication in his book *Vietnam: the Australian War*, Paul Ham says: "Dedicated to the Australian servicemen and women—and their families—who fought this politicians' war."[1] Veterans call it "The Lonely War."

From the end of the nineteenth century Australia had sent troops to fight in support of other countries. Australia was represented in China during the Boxer Rebellion from 1899 to 1901, the Boer War from 1899 to 1902, and the Malaya Emergency from 1950 to 1963, amongst others. Originally Australia responded to the call of the Mother Country sometimes without analyzing whether such wars were justified. Most were responses to countries where the British economic and personal interests were threatened. The Boer War demonstrated how far the British were prepared to go to expand and develop their empire—the huge "pink" areas in every schoolchild's atlas. The hostilities were initiated by the British who politically and geographically desired to build up their influence in the South of Africa; and economically to foster their need to control the gold mining areas held by the Dutch Boers. The cost of maintaining this huge empire was becoming more and more difficult. Their consequent decision to hold the "Boers to ransom" by imposing huge tariffs for importing and exporting goods to and from the coastal areas that they controlled, pushed the Boers into declaring war. As Britain was the home country to most Australians and questions were rarely asked—certainly not by political leaders of the day—colonial men went off on the

---

1. Ham, *Vietnam*, v.

first "Great Adventure"—thousands of miles from loved ones and from a vitally young sunburnt country, just to see the world and all its wonders.

After the Korean War and the Malaya Emergency when Australians had once again supported Britain, the tide turned to a support of the new Policeman of the World, the United States of America. When North Vietnam attacked the South, the United States went primarily to aid of the South Vietnamese to help once again to prevent the spread of Communism—a reaction to Stalin and the debacle in Europe with a divided Germany. At the end of World War II, Russia had cleverly increased its territories in Europe and an Iron Curtain had come down on many countries. In the east China was spreading its Communism through Asia and indoctrinating populations as it went—these were all the same fears people felt when North Korea invaded the south. Now the atlas where once "pink" countries had been prominent, was dominated by gargantuan areas of "red." Political leaders in Australia warned the people of the dangers of this growth of Communist converts through Asia and threatened that eventually they would come to Australia—"reds under beds" was the catchphrase of these times. In retrospect, it is hard to imagine that this type of thinking was so readily accepted but it generally was. In fact, all American presidents from Eisenhower onwards followed the "falling domino" principle. Accordingly, the United States, with its mindset, seemed to be a type of savior for those "Down Under," capable of halting the spread of indoctrination by the evil ones. Even if there was no fighting, it was a great security for Australia to have the powerful United States of America in Southeast Asia. An extremely popular book of these times was *You Can Trust the Communists (to Do Exactly as They Say)*, by Frederick Schwarz. Schwarz was a Queenslander who was recognized as an expert on Marxist-Leninist philosophy. He founded the Christian Anti-Communism Crusade (CACC) and from the 1950s onwards he spent a great deal of his time in the United States on speaking tours promoting his beliefs. Thousands of people attended and thousands more listened on radio and television. He befriended Ronald Reagan amongst others and, as a result, appeared to have some influence on political figures both in the United States and Australia. When his book was published in 1960 it became a "must read."

Vietnam was a different war—the military being a type of invader instead of a defender. To be able to send enough men, Australia reintroduced National Service and, in addition, a ballot system to establish which National Servicemen would go to Vietnam. Initially the reaction of the "Nashos" was mixed—many were prepared to go because it seemed a just war; some saw a way out of an aimless life that held few prospects; some wanted to follow in the footsteps of their fathers and grandfathers. But there was a number who refused to go. Some were given jobs in the army at home; others went to jail. Rolf Kling actually successfully trained with the SAS with the intention of going. He loved the training and the camaraderie but then he started to think things through: "I still had in the back of my mind that I was going there to kill people, and the one thing I did recognise was the SAS guys kill more people than the troops. In ambushes inadvertently, you knock over women and children. And I didn't really see myself wanting to do that. And I saw myself as different to the regs who were in the SAS. As much as they were friends of mine, I saw them as dogs of war. They wanted to go there and they wanted to do that. I was there because I had to be there."[2] He was in a squadron of 123 but the army decided to send 120. Anyone who didn't want to go could nominate to stay and he did. King went to the airport in Perth to see his comrades fly out to Vietnam. He became very emotional. Even though he was sure he had made the right decision and had had the opportunity to refuse to go, he felt he had let his mates down. He accepted that some of them would never return. For the next forty years he lived that moment over and over again. The sense that he had abandoned them made him feel a failure.

There were some who strongly felt the system unfair but out of their control—they went under silent protest. Doug English, a fanatically fit youth who worked at the *Sydney Morning Herald*, had no desire to fight in Vietnam, and his father, once a commando in Borneo, was angry that his son had been chosen by a lottery. Doug himself was also very angry, reporting that he went to Vietnam under protest and with a great deal of aggression. He fought with this constant attitude determined to kill as many Viet Cong as he could. He didn't feel any fear when he was out on patrol—just anger. But now this anger was directed at the enemy. "How dare you shoot at me?"[3]

There were few demonstrations against the Australian boys going compared with the situation in America—in Australia the anti-war movement did not grow until much later. The population generally thought National Service should never have been abolished as it made

---

2. Dapin, *The Nashos' War*, 385.
3. Dapin, *The Nashos' War*, 260.

real men of the younger generation. It wasn't until 1969 that the majority of Australians were in favor of bringing the men home.

Those in the regular army slowly came to regard the National Servicemen as their comrades, particularly the "gung ho" attitude they often brought to the military life and the bravery they continually displayed in ambushes. Australian soldiers witnessed horrors and atrocities but were forced to keep their feelings in check to survive. Generally, the nashos were sensitive to the people of Vietnam. During the battle of Long Tan, D Company were sent out on gathering information from the dead bodies of the VC. They were instructed, not just to look for bodies, but to check through every identifiable piece of body they could find, looking for any paperwork in the pockets. Diaries, wallets, identification markers—anything that would provide information about the Viet Cong and their strategies. They were warned to be careful moving bodies as these could be booby-trapped, so the men invented ingenious methods to carry out the search. During this exercise they buried about a hundred bodies each day. Dave Sabben "found a body, and it was severed through the nipple line. I found the lower part. He looked like he had been cut with a sheet of corrugated iron, like a ripple effect." [4] He searched vainly for the rest of the body so he could bury it complete. All the surrounding mud was red and very stodgy. During the same period Norm Wotherspoon was also burying Vietnamese, "and I realised that these were people who were younger than me—some were older—and this was actually their homeland. And, even though I hadn't been particularly religious, I said little prayers over the ones that I buried, and at the same time I was losing what little faith I had."[5] Up until then, Wotherspoon had accepted the fact that he had been sent to a foreign land to fight for a people he knew little about. But, actually seeing the reality of the results of that war, he decided that it was not normal to agree to what they were asked to do. The day he came to that realization dragged him into emotional depths like never before. He no longer just accepted what life threw at him but started to think and make decisions for himself. For the rest of his time in Vietnam, blankly following orders became far more difficult for him.

By the end of hostilities there were 200 National Servicemen dead—they made up 37 percent of the army and numbered 42 percent of the total fatal casualties. This was the real blight of the Vietnam War in

4. Dapin, *The Nashos' War*, 145-46.
5. Dapin, *The Nashos' War*, 146.

Australia—that so many who fought were selected by chance. Errol Noack, a reluctant conscript, was the first National Serviceman to be killed in Vietnam. When he left Australia, his last action was to take communion at his Lutheran parish. In his devotions he read the following words from John 16:22: "So you have pain now; but I will see you again, and your hearts will rejoice, and no one will take your joy from you." The Australian Regular Army, its reserve battalions, and the newly blooded national servicemen fought bravely together throughout. They were stalwart in their support and care of their comrades none striving only for personal glory but always fighting together as "mates" particularly in small unit formations. The Battle of Long Tan in particular is commemorated by Australian soldiers. Nevertheless, as in the United States, returning fighters were treated abysmally, a shame forever of the Australian public.

In August 2006, Prime Minister John Howard apologised in parliament to the Vietnam veterans: "He did not say he was sorry they had been sent to a war in which hundreds of young Australians had died and thousands been severely wounded. He showed no regret for the government's use of national servicemen to fight a foreign war. He was without remorse that many of the dead had been chosen by ballot. He was unrepentant that Robert Menzies had erroneously identified Chinese expansionism as the force behind Vietnamese Communism and mischievously labelled it a 'direct military threat to Australia.'"[6] Nor did Howard mention that, at that time, he was of an age to enlist and go as were many of the politicians of the day. He did not apologize for that. He only apologized for the poor reception that many received on their return. However, to the credit of the Australian government, whilst the US marines fought the biggest battles against the North Vietnamese army in the far north of South Vietnam, Australian soldiers were designated areas in the very south where they fought a type of guerrilla war against the local Vietnamese. The soldiers were told they were dealing with "hard core Communists" but possibly many of those killed were probably simple village people trying to protect their paddy fields and consequently their basic livelihoods. Thus, the Australians felt frustrated and many in the regular army wanted to move north to fight. The Australian government saw its role in Vietnam as internationally supportive rather than military. Although it had committed the country to this war, the government knew full well that there would be a dreaded political reaction if there were massive Australian

---

6. Dapin, *The Nashos' War*, 424–25.

losses similar to those of the US marine battalions. Americans lost more dead in some weeks that Australians did in a decade of war in Vietnam.

Nevertheless, Australians were involved in ferocious fighting—the battle of Long Tan being synonymous for ever with the Australian army. The military had learned the art of jungle warfare and the capability of living and fighting in humid conditions from its experience during the Malay Emergency. Those in command also studied the teachings of Mao Tse-tung in regard to guerrilla warfare. From this they learned that it was essential to prevent the local population becoming enmeshed with the guerrillas. Mao's instruction was in three stages. The first was the establishment of revolutionary cells in each hamlet, which enabled indoctrination of the peasants and also set up an infrastructure from which to operate successfully. The second was to group cells into working units—continual ambushes and surprise attacks on outposts help to expand and grow the revolutionary movement until the government becomes unable to contain it. The final stage is when such growth enables a strong united force to be able to stage conventional warfare against the government.

Delta Company, the unit that fought the battle of Long Tan, was superbly trained. The commander, Major Harry Smith, had always pushed his men beyond the military requirements. His soldiers became super fit. In running: "Where the battalion specified ten kilometres, Harry ordered twelve. Where it specified fifteen-kilo packs, Harry ordered twenty-kilo packs. Where an activity specified sandshoes, Harry ordered boots and gaiters: this was to strengthen the legs . . ."[7] Eventually the men reveled in being faster and stronger than those in other battalions. National Servicemen did not complain—because the army was an unknown to them, they reasoned this was normal training. The men were also trained well in night scouting—clothing fully covering the body, any equipment taped to prevent noise and reflection, expertise in signaling, and working in complete silence. Men were even forbidden to shave as this not only helped with camouflage but prevented infection from accidental cuts or the use of fouled water. Pretend Asian villages were constructed and soldiers were able to practice close-contact shooting skills, adding to their already honed long-range shooting abilities. There was also intense training in speedy boarding and disembarking into and from helicopters. Flight Lieutenant Bob Grandin, who had moved from a career of flying Dakotas, was impeccably trained in flying helicopters. Hovering was a

---

7. Grandin, *The Battle of Long Tan*, 51.

completely new challenge for him. "A real test was to hover over a mushroom patch with the crewman hanging out picking mushrooms for all to share, while you remained in the hover!"[8]

The battle of Long Tan was a great testing ground for Harry Smith's Delta Company. Another Australian company, Bravo, had been out on a daily patrol and had been forced to spend the night in the jungle. Delta Company was sent to replace it. Not long after Bravo had set out to return to its quarters, soldiers in Delta saw what they thought was a small number of Viet Cong. It was not until much later that these men were identified as soldiers of the North Vietnam army, taking over the area from the Viet Cong who had fled. In fact, warnings about the presence of the enemy had not filtered through to those that mattered! Whilst a concert was being enjoyed back at the base, Delta Company found themselves under attack with firepower quickly intensifying. This was the beginning of a three-hour battle between 108 inexperienced young men and 2,500 North Vietnamese. Led by seasoned commanders they proved the worth of their combat training, overcoming fear and uncertainty, and adapting their learned skills in small arms to face the seemingly hordes of a fanatical enemy, sometimes 245 feet away, sometimes only sixty-five feet. Accuracy was paramount. One of the leaders, Bob Buick listened as they called out to each other. "They were supporting themselves and their mates by calling out names. The courage, tenacity, skill and endurance displayed by the young men that day would live with me forever."[9] These youths had only begun army training eleven months before and yet they were able to immediately meld into a loyal band in the true "digger" tradition. Added to these challenges, in a short time the area was deluged with heavy monsoonal rains.

As the battle worsened artillery was called up, but this was initially too far away to be effective. Gradually, by rapid signaling—with the enemy sometimes successfully jamming the radio frequency—and the receiving of better grid references suggested by the New Zealand contingent, the artillery was able to achieve the desired effect on the North Vietnamese army. As the artillery continued to pound the enemy, men from the kitchens, the offices, the Q store, and the hospital, came from all over the base to keep resupplying the gun line from the ammunition dump. One soldier, "had been lying naked in the sick bay in the battery area at

---

8. Grandin, *The Battle of Long Tan*, 41.
9. Grandin, *The Battle of Long Tan*, 154–55.

Nui Dat trying to recover from a serious infection he had, when all hell let loose from the guns. He dashed, still naked from the sick bay to help those on the gun line by breaking 105 mm ammunition out of boxes."[10] Meanwhile Bravo Company, on hearing the barrage, had halted, and was impatiently waiting for permission to return to Long Tan and assist their mates. Over an hour later more ammunition was needed. After much haggling with the air force about flying restrictions in adverse weather, pilot Frank Riley asserted his authority as the commander and, after soldiers hastily loaded two helicopters, he led his crews to a successful drop at Long Tan.

Back at the base, "Adrian Roberts [commander of the armored personnel carriers] was under the troop shower when a runner arrived from Squadron Headquarters to say, 'The Major wants you with your map.'"[11]

At the same time as Bravo Company began their hike back to Long Tan, Adrian Roberts was leaving the Australian bases with ten armored personnel carriers packed with reinforcements of both men and ammunition. Each of the leaders at Long Tan brought to the battle their own special set of skills. Roberts had been brought up in the country in Western Australia. As a boy he had indulged a passion for exploring, going out each day and learning the lay of the land and gradually covering more and more of the bush until he was familiar with large areas of land. In Vietnam he used this gift to explore and get to know the land around the Australian base. He was the ideal person to take these huge vehicles to Long Tan for he knew the exits, the paths through the jungle, the best places to cross swollen rivers. He also had the assertive capability to overcome difficulty whenever it arose. The monsoonal rains and the raging battle were an added advantage. Poor visibility and deafening noise masked his advance from the North Vietnamese. More men and more ammunition clinched the defence at Long Tan. After three desperately long hours, the men had heroically persevered and the North Vietnamese withdrew into the jungle. All this time Harry Smith had quietly encouraged his Force. When asked by one of his men if he thought they would get through, he said: "I just knowingly winked back at him, confidently indicating I thought we would . . . It had not occurred to me we would

---

10. Grandin, *The Battle of Long Tan*, 190.
11. Grandin, *The Battle of Long Tan*, 129.

not survive. It was only after the battle I became fearful and frightened by what might have happened."[12]

When Delta Force returned the next day to the battlefield: "On the ground they saw tens, then scores, then hundreds of corpses, in grotesque positions, half-buried, dismembered, frozen in acts of blind self-sacrifice. Wild pigs snuffled about the field, feasting on the remains. Bodies were obliterated, fragments that were once part of a human being were found in limbless trees."[13] "The Australian dead lay where they fell, unmolested by the enemy, undisturbed by artillery. Most had their rifles by them, or in their hands. They had died fighting."[14] Of the missing, two were found wounded—one lying on his front in the mud, the second leaning against a tree. Bryan Wickens, a professional ex-British army soldier, formerly critical of conscripts, was so deeply impressed by the bravery of these men that he later in life changed his nationality to Australian. "The unbroken hiss of radio static could be heard. Vic Grice, an Australian radio operator, had died sitting up, with the 'squelch' of his radio off, like a cardiograph flat-lining. He appeared to be smiling."[15] The total number of Australian dead was eighteen; for the enemy there was an official estimate of 245. A document later discovered by Australians put the actual count by the Vietnamese at 878. The Australians buried the Vietnamese dead, and treated any wounded. There was no routine killing of wounded as one Australian journalist claimed. In fact, one journalist was trying to question soldiers as they went about their work—"Jack Kirby hung the reporter by the collar of his shirt on a rubber tree."[16] Years later, Bob Buick wrote: "I can still see the battlefield, smell and taste the air: the flyblown and maggoty bodies that fell apart, when dragged into a hole."[17]

In the aftermath, "the Viet Cong and North Vietnamese realised they were up against a far tougher adversary than hitherto thought . . . In fact, so heavy were the Vietnamese casualties from close-ranging Australian and New Zealand artillery that the Viet Cong were ordered never again to attempt a direct attack on Nui Dat: indeed, on no subsequent occasion during the war would the Task Force face a regimental

12. Grandin, *The Battle of Long Tan*, 185.
13. Ham, *Vietnam*, 252.
14. Ham, *Vietnam*, 252.
15. Ham, *Vietnam*, 252.
16. Ham, *Vietnam*, 254.
17. Grandin, *The Battle of Long Tan*, 237.

or larger offensive."[18] Sadly, medals and decorations were not awarded in the numbers they should have been and, in one instance, to the correct recipient. The men were not permitted to accept the foreign awards offered. A further consternation was when the Vietnam Veterans Association of Australia (VVAA) commandeered Long Tan Day, August 18, for the day of remembrance for all veterans of the war. Furthermore, in 1995, after requests for survivors of the Long Tan battle to be taken back to Vietnam to commemorate the struggle and remember those they had lost, a contingent was organized for this purpose. There was no consultation with the Long Tan survivors, nor did it include Delta Company. It was composed of various VVAA people, public servants, and politicians. One token survivor of Delta was included. What say those who sacrificed their lives at Long Tan to those who reveled in this "junket" trip? Would they not want their mates to be there? In the sentiment of Philip Caputo, recorded later in this book, only the veterans of Long Tan can pay real homage to those who were lost, "because of the small things that made us love you—your gestures, the words you spoke and the way you looked."[19]

> America's involvement in Vietnam began in secrecy; it ended thirty years later in failure, witnessed by the entire world. It was begun in good faith, by decent people, out of fateful misunderstandings, American over-confidence and Cold War miscalculation, and it was prolonged because it seemed easier to muddle through than admit that it had been caused by tragic decisions made by five American Presidents belonging to both political parties. Before the war was over more than 58,000 Americans would be dead; at least 250,000 South Vietnamese troops died in the conflict as well; so did over a million North Vietnam soldiers and Viet Cong guerrillas. Two million civilians North and South are thought to have perished as well as tens of thousands more in the neighbouring states of Laos and Cambodia. For many Vietnamese it was a brutal civil war; for others the bloody climatic chapter in a century old struggle for independence. For those Americans who fought in it and for those who fought against it back home as well as for those who merely glimpsed it on the nightly news, the Vietnam War was a decade of agony; the most divisive period since the Civil War. Vietnam seemed to call everything into question—the value of honor and gallantry; the qualities of cruelty and mercy; the candour of the American

---

18. Ham, *Vietnam*, 257.
19. Caputo, *A Rumor of War*, 224.

government; and, what it means to be a patriot. Those who lived through it have never been able to erase its memory, have never stopped arguing about what really happened, why everything went so badly wrong, who was to blame and, whether it was all worth it![20]

How did it all go so badly wrong? Did those who made momentous life-changing decisions learn anything from the bloodied past, or was their hubris too great to face and admit their erroneous policies and devastating strategies? In fact, by 1965 the war was acknowledged by political leaders in the United States to be unwinnable, but they nevertheless continued to send their youth into battle. Whilst Lyndon B. Johnson was officially committing troops on the ground in great numbers, a Top Secret document was being compiled by John McNaughton, the Assistant Secretary of Defense. In this analysis McNaughton listed by percentage the reasons for continuing the conflict:

> 70%—to avoid a humiliating United States defeat (to our reputation as a guarantor).
> 20%—to keep SVN (and then adjacent) territory from Chinese hands.
> 10%—to permit the people of SVN to enjoy a better, freer way of life.
> ALSO—To emerge from crisis without unacceptable taint from methods used.
> NOT—To "help a friend," although it would be hard to stay in if asked out.[21]

From the beginning the Americans, like the French colonials before them, fought the war their way, doing little or no groundwork with the Vietnamese themselves and not allowing for the vastly different culture in which they were enmeshed. They were rarely sensitive to the inhabitants, calling them "gooks" (monkeys) whilst completely oblivious to the fact that most Vietnamese labeled them as "Khi Dot" (big monkeys). Even though the Americans found, as the French had, that it was almost impossible to establish if a Vietnamese was a Viet Cong, they nevertheless were not always astute enough to identify VC spies in their midst when there were "alarm bells." One of the Vietnamese journalists working for one of America's biggest weekly news magazines was actually a Viet Cong

---

20. Burns and Novick, *The Vietnam War. Episode 1*. Film.
21. McNaughton, "Proposed Course of Action," 694–702.

colonel. "He had been born in the south and lived there, although his father had elected to go north when the 1954 Geneva Accords divided the country into communist and non-communists—a clue that should have been picked up by the CIA perhaps."[22] He originally worked for the Vietnam Press, "where he was so skilful at gathering information that he was sent to the United States to study journalism at university. In 1960 he returned to join Reuters as a reporter, and soon developed a reputation as a very good one . . . He became very popular because of his political and military knowledge and good sources."[23]

As the war progressed the United States became a hotbed of opposition to this war. In Vietnam men of the military originally embarked willingly on this idealistic journey. As Lieutenant General Harold G. Moore commented on this idealism in the introduction to his book on his experiences in the US war involvement in Vietnam, John Fitzgerald Kennedy had said the following words in his inaugural address as President: "Let every nation know, whether it wishes us well or ill, that we shall pay any price, bear any burden, meet any hardship, support any friend, oppose any foe to assure the survival and the success of liberty. This much we pledge—and more."[24] Moore calls his generation "Kennedy's young stalwarts'" and the generation who was chosen to put that pledge into practice in the defense of freedom. But, he also points out that the man who made that speech on their behalf is no longer there to witness its fulfillment. John F. Kennedy "waited for us on a hill in Arlington National Cemetery, and in time we came by the thousands to fill these slopes with our white marble markers and to ask on the murmur of the wind if that was truly the future he had envisioned for us."[25] There was an idealism when completely unseasoned men arrived in Vietnam—although their energy and conviction was initially overwhelmed by the intense tropical heat and humidity, the treacherous jungle vegetation, the constant swirling dust, and the ever-present fear of the sniper's bullets—some saw the surreal beauty of this remote land. Particularly at sunset the calm China Sea diffused into the pastel colors of the sky, and the strip of white coastal sand looked to some like the edge of the world.

22. Lunn, *Vietnam*, 255.
23. Lunn, *Vietnam*, 255.
24. Addis, ed. *I Have a Dream*, 128.
25. Moore and Galloway, *We Were Soldiers Once*, xix.

The military fortunately had learned some lessons from the war in Korea. To ensure that the armies were not bogged down and delayed by transporting equipment and men along jungle tracks and through jungle vegetation, an innovative plan of providing huge helicopters to do just that was embarked upon. Bigger, faster, and better helicopters were designed and built and new systems of training developed. Captain Paul Winkel related that pilots trained from July 1964 until they arrived in Vietnam, concentrating on precision flying, radio work, navigation, reporting, and foul-weather flying. The constant emphasis was on timing and co-ordination with the various branches of the military: the artillery, the infantry, the gunships. The men engaged in endless practice for months before they actually went into the battlefield. He commented, "Many of us are alive today because we learned our lessons well."[26]

Employing such helicopters was a revolutionary idea, which achieved its purpose but using air power in another way did not: the United States sent planes over the jungle to drop chemical defoliants to clear the hiding places of the Viet Cong. Sometimes this was a successful enterprise but it was dependent on which chemicals were used: "The only thing that upset anyone in the Saigon military about this gruesome operation was that it was yet another brilliant theoretical idea that didn't work. In tropical jungle no sooner did the vegetation die than the sun hit the ground for the first time in centuries and, within months, the regrowth was higher than head height again. And now it was denser at ground level than before, when the canopy of the higher trees had restricted the undergrowth. The guerrillas became harder to find."[27] Of course there were also chemicals that were so deadly that the earth itself died so that there was no response to light and warmth. In 1965 alone, defoliants destroyed enough food to feed 245,000 Vietnamese people for a year. This sort of action led many of the peasants to hate the invaders, and extend support to the Viet Cong.

The use of mustard gas in World War I left the soldiers who survived it in agony, living the rest of their lives in distress, struggling for each breath. A British officer gave an account of a visit to victims of gassing to a reporter from the *Daily Mail*, which was published on May 7, 1915:

> Their faces, arms, and hands were of a shiny grey-black colour, with mouths open and bead-glazed eyes, all swaying slightly backwards and forwards trying to get breath. It was the most

---

26. Moore and Galloway, *We Were Soldiers Once*, 42.
27. Lunn, *Vietnam*, 111.

appalling sight, all these poor black faces, struggling, struggling for life, what with the groaning and noise of the efforts for breath. There is practically nothing to be done for them except to give them salt and water to try to make them sick. The effect the gas has is to fill the lungs with a watery, frothy matter which gradually increases and rises till it fills up the whole lungs and comes up to the mouth; then they die. It is suffocation, slow drowning taking in some cases one or two days.[28]

Though banned in future wars, men throughout successive wars had developed other heinous toxics:

... the Vietnam War came up with many unpleasant ways to die—it was the pictures of billowing red clouds of burning napalm and victims with their burnt skin hanging off in tatters that became the enduring images of that war. Napalm is gasoline thickened by various additives. Although it was developed in World War II for use in flame-throwers, during the Vietnam War Dow Chemicals manufactured a version that was thickened into a gel. When a canister was dropped by plane, it exploded near the ground, covering the target with a sticky petroleum jelly that burnt at 1,800 degrees Fahrenheit.[29]

It has been estimated that some 400,000 tons of napalm bombs were dropped, not only on enemy troops, but on innocent civilians as well. The publication of images of these actions steadily turned the tide of public opinion against the war.

In addition, Agent Orange, for example, killed and maimed not only people on the ground but also future generations. Just as the atomic bombs in Hiroshima and Nagasaki caused cancers in the people of these cities and produced mutant babies—some with deformities so wretched that they could not survive—so future generations of children in Vietnam were affected. In 2006 Christopher Hitchens visited Vietnam with the intention of writing a report on the effects of herbicides used in the conflict: "What he saw almost broke his faith in the power of words to describe the things before his eyes: tiny legs and arms bent at impossible angles; children's faces that seemed too big or small for their skulls; twitching children lying tethered to their cots on the floor."[30] Air power was certainly a harbinger of devastating evil.

28. Hamilton, *The History of World War I in Photographs*, 47.
29. Cawthorne, *Vietnam*, 93.
30. Ham, *Vietnam*, 660.

With this enormous fleet of helicopters, the military procedure was to establish battalions in various base camps in the north. Combat troops were sent into the jungle to seek out the North Vietnamese army and the Viet Cong and destroy them. Because of the difficulty in locating the enemy they were regularly ambushed with horrific losses. They were pitted against fanatical fighting men who carried in their hearts the dictum of Ho Chi Minh: "Nothing is more precious than freedom and independence"[31]—the same words that motivated the Vietnamese when fighting and defeating the French colonialists in years gone by. Fighting battles in jungles and struggling to take over specific land points such as strategic hills, once the Americans succeeded in destroying and routing the North Vietnamese, they then moved out to other suspect areas. In most instances the North Vietnamese merely reclaimed the abandoned hills they had previously held. Because this was a war without a designated front, success could not be measured by territory gained—the Americans gauged their victory by body counts. These were generally exaggerated to boost morale for the army and the American public at home. Frustratingly for the fighting men, they would often find themselves fighting again for the same territory they had gained and lost months or even years before.

In all new areas of conflict, it became almost impossible to organize a fighting front with the enemy approaching from all flanks, thus in the jungle undergrowth groups of soldiers often became separated from the main body and were forced to fight large numbers on their own to survive. When men of the 2nd Platoon at Ia Drang, who had been fighting a lone battle against extreme odds, were finally located they were half buried in shallow ditches they had dug with their weapons and their hands. They had fired at the enemy for days and nights from this prone position and were all in a state of shock. The rescuers had to mentally coax and physically force them to stand up to begin the walk back to safety. All around them, as close as a few feet, were innumerable dead Vietnamese. One soldier who had become separated from his battalion survived because of the action of an enemy soldier. After hiding in the jungle alone for some five days, "a North Vietnamese soldier on the tail end of a passing column looked into the hole in the brush and saw the American . . . 'Four walked by me and the last one looked me right in the eye. He stopped and pointed his rifle at me. I raised my wounded hand

---

31. Moore and Galloway, *We Were Soldiers Once*, 50.

and shook my head no. He lowered his rifle and walked away. So young. He was just a boy, not more than sixteen or seventeen.'"[32]

As in all wars, soldiers suffered the loss of close comrades, men they had trained with and had become "brothers in arms." Those who survived lived lives embedded in the past, with memories they could not erase. In the battle of Ia Drang, Alpha Company's Sergeant Hansen relates how when carrying out a trooper in a poncho: "The man on the left corner of the litter was shot in the back. He went down immediately, . I comforted him, then got Kirsch out. Kirsch was gut-shot but survived. When I got back to Henry, he was dead. I think about him often, dying alone on that open field.'"[33] During any break in fighting, helicopters flew in to collect the dead and wounded. Men who loaded the bodies had a horrific duty to perform especially when those dead were their serving comrades. Sometimes there would be so many that it required more than one of the largest helicopters available—aircraft capable of up to fifty men. One of the soldiers engaged in this duty remembered: "We were picking up our dead and placing them in the choppers. Some of these guys I had known for two years, yet I could recognize them only by their name tags. Their faces were blown off."[34] The loaders worked in silence: there was nothing that could be said. Often, they were picking up bodies from a previous night. Even in such a short period, because of the humidity bodies were already rapidly decomposing and the stench was overpowering. The daylight revealed bodies in pieces, bodies hanging from trees, bodies buried in rubble. Once the intact bodies were recovered, the horrific task of collecting body parts was undertaken. Men prayed they would never have to experience this again, but of course many had to. Specialist Jon Wallenius recounted his experience of loading a helicopter: "Bodies were loaded floor to ceiling. When the ramp finally closed blood poured through the hinges."[35] Another specialist described how, when waiting at the Iz for choppers to Phu Bai, "one last shell came in, landing in the middle of a pile of full body bags, making a mess that no one wanted to clean up, 'a real shit deal.'"[36] When you read of these experiences it becomes beyond

32. Moore and Galloway, *We Were Soldiers Once*, 323.
33. Moore and Galloway, *We Were Soldiers Once*, 136.
34. Moore and Galloway, *We Were Soldiers Once*, 202.
35. Moore and Galloway, *We Were Soldiers Once*, 341.
36. Herr, *Dispatches*, 57.

comprehension to understand how men could live with these memories for the rest of their lives.

Private First Class David A. Lavender would constantly recall his feelings as men died around him. These men were his buddies: men he had been with for two years. They were all only young—in their early twenties—and living, eating, sleeping, and training together. They had all become like brothers. "Hearing these fellows scream, hearing them killed, stuck in my heart and mind ever since."[37] Specialist Jack P. Smith, one of Charlie Company's wounded, remembered: "In the morning the place looked like the devil's butcher shop; there were people hanging out of trees. The ground was slippery with blood. Men who were my closest friends were all around me, dead."[38]

While all this suffering and death claimed American and Australian lives the enemy also was struggling with the same carnage, devastation, and torment. In addition, in this war, civilians, men, women, and children were slaughtered—sometimes as a result of nearby conflict, but very often deliberately because of the fear they might be harboring Viet Cong. Many villagers faced the Americans by day and the VC by night. The worst reported incident was in the hamlet of My Lai. Because of inaccurate US intelligence the army was led to believe that various villages were harboring Viet Cong soldiers. Even though observation helicopters had flown over the surrounding area and reported no incidents of enemy fire, Charlie Company of the 1st Battalion, 20th Infantry Regiment of the Task Force Barker was sent into My Lai to locate the Viet Cong. The soldiers moved through the hamlet murdering civilians, both old men and infant children, and raping and killing women. Three helicopter pilots, led by Hugh Thompson Jr., witnessed the massacre of approximately seventy to eighty villagers, slain with rifles, bayonets, and grenades. According to one of the pilots, Larry Colburn:

> Then we saw a young girl about twenty years old lying on the grass. We could see she was unarmed and wounded in the chest. We marked her with smoke because we saw a squad not too far away. The smoke was green, meaning it's safe to approach. Red would have meant the opposite. We were hovering six feet off the ground not more than twenty feet away when Captain [Ernest] Medina came over, kicked her, stepped back, and finished her off. He did it right in front of us. When we saw Medina

37. Moore and Galloway, *We Were Soldiers Once*, 285.
38. Moore and Galloway, *We Were Soldiers Once*, 337.

do that, it clicked. It was our guys doing the killing. The bodies were marked with smoke—you find yourself feeling that you indirectly killed them. I'll never forget one lady who was hiding in the grass. She was crouched in a fetal position. I motioned to her—stay down, be quiet, stay there. We flew off on more reconnaissance. We came back later and she was in the same position, right where I'd told her to stay. But someone had come up behind her and literally blew her brains out. I'll never forget the look of bewilderment on her face.[39]

The helicopter crew managed to extract a small child, alive, from the hundreds of bodies on the ground and also organized another helicopter to transport people hiding in a bunker to a safe location. Of the officers and their men who were directly involved in the massacre, the only marine arrested and charged was the platoon leader, Lieutenant William Calley. Calley was sentenced to life imprisonment but this was reduced to five years on the intervention of President Nixon. He actually only served three and a half years of house arrest and was then released. Hugh Thompson made an official report to the army and testified to Congress on his return home. His commanders in Vietnam covered up the massacre and attempted to bribe him with a medal, which he threw away in disgust. Thompson was ostracized both in Vietnam and at home, causing incredible ongoing distress, which ruined his life and his marriage. It was not until thirty years later that he and his crew were recognized for their integrity and courage.

The US government continually denied the terrible toll inflicted on civilians in Vietnam, calling it "collateral damage." In the same way it denied that President Nixon had begun sending troops into neighboring Cambodia to eliminate Viet Cong operating from border villages. American interference in the politics of this country eventually led to the growing strength of the Khmer Rouge. In the 1970s civil war escalated and the United States began to openly bomb strategic areas in Cambodia. US diplomats continually downplayed the "collateral damage" caused, denying the reports of Reuters and other journalists. Refugees fled to the safety of the major cities: "The American embassy in Phnom Penh—and Henry Kissinger's team in Washington—insisted that the refugees were fleeing only one thing: attacks by the brutal Khmer Rouge. But, in fact, they were fleeing both the Khmer Rouge and the American bombs."[40]

39. Colburn, "They were butchering people," 346–47.
40. Schanberg, *Beyond the Killing Fields*, 5.

Many who didn't flee joined the Khmer Rouge in anger about the bombing—bombing that involved the use of cluster bombs containing napalm. When the Khmer Rouge won this five-year war all journalists were trucked out to Thailand. The Khmer Rouge then proceeded to kill millions of its own people in what became known as the Killing Fields.

The war in Vietnam was a lonely war. In World War I men from villages and hamlets throughout Britain enlisted together. These became known as the "Pals Regiments," but there was a heavy cost when they went into battle together and villages at home mourned the loss of almost the whole of their youth in one operation. During World War II the five Sullivan brothers, who served together on the USS *Juneau*, were all lost in action on its sinking in early November 1942. During and after both wars, steps were taken to ensure that such tragedies did not reoccur. Nevertheless, men who came together, trained together, and were shipped overseas together, remained together for the duration. They became as brothers, with a relationship that some described as so close that it was closer than any other known relationship—even that of a marriage. A soldier in World War II related that he and three others who enlisted in Brisbane at the same time, because of their close camaraderie, vowed they would endeavor to stay together until the end of the war. When boarding a ship in Crete to evade the Germans they were the last to board. As they did so another soldier tried to push in ahead and, to keep together, one of the four pushed him off the pier. This soldier worried about the interloper's fate for the rest of his life.

By the time of the Vietnam War procedures for sending men to a war zone had changed dramatically. Although many did train together in the United States and stayed together in battle, on the whole, the Vietnam War was different. Soldiers carried out a tour of duty of a specified time. They came often alone, to fill gaps in the fighting corps, and left alone once their tour was completed, usually severing any bonds with a unit or fighting comrades. Relief about completing duty safely carried with it a "survivor" guilt at leaving mates still involved in days and nights of ongoing peril. Many returning soldiers were reluctant to ever attend reunions of veterans in case they discovered that those they fought with had not returned home. In former wars men traveled home by troopships where, being with their compatriots on board for days or even weeks: "the warriors could relive their feelings, express grief for lost comrades, tell each other about their fears, and, above all, receive the support of their fellow soldiers. They were provided with a sounding board for their own sanity."[41] Soldiers returning from Vietnam were denied this essential ritual. Often alone, they were flown back and arrived in the United States sometimes even on the same day they left the field of battle. Other countries, such as Australia, did not make this mistake, ensuring that soldiers were given the best opportunity to readjust to the strange arrival in a country at peace. Britain also was vigilant in this regard—those returning from the Falklands conflict, for example, were sent home by ship rather than plane and then debriefed at home stations in intact units before reuniting with families.

Vietnam also became a war where journalists abounded. The American authorities privately regretted allowing this to happen, particularly when the war began to accumulate devastating numbers of casualties with little strategic progress. To control the information sent to the world the military held daily press conferences in Saigon where they gave the "official" state of affairs for the day. Any reporter who strayed from this view was in danger of losing his or her accreditation and even of being sent home. But reporters were able to get to the actual battle zones and knew exactly what was happening. Nevertheless, the army continued to either bury or falsify bad news. Consequently the US military was the butt of much cynical and delving questions at these press affairs. But whether these same journalists were able to broadcast honestly was a test that was frequently thwarted. After the battle in A Shau Valley, an Australian journalist, Bruce Piggott, reported that forty-five helicopters had been shot down in the assault. The US military claimed, as it was far too sensitive a report to be seen by the enemy, that the official count was fifteen helicopters lost. The military were aware that this report may not be believed and also realized that if some journalist was eventually able to reveal the actual figures it would become a much bigger issue, especially when a cover-up was attempted. So, very cleverly, after a period of about twelve hours, the military released the report again and, after another day, released it once more. The objective, which was achieved, was to influence the agencies, such as Reuters, to think: "Shit, we've got this bloody fifteen helicopters from the A Shau Valley again. We've had it three times this week."[42] It was a brilliant (and successful) attempt to bury the story. The press had so many reports to file and get into print that editors had to be selective in what they accepted.

41. Grossman, *On Killing*, 272.
42. Lunn, *Vietnam*, 86.

When Reuter journalist Hugh Lunn went to view the results of an incident at Tam Ky prison he saw where: "Some ARVN soldiers arranged the dead guerrillas—in one-man bunker holes like flowers in flower pots. I watched as tiny-tots unwrapped green sweets and put them in the open mouth of one grotesquely twisted Viet Cong."[43] After filing his report he discovered it appeared in the press as follows: "Children, used to war, stuck twigs in the mouth of a dead guerrilla."[44] Reporter Jim Pringle, when he came across a number of dead children, wrote: "Viet Cong child soldiers lay like broken dolls along the banks of this canal today and an American sergeant said: 'If they're old enough to pull a trigger they're old enough to die.'"[45]

Although there were many journalists who opted to remain in relative safety, often in the numerous bars of Saigon, gleaning their news from various local sources, there were others who successfully hitched rides on helicopters going out with armaments and supplies, and coming back with the dead and the wounded. By managing to get to the scene of battles and ambushes they were able to relate the real situation—they felt that the American public deserved to see the real picture (but no doubt they wanted to be the "first with the latest"—they were often thwarted in this because of the lack of radio communication, etc. available to them.) Lieutenant General Harold Moore was one who was supportive of them being there. He believed, probably in contrast to official US reporting, that people at home had a right to know what their sons and husbands were doing in the jungles of Vietnam. He always welcomed journalists to his brigade; in fact, he later collaborated with Joseph Galloway, a war correspondent he knew in Vietnam, to write his majestic work on the decisive battle at Ia Drang. He had two provisos; no releasing of information that would endanger any of his men, and keeping well in the background so that operations could not be jeopardized.

Nevertheless, the constant presence of journalists in war zones can sometimes lead to extreme reporting. "War today appears daily on television and print media. Journalists can portray situations in the most vivid ways. The object is to stay on top in a fiercely competitive race towards the ever more spectacular. The law of the jungle. All methods are justified. What this leads to is the photograph Eddie Adams took in Saigon

---

43. Lunn, *Vietnam*, 100.
44. Lunn, *Vietnam*, 100.
45. Lunn, *Vietnam*, 95.

in 1968: the Chief of the South Vietnamese national police holds his gun to a suspect's head and shoots him down in the street. Death on camera, the execution victim's face in close-up. An execution that would not have been carried out, Susan Sontag tells us, if journalists had not been available to witness it. It is the logical conclusion: the photojournalist is no longer a witness of the tragedy. Not merely a voyeur. Not merely, even, an accomplice. He is its perpetrator."[46]

The soldiers definitely did not need the presence of "gung ho" journalists flying in and flying back to a relative safety—it was probably soul-destroying to most. All the day-to-day harrowing experiences of killing and grievous affliction created a constant extreme suspense of not knowing what was going to happen in the next hour, in the next minute, and made it impossible to grasp any sort of normality—you had to learn to "slow yourself down when your heart tried to punch its way through your chest, get swift when everything went to stop and all you could feel of your whole life was the entropy whipping through it . . . You could be in the most protected space in Vietnam and still know that your safety was provisional, that early death, blindness, loss of legs, arms or balls, major and lasting disfigurement—the whole rotten deal—could come in on the freakyfluky as easily as in the so-called expected ways."[47] The strain, the constant terror, and the unbearable sights showed in the eyes of each combatant: "He had one of those faces, I saw that face at least a thousand times at a hundred bases and camps, all the youth sucked out of the eyes, the color drawn from the skin, cold white lips . . ."[48] "People retreated into positions of hard irony, cynicism, despair, some saw the action and declared for it, only heavy killing could make them feel so alive. And some just went insane, followed the black-light arrow around the bend and took possession of the madness that had been waiting there in trust for them for eighteen or twenty-five or fifty years. Every time there was combat you had a licence to go maniac, everyone snapped over the line once there and nobody noticed, they hardly noticed if you forgot to snap back again."[49] Some had even lost the hope of going home and being with loved ones ever again, "Once or twice, when the men from Graves Registration took the personal effects from the packs and pockets

---

46. Maspero, *Out of the Shadows*, 117–18.
47. Herr, *Dispatches*, 19.
48. Herr, *Dispatches*, 21.
49. Herr, *Dispatches*, 53.

of dead Marines, they found letters from home that had been delivered days before and were still unopened."[50]

After the Americans finally withdrew from Vietnam, the country was taken over by the North Vietnamese. Those in the south suffered extreme hardship with any of the populace who had been loyal to the United States or had served in the South Vietnamese army being executed or re-educated in the Communist camps. Not only had many South Vietnamese lost their homes and possessions during the war years but now they had lost their freedom from the blight of Communism.

Furthermore, when the peace treaty was signed, the North Vietnamese provided the Americans with a list of prisoners they were holding. This list of 591 was vastly short of the figure established by the US intelligence agencies who, for example, listed some 311 prisoners being held in Laos alone, where the North Vietnamese list had only nine for Laos. Over the following years a substantial amount of evidence has been accumulated proving that there were men left behind: "Two defense secretaries testified to the Senate POW Committee in September 1992 that prisoners were not returned . . . Over the years the DIA received more than 1,600 firsthand sightings of live American prisoners . . . In the late 1970s and early 1980s listening stations picked up messages in which Laotian military personnel spoke about moving American prisoners from one labor camp to another . . . A series of what appeared to be distress signals from Vietnam and Laos were captured by the government's satellite system in the late 1980s and early '90s."[51] In addition, during the war period, motion sensors had been dropped in the jungle. All US airmen had been trained to use these: "in 1974, a year after the supposedly complete return of prisoners, the gathered data showed that a person or people had manually entered into the sensors . . . 'no less than 20 authenticator numbers that corresponded exactly to the classified authenticator numbers of 20 U.S. POWs who were lost in Laos.'"[52] A final piece of damning evidence was the discovery in 1993, in a Moscow archive, of a transcript of a briefing a North Vietnamese general gave concerning the fact that there were many more POWs being held than originally stated.

Succeeding presidents and the senate have discredited all the evidence supplied. People who have fought for some action to be taken have

50. Herr, *Dispatches*, 69.
51. Schanberg, *Beyond the Killing Fields*, 197–98.
52. Schanberg, *Beyond the Killing Fields*, 199–200.

been consigned to oblivion. Senator John McCain, who was a Vietnam POW himself, and Senator John Kerry combined to bury incriminating documents and successfully brought before the senate legislation that makes any investigation impossible to proceed. The amazing element in all this is the ongoing collusion of the press. In 1954 France paid ransoms to the Vietnamese to enable it to bring *all* its POWs home.

Adrian Roberts, an Australian Troop Commander at Long Tan, writes: "I am not a pacifist. I realise that war will always have a place in human activities. But, when I reflect on the ultimate futility that was Vietnam, I can only hope that the leadership of the day thinks with rigour and has morality before committing its youth to such a folly in the future."[53]

---

53. Grandin, *The Battle of Long Tan*, 270.

16

The Raging of Wars Never Ceases

So, THE PATTERN CONTINUES—AT any one time there are some eighty wars being waged in the world. Are leaders committing their countrymen to war for the same reasons we have seen in the past—for power and authority, for defense of their homeland, for territorial gain, for the freedom of tyranny by an invader? When does the sending of troops to a foreign land become interference in another country—when do freedom fighters begin to be called terrorists? Kuwait, Iraq, Afghanistan—are any of these another Vietnam?

In January 1991, the United States led a sanctioned United Nations coalition to reverse the invasion of Kuwait by Iraq. The President, George Bush Snr., left Saddam Hussein in power in Iraq as the aim of freeing Kuwait had been achieved but, in doing so, he left an unanticipated "Iraq problem." US presidents who followed him had no military experience and were all devastatingly weak on foreign policy. Consequently, this lack of expertise, combined with thwarted ambitions, took the United States on the path to a second war in Iraq. George Bush Jr. and his cohorts, Donald Rumsfeld and Dick Cheney, were determined to depose Saddam Hussein and used the events of 9/11 to push their case for the harboring of terrorists and the concealment of weapons of mass destruction in Iraq. By manufacturing evidence to push their cause, and by a flagrant disregard for a truly legal approval by the United Nations, the political leaders sent thousands of young soldiers to serve their cause and, in the process, many of these young men and women sacrificed their lives. The combatants killed innocent civilians, destroyed cities and towns, and allowed the cultural heritage contained in a country regarded as the "cradle of civilization" to be desecrated. As one US marine stated: "I don't know whether or not George Bush went to war with a noble heart. Only George knows ... Because he and we, knew about the torture and rape cells, he had to choose whether or not to allow torture, rape and horrible deaths to go unchecked. Whatever his true motives, it is clear that the president chose to do what the United Nations chose not to do."[1] "Wake led, for he knew the road and the road wanted knowing."[2]

Deceit to the public, ulterior motives, truth concealed? "Greg Thielmann, a former State Department expert on weapons proliferation, said he thought that 'the American public was seriously misled. The administration twisted, distorted, and simplified intelligence in a way that led Americans to seriously misunderstand the nature of the Iraq threat. I'm not sure I can think of a worse act against the people in a democracy than a president distorting critical classified information'"[3]

In today's climate, the waging of a war can often be traced to economic ambitions—the control of oil, for example. The Middle East is the major source for the world's crude oil. Even the sanctions imposed on Iraq didn't prevent Saddam Hussein from selling his product to neighboring Syria. With the second invasion of Iraq all oil contracts (mostly held by the French) were canceled and put on the open world market. Whether the invaders succeeded in gaining some of these contracts has become a serious matter of conjecture and a situation very hard to ascertain clearly. When the United States eventually pulled out of Iraq, they left a dead dictator, an unstable government, a ruined country, a divided nation, desperately grieving and damaged peoples, and the loss of priceless antiquities by "organized" looting. US troops allowed the ransacking of museums and libraries—many thousands of irreplaceable artifacts were taken; even the card catalogue of the Baghdad Museum was destroyed so it is impossible to establish exactly what has been lost. The occupation forces did, however, secure the Ministry of Oil, safeguarding all its documentation and its detailed inventory of Iraqi oil reserves.

Participants in modern warfare will still suffer as their forebears, but troops in major conflicts can be assured of a base to return to with food, water, clean uniforms and, most of all, medical help in the field—no

---

1. Marlantes, *What It Is Like to Go to War*, 58.
2. Buchan, "Mr Standfast," 510.
3. Burrough et al., "The Path to War." No pages. Online.

longer months of tenuous survival in flooded trenches. However, even today, there are some conflicts where warring countries do not prioritize the needs of their fighting men and women. In the Chechen wars, Russian soldiers suffered horrifically from lack of support and care. Seemingly learning little from the poor maintenance of troops in both world wars, the Russian government still fails in its responsibility to the lower ranks of the army. Cleanliness, medical facilities, and food supplies are often, according to journalist Arkady Babchenko, incredibly substandard for a fighting army.

In 2009, former war correspondent, Sydney Schanberg wrote: "To me, now a septuagenarian, it seems that our planet—and maybe Washington in particular—has become almost comfortable with regular wars. President Eisenhower's warning to America to beware of 'the military-industrial complex' has been brushed aside. We Americans are notoriously deficient about taking lessons from our own history."[4]

---

4. Schanberg, *Beyond the Killing Fields*, x.

17

Death and Killing

The following section of war, death, and killing primarily consists of a number of quotations, for who better can describe these experiences than the participants themselves?

War

We stood there watching the bombardment in silence. It's at these times, when houses whirl among tons of earth in the air, fly apart in fragments and leave behind craters the size of ponds, and the ground trembles for two miles around from the impact of the massive shells, that you are especially aware of the frailty of the human body, the softness of bones and flesh and their defencelessness against metal. Heavens above, is this whole inferno just meant to kill people, or will it split the earth in two? You realize how brittle you are and that there is no way you can resist this avalanche that is tearing a whole village to shreds. And the realization of how easy it is to kill a person paralyzes you and leaves you speechless.[1]

God is our refuge and strength,
  a very present help in trouble.
Therefore we will not fear, though the earth should change,
  though the mountains shake in the heart of the sea;
though its waters roar and foam,
  though the mountains tremble with its tumult.

---

1. Babchenko, *One Soldier's War*, 213–14.

There is a river whose streams make glad the city of God,
  the holy habitation of the Most High.
God is in the midst of the city; it shall not be moved;
  God will help it when the morning dawns.
The nations are in uproar, the kingdoms totter;
  he utters his voice, the earth melts.
The LORD of Hosts is with us; the God of Jacob is our refuge.

Come, behold the works of the LORD;
  see what desolations he has brought on the earth.
He makes wars cease to the end of the earth;
  he breaks the bow, and shatters the spear;
  he burns the shields with fire.
'Be still and know that I am God!
  I am exalted among the nations,
  I am exalted in the earth.'
The LORD of Hosts is with us; the God of Jacob is our refuge.
(PS 46 NRSV)

Death

"The dark is impenetrable; you can't even see the hand in front of your face. It seems there is no sky, no ground, no life, no light, no joy, no love, and no heroism. Just night and death. Because night is the time of death. Every time the sun goes down life dies."[2]

And when death does come there is no distinction. Many soldiers involved in collecting, identifying, and recording body counts have similar opinions on what they see. Philip Caputo, in particular, records in his book how he discovered that, strangely, all the bodies he dealt with looked the same. Their skin had a tallow-like texture, sometimes pale eyes are open, and usually their lips are parted as if they were about to speak when death struck. Bodies even smell the same if they have been dead for a similar amount of time. Obviously, the stench is far more potent if the body is old and beginning to rot. All agree that a person who dies in relative peace, at home or in a modern hospital, is a reason for grief and sorrow; someone who dies on the battlefield, suddenly in the most horrifying and grotesque manner, perhaps with internal organs spilt in the midst of the blood and mud, becomes a life-shattering experience, which can rarely be erased.

---

2. Babchenko, *One Soldier's War*, 170.

Some soldiers died instantly, some took days to die, or even returned home to die within a few months. Many died stoically but many also died screaming in agony. When a shrapnel shell burst in front of one young subaltern he was absolutely riddled with mortal wounds: "He lay in my arms until he died, shrieking in his agony and said he hoped I would excuse him for making such a noise as he really could not help it."[3] "From the darkness on all sides came the groans and wails of wounded men; faint, long, sobbing moans of agony, and despairing shrieks. It was too horribly obvious to me that dozens of men with serious wounds must have crawled for safety into shell holes, and now the water was rising above them and, powerless to move, they were slowly drowning."[4] Probably the most horrible death to witness was of men enveloped by mustard gas. Often, soldiers were taken unawares, with no time to make preparations. They sat or lay as the gas hit and, when they vomited, pieces of corroded lungs were regurgitated. If they died quickly it was a blessing but few did, often spending days slowly suffocating to death. Many pleaded for others to end it all for them quickly.

Is Dying More Wretched Than Killing? Is Killing More Glorious Than Dying?

Many soldiers in the American Civil War embarked on battle expecting to die. Their death would help the cause! This steadfast attitude helped them to come to terms with the necessity to kill and in so doing, alleviate their guilt for the slaughter around them. John Weissert of Michigan, pledging that he was prepared to die for God and country, wrote: "I did not go to war to murder. No! and . . . Our dear Lord knows it and he will stand by me."[5]

Dying a good death, whether in times of peace or war, was part of the strongly prevalent mid-nineteenth century Christian belief. To die honorably and gladly was an example of defeating the devil and his devious wiles and, in glorying in the salvation of the risen Lord. In fact, because of the times, Civil War soldiers were no doubt far better prepared for death than soldiers of modern times. Added to the horrors of the actual fighting, the lack of medical knowledge or expertise and the

---

3. Stephenson, *The Last Full Measure*, 207.
4. Stephenson, *The Last Full Measure*, 209.
5. Faust, *This Republic of Suffering*, 6.

prevalence of filth and contamination on the battlefield made survival a doubtful prospect.

Of course, there were also examples of strongly held scepticism that prevented a soldier from embracing Christ, fearing such action would give way to fear. Then there was the twisted Christianity that held to a doctrine of universalism. "David Cornwell of the Eighth Illinois [reasoned], 'I couldn't imagine . . . the soul of a soldier who had died in the defense of his country being consigned to an orthodox hell, whatever his opinion might be of the plan of salvation,'"[6] which rather cancels out the sacrifice on the cross!

Duty to one's country became merged with duty to God—all pointing to a glorious death "in the cause." Dying for one's fellow soldiers and for those loved ones at home exemplified the sacrifice of Christ dying for mankind even if one's understanding of Christianity was slightly flawed or incomplete. But killing was a much harder concept to embrace. Killing was violating the Ten Commandments of the Old Testament and the teaching of Jesus in the New Testament. An added dilemma was that in the American Civil War one was fighting one's own countrymen (subsequently the wars in Korea and Vietnam). As in all wars some men believed all death was murder—and, as in all wars, these initial feelings dissipated as comrades fell, creating a strong sense of vengeance that pushed soldiers to acts of endless slaughter on such a scale that had never before been contemplated. And, as in all wars, after the battle, men had to come to terms with what had taken place and their part in it. General Grant after Shiloh: "I saw an open field . . . so covered with dead that it would have been possible to walk across the clearing, in any direction, stepping only on dead bodies without a foot touching the ground."[7]

Killing

No matter how men and women are prepared for battle (and prepared to kill), the reality is shattering to the psyche. However, in some cases, the "warrior" seemed to embrace killing and even find some joy in it. Henry de Man wrote of his personal experience in World War I: "One day . . . I secured a direct hit on an enemy encampment, saw bodies or parts of bodies go up in the air, and heard the desperate yelling of the wounded

---

6. Faust, *This Republic of Suffering*, 25.
7. Faust, *This Republic of Suffering*, 58.

or the runaways. I had to confess to myself that it was one of the happiest moments of my life."[8] Again, in World War I, a British soldier was escorting six German prisoners to the rear. Less than an hour before he had lost his close friend. He had no compunction in making the use of a couple of bombs to help ease his grief. When soldiers went through horrific periods of trauma such retaliations brought a momentary surge of relief. Sometimes these reactions brought guilt and remorse later but for many it was a way of coping with the constant danger surrounding them and their units.

During World War II two brothers were severely reprimanded for throwing grenades into a cave where there were Japanese soldiers. Years later they showed no regret for failing to allow these men to surrender. They had lost mates in battle and heard of the barbarity inflicted on prisoners of war. The Japanese fought ferociously, seemingly with a brutal almost primitive hatred of their enemies and combatants found it difficult to respect them as worthy opponents. One of the known practices of the Japanese was bayoneting an enemy to death, then severing his penis and thrusting it in his mouth as the ultimate insult—a common practice of some ancient warriors. Yet, incongruously, the Japanese were obsessed with their own honor and that of their families—so when Japanese soldiers refused to surrender because of the loss of honor this became a justification for many to kill rather than take prisoners. A survey once found that, whereas only 10 percent of American soldiers were willing to kill German soldiers, almost 43 percent found no problem in killing the Japanese.

Roscoe C. Blunt Jr. remembered traversing a mined field on the border between Holland and Germany, on November 19, 1944:

> ... My heart jumped into my throat when it finally occurred to me I was running full tilt in a field infested with hundreds of wooden Schu mines. 'Mines! Mines!' I screamed at the other GIs around me, but for the legless GI I had just passed it was too late. I skidded to a stop and stared at the ground. Some were buried shallow, the rest just planted on the surface in no particular pattern ... I was pushing my feet along the ground, not wanting to lift them, when an explosion about 100 feet to my left signalled another victim ... This man didn't have to worrying about being an amputee—both his legs and groin area had been blown away and he was dead before he hit the ground. I was instantly sickened when I shot a glance in his direction and saw his body

8. De Man, *The Remaking of a Mind*, 198.

still twitching on the ground, even in death. The sight of this second shattered body unnerved me. This was a rotten war, a stinking way to die."[9]

No matter how men died, each time it was a "stinking way to die": Donald Burgett watched parachutists exiting a plane at a dangerously low level: "Seventeen men hit the ground before their chutes had time to open. They made a sound like ripe pumpkins being thrown down to burst against the ground."[10]

In Vietnam an Australian reported how he discovered the unbelievable power of his weapon when he hit the target—he was overwhelmed in awe. In a similar vein Philip Caputo related: "Under fire, a man's powers of life heightened in proportion to the proximity of death, so that he felt an elation as extreme as his dread. His senses quickened, he attained an acuity of consciousness at once pleasurable and excruciating. It was something like the elevated state of awareness induced by drugs. And it could be just as addictive, for it made whatever else life offered in the way of delights or torments seem pedestrian."[11] A number of soldiers initially found killing "glamorous" and likened the experience to the thrill of an orgasm. They felt like warrior gods, untouchable and infinite. Sometimes when a man knew his shooting had been accurate he felt proud; it was as if he had gotten away with an act condemned by daily life back home. "People could take immense delight in breaking the highest moral law."[12] And, there comes a point when fighting and killing descends into callousness and then callousness descends further into savagery. "I wanted to level the village and kill the rest of the Viet Cong in close combat. I wanted us to tear their guts out with bayonets."[13]

Americans at war often held in their minds images of cinematic heroes. Many combatants, on first going into battle in the Pacific in the 1940s, tried to imitate the escapades of Errol Flynn, Gary Cooper, and Victor McLaglen amongst others. Vietnam War soldiers used images of John Wayne and Audie Murphy. A young girl, Carol McCutchean, was known to have joined the Women Marines because she was thrilled by John Wayne movies. Soldiers remember seeing some of their buddies

---

9. Stephenson, *The Last Full Measure*, 301.
10. Stephenson, *The Last Full Measure*, 283.
11. Caputo, *A Rumor of War*, xv.
12. Bourke, *An Intimate History of Killing*, 32.
13. Caputo, *A Rumor of War*, 268.

putting on a performance of bravado if they sensed a television crew in the area. Certainly, it was a foolhardy thing to do and probably there were a few who, throwing caution to the wind, reaped the drastic consequences. No doubt for some youths though it was an outlet, helping them to cope in the midst of all the terror, for just one more day.

But killing, and the aftermath, slowly but surely changed most of the attitudes—whether it destroyed men on the one hand or whether it made them indifferent on the other: "I hadn't budged an inch or said a word, just stood glued to the spot almost in a trance. The corpses were sprawled where the veterans had dragged them around to get into their packs and pockets. Would I become this casual and calloused about enemy dead? I wondered. Would the war dehumanize me so that I, too, could 'field strip' enemy dead with such nonchalance? The time soon came when it didn't bother me a bit."[14] As he was crawling through the jungle undergrowth, Philip Caputo panicked: "Please don't let them hear me or see me, I prayed silently. Please let everything go right. Let me get them, all of them. Guilt washed over me because I was asking God to help me kill. I felt guilty, but I prayed anyway."[15] "I had killed before, or at least tried to kill those people who shot at me, but my killing was different, on a lesser scale and under my control. The death I administered was not grotesque—just a small hole in the body and that was it. My kind of death was fair; it gave them a chance to hide from the bullet behind a wall, just as I had hidden from their bullets. But to hide from a large-caliber canon was impossible. This caliber could reach you everywhere: it crushed walls and killed terribly, with a roar, tearing off heads, turning bodies inside out, blowing the flesh off a person and leaving bare bones inside their tunics."[16]

Soldiers were driven to actions they would never have thought possible in ordinary life. One of these was the practice of trophy collecting. Sometimes this just took the form of black humor when corpses were used in pranks. During World War I soldiers used to comb the hair of corpses and put cigarettes in their mouths. A lesser evil was collecting German helmets and firearms to take home. In World War II, in the Pacific theater, there were particularly brutal types of trophy collecting:

> He came up to me dragging what I assumed to be a corpse. But the Japanese wasn't dead. He had been wounded severely in the

---

14. Sledge, *With the Old Breed*, 64.
15. Caputo, *A Rumor of War*, 264.
16. Babchenko, *One Soldier's War*, 230.

back and couldn't move his arms; otherwise he would have resisted to his last breath. The Japanese's mouth glowed with huge gold-crowned teeth, and his captor wanted them. He put the point of his kabar on the base of a tooth and hit the handle with the palm of his hand. Because the Japanese was kicking his feet and thrashing around, the knife point glanced off the tooth and sank deeply into the victim's mouth. The Marine cursed him and with a slash cut his cheeks open to each ear. He put his foot on the sufferer's lower jaw and tried again. Blood poured out of the soldier's mouth. He made a gurgling noise and thrashed wildly. I shouted, 'Put the man out of his misery.'[17]

During the Vietnam War there was a craze for cutting off the enemy's ears and displaying them usually in grotesque ways.

From the time when men landed on the shores ready to go into battle—fit, eager, and idealistic—to the time when they became battle-weary, desperately filthy, covered in seeping boils, ringworm, foot rot, and continually starved of good food and sleep—soldiers' attitudes changed dramatically. They became hardened and slightly insane. In contrast when Philip Caputo returned home and was asked how he felt when he went into combat for the first time he was unable to reply truthfully in case people thought he was a war lover. "The truth is, I felt happy. The nervousness had left me the moment I got into the helicopter, and I felt happier than I ever had."[18] But, as the months progressed, Caputo became aware that he had a tendency to suddenly fall into a deep depression. He became embittered and frequently exploded in anger for no apparent reason. Because he dwelt on friends who had died in the conflict, he came to the conclusion that his demeanor was caused by deep grief. He questioned whether his friends had died in vain: for nothing: " if not for nothing, then for nothing tangible."[19]

During the fighting many men, from initially feeling pity and guilt over the bodies of those youths they had killed, slowly but surely began to lose their moral aptitude until the only good enemy was a dead enemy—even if there was only a suspicion and not any proof that he was the enemy. This was when men began to feel a deep emptiness, a complete sense of futility, and an intense fear that they would never again feel normal. These feelings, like the feelings of grief for lost mates, also

---

17. Sledge, *With the Old Breed*, 120.
18. Caputo, *A Rumor of War*, 81.
19. Caputo, *A Rumor of War*, 201.

Death and Killing

compacted on their return home, when they began to relive memories and brood incessantly without any support or outlets.

The only fighting men who seemed to see killing as a hunter's challenge without incurring any obvious signs of genuine remorse, were the snipers. Snipers were particularly prevalent in the ranks of North Vietnam army and Viet Cong but there were many hardened men who skilfully operated as snipers with the American and Australian contingents. "Sniping, too, came to be regarded as a 'dirty' and dishonorable trade. There was something not quite proper about killing with 'eager hand'. Snipers belonged to the 'Hate Squad.'"[20] Even snipers themselves admitted that they were nothing better than murderers—coolly and expertly shooting defenceless men. Most believed that only perverted people engaged in this form of killing. The officers also resented the snipers because they were free to act of their own free will without waiting for orders. There always existed a bellicose feeling between the ordinary soldier and snipers. It usually resulted in snipers being kept separate from the rest of the battalion. Further resentment developed, however, when for their own protection they were exempted from regular duties.

One American sniper from the war in Afghanistan knew that he was regarded as a member of "Murder Inc.," but felt he was involved in a battle of good and evil where he could be justified in eliminating, in particular, those who were engaged in battle for the Taliban as snipers. He likened his actions to those of the shepherd boy David who, with the blessing of his God, went out and slew Goliath. This present-day combatant believed that God saw the need in the world for soldiers and was always with him when he carried out his duty. By being meticulous and faithful in his actions he never killed in an unplanned fury of action but always followed a carefully planned path to a "righteous" kill. He will always carry horrific memories, as do so many others, but he says: "I was driven by the certainty that someday I will have to stand in front of the Lord, and he's going to know that either I shot some people who didn't need to be shot or I only shot people who needed to be shot."[21]

"Killing produced transformations that were not readily reversible: the living into the dead, most obviously, but the survivors into different

---

20. Bourke, *An Intimate History of Killing*, 66.
21. Langewiesche, "The Distant Executioner." No pages. Online.

men as well, men required to deny, to numb basic human feeling at costs they may have paid for decades after the war ended . . ."[22]

How Hard Was It to Do Your Duty and Kill?

There are huge psychological, sociological, ethical, and theological pressures on the average person to go out into the field of battle and kill. Although there is evil as well as good in each human being, the extremes of evil are not the norm. Obviously, there are in society hard-core criminals and sociopaths and there are many complex reasons why some people are in this mold. Such persons with a predisposition to kill were deliberately chosen by the Nazi hierarchy to commit atrocities and guard the prison camps from hell. In addition, those who carried out these heinous acts were for ever bound to their masters, trapped by their very deeds. But the average warrior has to be conditioned to kill. Studies have shown that many soldiers do not shoot directly at the enemy. Many had it down to a fine art—it is not necessary to fire unusually high (which would be obvious) to achieve an intentional miss. In the nineteenth-century wars the hit ratio was extraordinarily low. Even with better weapons hit rates only improved slowly—in World War II, US soldiers only attained a successful firing rate of 15 to 20 percent. In addition to deliberate misses, in the midst of battle, many soldiers delegated themselves to other tasks such as running messages, providing ammunition, tending the wounded, scouting for targets. When soldiers retreated to a quiet sector their relief at being out of immediate danger was potent, but so also was the relief that being away from the danger eliminated the duress of having to destroy another human being.

By the time of the Vietnam War, the United States had instigated methods specifically to condition men to kill. One of the most powerful of influences for the soldier was the authority of a respected leader and this factor was used by the constant presence of a leader with whom they bonded. When leaders were not physically nearby the firing rate was found to lower significantly. Another successful method, which helped to assuage some guilt, was group absolution. The accountability of the group rather than of the individual aids in reducing personal responsibility. There have always been examples of lone soldiers either actively or passively refusing to kill: "Michael Kathman, a tunnel rat crawling alone

---

22. Faust, *This Republic of Suffering*, 60.

in a Vietcong tunnel, was alone when he switched on the light and suddenly found 'not more than 15 feet away . . . a [lone] Viet Cong eating a handful of rice . . . After a moment, he put his pouch of rice on the floor of the tunnel beside him, turned his back to me and slowly started crawling away."[23] A relieved Kathman crawled back in the opposite direction. He had found no hatred for the young Viet Cong. Despite brutal training, there were still men in Vietnam who found it hard to hate the Vietnamese—unlike the hatred that seem to naturally abound with the Germans and Japanese in World War II.

Men, particularly Marines, were rigorously trained in servility by drill sergeants in boot camp—hazing, harassment, drill, shouting and cursing, punishments for minor actions, and constant almost sadistic stupidity. During Vietnam War training, the emphasis was almost exclusively on stressing the fact that soldiers were going to war to kill. "We'd run PT [physical training] in the morning and every time your left foot hit the deck you'd have to chant 'kill, kill, kill, kill.' It was drilled into your mind so much that it seemed like when it actually came down to it, it didn't bother you, you know?"[24] Even though, from childhood, humans are taught that killing is wrong, such continual training leads from morality to confusion to acceptance. Soldiers are dropped in a mire of contradictions whereby they survive the conflict through their training but then have to face the suffering and responsibility in the aftermath.

Just as the Nazis categorized the Jews as subhuman to build a guilt-free method of treatment of them, so in later wars the enemy was typecast as being lesser socially, racially, religiously, culturally, and even morally. Thus, the peasants, the colored, the poorly educated, and Islam amongst others, also became subhuman. They were not fathers, mothers, brothers, sisters; they were Japs, Krauts, huns, gooks, slopes, dinks, reds, terrorists, radicals, apes, boongs, coons, towel heads, imperialist pigs, crispy critters (incinerated by napalm), etc., making it psychologically possible for soldiers to accept that their lives were not of a high value. Unbelievably, the words of a British rector, expressed in a sermon preached in 1915, were often quoted during the Vietnam conflict: "we are fighting for dear life against enemies who are not Christians, not human beings, but reptiles."[25] In the same way the language of fighting men is a language of

---

23. Grossman, *On Killing*, 155.
24. Grossman, *On Killing*, 251.
25. Bourke, *An Intimate History of Killing*, 292.

denial: soldiers do not kill, "instead the enemy was knocked over, wasted, greased, taken out, and mopped up. The enemy is hosed, zapped, probed and fired on."[26]

Then the next step from killing in combat is committing atrocities: "wilful killing, torture, or inhuman treatment of, or wilful causing great suffering or serious injury to the body or health of persons taking no active part in the hostilities, including members of the armed forces who had laid down their arms or who were not combatants because of sickness, wounds, or any other causes, was a war crime . . . In addition, the maltreatment of dead bodies, firing on localities which were undefended and without military significance, and plunder, were defined as war crimes."[27] It is obvious that the bombing of cities and towns of no military significance was also a war crime but no prosecutions appear to be brought to bear on the pilots who carried out such actions. Although trials for war crimes in World War II involved German and Japanese defendants it is fact that atrocious actions were committed by both sides during this war and in preceding and following wars. One of the most common examples was the shooting of unarmed prisoners of war, which occurred on both sides. What happened in Vietnam at My Lai under the leadership of William Calley was neither a unique nor an isolated incident. Rifleman Barry Kavanagh from Australia remembered a night when, "his platoon heard 'some scuffling in the bushes,' and so they opened fire. In the morning, 'we discovered it's a party of schoolgirls who had been missing from a nearby village. The big Aussies shot the ones who were still alive so no one would start a nasty scandal.'"[28] An American Special Forces paratrooper recounted: "A lot of us wiped out whole villages . . . we were [all] afraid that we were gonna be the next ones that was gonna be court-martialled or called upon to testify against someone or against themselves."[29] The war in Vietnam seems to have been labeled as particularly vicious probably because combatants were more willing to admit to atrocities; they opened up more about the whole experience of this new type of war where there was no relief from the constant fear of the ever present hidden enemy. The participation of more war correspondents and the whole disenchantment with the

26. Grossman, *On Killing*, 92.
27. Bourke, *An Intimate History of Killing*, 176–77.
28. Bourke, *An Intimate History of Killing*, 178.
29. Bourke, *An Intimate History of Killing*, 179.

conduct of the war back home also contributed to the uncovering of these gruesome details.

The most frightening result of the sentencing of William Calley was the reaction of hundreds of war veterans in the United States. "In protest against Calley's conviction, veterans of the Second World War and the Korean War tried to surrender to police in several cities on the grounds that, 'if this man is guilty, he is guilty for the same things we did. We shot up villains under orders and killed civilians too.' The wholesale slaughter of prisoners was a particularly serious problem in the Pacific theatre of war."[30] In fact there, soldiers were bribed, to be persuaded to keep prisoners alive.

There are also varying reactions to killing dependent on the theater of war. Killing from a distance, on the whole, became more bearable. Studies have found that navy and air force combatants suffer less guilt, anxiety, and depression than army personnel. Rather than a personal confrontation with the enemy, "modern navies kill ships and airplanes. Of course, there are people in these ships and airplanes, but psychological and mechanical distances protect the modern sailor ... A similar phenomenon has occurred in aerial combat."[31] In fact, in these branches of the military, killing the enemy has not presented the problems that occur in land conflict. If the enemy can only be seen with the aid of mechanical means such as binoculars or radar, the hesitation in "pressing the button" or "pulling the trigger" is not common. Men and women can almost pretend they are not killing other human beings. "On the whole, however, distance is a sufficient buffer: gunners fire at grid references they cannot see; submarine crews fire torpedoes at 'ships' (and not, somehow, at the people in the ships); pilots launch their missiles at 'targets.'"[32] "What do we do when, in an honest moment, the former pilot looks right into your eyes, completely vulnerable, and says in a near whisper, 'I loved it. I lit up the entire fucking valley.'"[33] "According to one American survey conducted during the Second World War, three quarters of combat air crew were willing to perform further combat duty compared with only two fifths of combat infantrymen."[34] Obviously, there are exceptions as

30. Bourke, *An Intimate History of Killing*, 184.
31. Grossman, *On Killing*, 59.
32. Grossman, *On Killing*, 108.
33. Marlantes, *What It Is Like to Go to War*, 218.
34. Bourke, *An Intimate History of Killing*, 57.

in the intensive bombing of civilians in Hamburg and Dresden by British and Australian pilots at the end of World War II. An Australian pilot was traumatized by guilt for so many years that he eventually committed suicide in the 1980s in a quiet suburban park.

One of the most brutal methods of conditioning in the US military came to light with the developing work of Dr. Narut, a US navy psychiatrist who was training military assassins to overcome their resistance to killing. "Men were shown a series of gruesome films, which get progressively more horrific. The trainee is forced to watch by having his head bolted in a clamp so that he cannot turn away, and a special device keeps his eyelids open."[35] Subsequently the US government denied this experimentation by Narut but evidence and published articles appear to support the work.

The extremes of desensitization are frighteningly real in today's modern world of warfare. Now bomber crews fly from the United States and back to bomb countries like Iraq or Libya. Someone can now press a button to launch a cruise missile from a navy ship hundreds of miles from a target. People can operate drones from computer consoles at their place of work in America—they can do this in their normal day commuting back and forth to wives and children in wholesome attractive suburbs. In recent years there have been two instances of commercial jetliners being destroyed "by mistake," by ground missiles; one in the Ukraine, another over Iran. In 2012, "Mamana Bibi, a sixty-eight-year old woman picking vegetables in her family's large, open land in northern Waziristan, Pakistan, was killed by a United States drone aircraft. She was not a terrorist but a midwife married to a retired schoolteacher, yet she was blown to pieces in front of her nine young grandchildren . . . Nobody has come to investigate nor has anyone been held accountable. Quite simply, nobody seems to care."[36] With modern cell phones, a soldier in Afghanistan can call his girlfriend at night after a day of experiencing death and killing and yet have a somewhat normal conversation with her.

In today's world children are exposed to killing and death through watching film and television, and through actively participating in killing and death through computer programs. They experience the thrill of a successful kill and the ego-building in achieving a high score in the game.

---

35. Grossman, *On Killing*, 307.
36. Armstrong, *Fields of Blood*, 358.

They are being conditioned to participate in violence as a way of problem solving in life but they are not exposed to the realities of what follows:

> Walk through a burned-out village where the dogs haven't been fed and you *hear* them eating the dead. If this doesn't snap through your conditioning, then *smell* human meat rotting. *Listen* to the wailing of the orphaned child and go mad with it because you can't get it out of your ears until you either walk away or do away with the child. Pick up chunks of body and *feel* the true meaning of dead weight. These senses aren't filtered and dulled by visual media. These channels are much more directly open to the heart. This is another reason why computer-game warfare has no natural checks on its violence.[37]

Perhaps if there was a technology that could introduce the sounds, the smells, the weeping, and the physical feel of killing, video games might lose their impact? Or perhaps the video player would eventually become conditioned to these too, and dismiss them. The real experience of combat might be the only deterrent, but we cannot proceed continually on this destructive and horrific path.

Would future governments be prepared to spend the same amount of money, and expound the same amount of time and energy, to train men and women to deal with the results of the killing that they have been trained and conditioned to do? Probably not—after all, the aim is to defeat the enemy by killing as many of them as is possible. If men and women suffer from their success this is just an unfortunate by-product.

Dealing with the Aftermath of Killing—Immediate

Just as Elisabeth Kubler-Ross's stages of dealing with dying follow a specific pattern (which nevertheless should not be acknowledged as a hard and fast rule), so there appears to be a list of responses to killing in war. These would not necessarily appear in the psyche of every combatant and some stages would be more prevalent than others. Grossman in his work *On Killing*, lists them as follows: Concern about the act; Automatic reaction without thought; Exhilaration and satisfaction; Guilt, remorse and revulsion with the success; Rationalization and acceptance to be able to continue. Where in this list is Mourning, for mourning is not guilt or remorse but a step on its own. Somewhere in there also could be

---

37. Marlantes, *What It Is Like to Go to War*, 77.

inserted, Numbness. Marlantes, in his book, *What It Is Like to Go to War*, comments that when a successful battle is over, there is no elation, just numbed exhaustion. When a soldier is on the verge of attacking, the feeling can definitely be exhilaration at the prospect as well as exhilaration at its success. Adrenaline kicks in with combat. It is like experiencing a high with cocaine or heroin but the problem is that it has all the coming down that drug-taking involves. And, in between, when there are so many functions to address for this success, your feelings are unconsciously suppressed, in fact, Marlantes says your brain is "jammed."

Dealing with the Aftermath of Killing—Long Term

The initial priority is the provision of better psychological and spiritual preparation for the return to home and families. In the decommissioning process there should be preparation for wives and families as well as the returning combatant. It has been noted that returning in groups has worked best in the past as had debriefing after action. In World War II families were desperate to see their husbands and sons return immediately from the prisoner of war camps in the jungles of Asia. The authorities would not allow those who had been released to go home until they had undergone strict medical checks and had some necessary convalescent time. The prisoners themselves were too ashamed of their gaunt appearance to contemplate going straight back to Australia, so families had to endure a frustrating but necessary time of waiting.

Returning soldiers need to be welcomed back into their community, restored to the family they love, and thanked by people for risking their lives and their sanity for them. Parades or, better still, solemn processionals, help to restore some dignity and promise. "There is also a deeper side to coming home. The returning warrior needs to heal more than his mind and his body. He needs to heal his soul."[38] There is an essential need for counseling for veterans and their families, for religious services of affirmation, and for help from the military in integrating men and women back into society. Chaplains could conduct the religious services on the bases before demobbing and also get in touch with pastors in the veteran's community to help with all the problems that are bound to arise when the link with the military is finally severed. There is no doubt that the spiritual needs of a man going through the constant memories of

---

38. Marlantes, *What It Is Like to Go to War*, 196.

killing and carnage are hard to be tackled, particularly by pastors and priests who have had no experience of war. Here is the opportunity for ongoing work of military chaplains who can give guidance and support for the future. Down talk, in groups, with older veterans, in a safe place, can begin the healing of shame and fear. Honesty has to be acknowledged; not necessarily applauded but not condemned. It is all part of the healing process that each person needs. Years later, after suffering from post-traumatic stress disorder and a broken marriage, Karl Marlantes says: "My feeling now? Oh, the sadness. The sadness. And, oh, the grief of evil in the world to which I contributed."[39]

Post-traumatic Stress Disorder

Post-traumatic Stress Disorder has been present in many combatants returning from wars for over a hundred years—probably for as long as wars have existed, but known under different medical terminologies. During World War I it was called shell shock or, officially, LMF (lack of moral fiber); in World War II and the Korean War it was called combat neurosis and combat fatigue; and, after the Gulf War there was Gulf War Syndrome. In 1980, the American Psychiatric Association finally recognized that the mental health issue, Post-traumatic Stress Disorder, as it was called in relation to the Vietnam veterans, was a true mental illness and it was acknowledged that if the condition persisted for more than two years, it was almost impossible to cure. It was seen as a response to continually experiencing situations that were grossly abnormal.

On the battlefield and in the jungles of Asia, soldiers cannot afford to allow fear, guilt, or grief to be emotionally felt. Combatants must suppress all such feelings to be able to function. Men and women become desensitized, feeling nothing even when they kill or a mate beside them is slain with brains and blood splattering everybody in the vicinity. Sometimes soldiers descended into black humor to combat the horror; distressingly sometimes they took part in heinous acts against the captured enemy or even the civilians caught up in the fury of it all. But the finality of battle service and the strange homecoming when veterans feel isolated in a community, which functions as if war and killing don't exist, means that all those suppressed powerful feelings come shrieking to the surface. Trying to sustain normality in public when someone momentarily leaves

---

39. Marlantes, *What It Is Like to Go to War*, 31.

a bag on a table, or watching a child throw a tantrum in the supermarket, or hearing a vehicle backfiring in traffic, can be an impossible feat. Men are trained to fight and kill but they are not "detrained" to live and once again relate to family and friends who have little real understanding of war. A huge responsibility rests with the military which they served.

Unfortunately, in Australia, the military has been slow to acknowledge the seriousness of PTSD amongst its veterans, attempting to find other causes, such as car accidents, childhood abuse, personality disorders, alcoholism, etc. Since PTSD has been prevalent in a vast number of Vietnam veterans it is difficult to agree with the premise of pre-existing conditions. The troops sent to this country were very carefully screened and selected; the National Servicemen in particular, were regarded as the finest of Australian youth at the time and after training was completed, comments were published claiming them to be some of the best soldiers Australia had ever sent into battle. Surely the screening would have picked up any suspect personality traits? In fact, one seasoned soldier has stated that every man or woman involved in conflict from any war suffers PTSD. Those who state they don't experience trauma are, in his opinion, lying. Their experience may be mammoth and ongoing or it may be at the other end of the spectrum as almost bearable, and only periodic. His experience was an impossibility to sleep without constant nightmares, thrashing around in bed and falling to the floor in the process. He is now in an aged care facility and is able to sleep for the first time since he returned from Vietnam. At night three or four dementia patients often wander up and down the passage outside his door. He feels that it might be the sense that there is a soldier on sentry duty outside that gives him a peaceful night.

For those of us who attended school in the late forties and fifties, remember there were the teachers who seemed to be on a short fuse most of the time. They threw chalk and blackboard erasers at the students, they punched boys or clipped their ears, they shouted at the girls, they slammed down desk lids. Then, also notice that most of the women teachers were spinsters—a greater number of spinsters than should have been normal. How many of these had once worn an engagement ring or enjoyed the company of a special boy? Surely, all this is one of the results of World War II. At an Anzac March just after the end of this war in Mundaring, a small country town in Western Australia, a mother explained to her young son that the group of ladies standing outside the post office watching the men march by, were women whose fiancés and boyfriends failed to return from the battlefields.

With the Vietnam War, the problems for returned soldiers became more obvious to those at home. No longer did society hide everything. Problems of living were often exposed and discussed. In addition, the more modern wars were vastly different with no designated front line. They were fought in jungles where the enemy could be hidden, in front and behind, so that soldiers were always on constant alert from all directions. This meant that there was no relief for emotions and senses. Consequently, veterans could no longer struggle on using their own devices. When they came home they needed acknowledgment and medical help, and this was mostly lacking.

In the absence of the right medical help, veterans used alcohol, cigarettes, and drugs to combat their neuroses—intense mood swings, aggression to wives and children, paranoid attitudes to the smallest problem, insomnia, horrific nightmares, delirium, sweat-drenched sheets, verbal and physical abuse, and the inability to socialize, finding normal day-to-day life inane and pointless. Men often slept with a revolver and wives were continually awoken to endure attempted strangulation and warnings to "move out." Broken marriages and estrangement from children and extended family members followed in many cases. There were some who managed to get through with the patient help of their wives but family life was nevertheless not normal. The children of some veterans of the Vietnam War experienced an abnormal life of constant moving—traveling from one state to another, transitioning from city to country, attending countless numbers of schools, and never being able to establish permanent friendships and roots. Their fathers were never able to settle for long in any one locality. Other veterans choose to live in the Australian bush, for example, or at least in a quiet rural area. Some even settle in a country far away from their original field of combat.

Often men were confronted with unwanted visions of soldiers they had killed, which compounded all the remorse. When they failed to get rid of the hate, the guilt, the anger, and their unexplainable violent behavior, they succumbed to alcoholism and even suicide. It is estimated that well over 200 veterans in Australia have suicided since 1986 and many more have been constantly on suicide watch. The nature of recent wars, with no established fronts and higher weapon technology, has forced each man or woman to rely more on their individual psyches than ever before. David Grossman, the author of *On Killing*, also believes that PTSD has been more prevalent in recent wars because of the more sophisticated training in killing—as noted previously, in World War II only 15 to 20 percent of riflemen actually fired directly at an enemy soldier; 55 percent did so in the Korean War; and 90 percent in Vietnam. Men, who somehow got through combat without actually killing or knowing implicitly that they had killed, were more likely to come through with fewer mental health issues. PTSD will continue to be a problem with men and women returning from Iraq and Afghanistan.

The Desperate Need for Better Preparation in the Future

To forestall the worst of these resultant patterns, Karl Marlantes strongly advocates the need for men and women to be spiritually prepared for death and killing before they transfer to the combat zone. In this present hedonistic, alien culture it is extremely difficult to have a strong grounding in what one believes, so being thrust into a situation where one needs to rely on oneself alone is overwhelming. The soldier needs to put on a spiritual armor—it is no use trying to put this on after the event: they need it to endure the battle. Those who die without a faith are grasping at the futility of it all. On the whole those who die with a faith cope with death better. But, above all, the dying soldier needs honesty and prayer. Americans make it a practice to take their dead home but Marlantes contends there is a place for burying the enemy's dead and even praying over their graves. This might allow for soldiers to partly come to terms with the killing of the enemy; or enable them to vent their anger for the deaths of their mates at enemy hands. Comfort comes from silent support, but it also comes from duties designed to help the bereaved (or the guilty) work through frightening emotions that have never been encountered before. After the action is the time to debrief both with words and with actions. To do this immediately can set the pattern for facing the suffering as time goes on. Suffering moves in waves, from despair to faithful acceptance, from faithful acceptance to despair. Expressing themselves to each other—when the numbness has started to pass—is the first step to a possible healing.

Then, on examining the role of religion in the theater of war, Marlantes emphasizes the need for a wise and honest chaplain to spend time just listening and allowing men to unwind and talk about their terrors—a chaplain who is willing to be part of a team lending a hand with medical emergencies and zipping up body bags. In all wars there seems to be an indecisiveness on the part of chaplains—they need to find what the men really need, and some don't. Marlantes recounts how, amidst bad weather and through dense jungle-covered mountains, a helicopter managed to get through to a battalion with vital supplies and a welcome batch of mail. Also on board was the battalion chaplain. "He had brought bottles of Southern Comfort and some new dirty jokes. I accepted the Southern Comfort, thanked him, laughed at the jokes . . . Inside I was seething."[40] He couldn't understand why he felt so angry when the chaplain had risked danger to bring the men some cheer. It wasn't until years later, when he had that time to reflect on all the horrors of war, death, and killing, that he realized why he had experienced that anger. He was in turmoil because he was directly involved in that killing. "I was struggling with a situation approaching the sacred in its terror and contact with the infinite, and he was trying to numb me to it. I needed help with the existential terror of my own death and responsibility for the death of others, enemies and friends, not Southern comfort. I needed a spiritual guide."[41] On his return home, Marlantes was able to find some peace with his demons, when a friend who was a Roman Catholic friar, conducted a Mass for the Dead for him.

40. Marlantes, *What It is Like to Go to War*, 7.
41. Marlantes, *What It is Like to Go to War*, 7.

18

Christianity Must Play an Effective Part

THE CHAPLAIN TO THE armed forces in today's world needs to perform a vital service in a world far different from that of past wars. His or her role is now formalized, and training by both the army and the church denomination must be relevant in all its aims and objectives to be effective in these days of complete uncertainty.

The chaplain in the Australian Regular Army (or attached to the Army Reserve) is a commissioned service officer responsible for the provision of spiritual, religious, and pastoral support to all members of the services and their families, in peacetime as well as during times of conflict. He or she is a commissioned member of the military and in this way the situation of life and work varies considerably from that of the ordained man or woman in the civilian clergy. This obviously can cause ambiguity in many areas of work and particularly creates tension in relation to the two institutions that he or she serves, i.e., the church and the state. For example, each chaplain is required to be an active member of his or her denomination; each is appointed and commissioned to this work by his or her denomination; and, whilst answering to the doctrines and practices of that denomination, a duty to obey the orders of the military is a necessity. Whereas the civilian minister/pastor/priest serves their specific congregation, the military chaplain is required to go beyond denomination to act as part of a unified, multi-faith team, providing leadership in the practice of faith and religious observance. Provision of a religious ministry to members of his or her own denomination is an essential, but facilitating advice to people of all faiths is also needed.

True, the military chaplain has similar duties as the civilian minister or priest. He or she must provide spiritual ministry, religious ministry, pastoral care, advice, and counsel, and lead men and women to a mature spiritual understanding through character formation and development. The last mentioned requirement would be a natural progression in the church from preaching in the pulpit, encouraging participation in weekly worship, in home groups, Bible studies, and church organisations or clubs, and eventually for the more spiritually mature—evangelization. In the military, however, a much more formal attitude is necessitated. Character Formation and Development courses are conducted. It becomes the army chaplain's functional responsibility to become a specialist in training army personnel so that they may develop their own interpersonal skills, be motivated to be responsible for moral judgments, and be enabled to set exemplary standards for those serving with them and under them. Leadership is a vital component in all these programs.

As in all ministries, pastoral work is vital: ministering to all family members through personal contact and delving into all aspects of military, domestic, and emotional stress as needed. The military chaplain does live in a different world: even in peacetime the surrounding atmosphere is governed by regulation and periodic observances. On the battlefield the world is far removed from that in the home country with adjustments difficult to comprehend by the ordinary person. The pastoral work here is crucial to the well-being of the serving man or woman. The military chaplain on the home front is also the link for the families waiting and worrying about their loved ones.

Chaplaincy services including memorial and commemoration services are held both at home and in the field. The chaplain is responsible for all the resources necessary for a comforting and spiritual uplifting memorial whether in a formal or an ad hoc situation. The chaplain is there to serve all individuals for whom they are responsible and in whatever situation they are in. This is in addition to training and character development and pastoral care and advice. The liturgy of church services and the words and actions of memorials are a vital part of the comforting healing process of loss. Vigil services and formal or informal leave-takings when coffins are placed on aircraft for the journey home brings spiritual comfort—not closure, which is a much abused term, but the strength to continue.

As it can be seen, there is often present a question of ambiguity in whom is the master to serve. The military chaplain is doubly commissioned by the church and the state. Is it possible to have total obedience to the military and proper obedience to God? A Christian has to live in the world but not of the world. How then does the military chaplain live in a world of conflict and killing and not become part of it; not of the killing but as the servant of the military that makes the decision to kill? Does he or she then lose his or her credibility? The chaplain is there to represent Christ, the peacemaker; the chaplain has a non-combatant role; the chaplain proclaims the gospel and supports the cause. There are two roles—that of priest and that of an officer—the problem is when one conflicts with the other and it becomes a moral dilemma. David Martin, in his work *Reflections on Sociology and Theology*, reflects: "The dangers are real in so far as his or her Christianity is likely to be absorbed by the specification of the role rather than being able to transform it."[1] Because of this tension, Martin sees that, whereby the chaplain is doubly commissioned, he or she has a social role, which could cease to become distinctively Christian. One of the major problems for the soldier is ethics versus military authority. Soldiers have to obey orders and then have to live with the results of following those orders, some of which may be contrary to moral or Christian standards. An example is the situations that daily arose in Vietnam when villagers were often automatically regarded as Viet Cong or Viet Cong sympathizers with resultant unlawful massacres. Soldiers in all wars come to the chaplain for counsel after becoming part of barbaric assaults. In past wars many chaplains have had no problems reconciling their religious ethic with the moral universe of the military. Today the preparation of chaplains for the battlefield is far more in-depth and thorough. Chaplains have often been accused of hypocrisy—that they have encouraged soldiers to kill, while highmindedly refusing to bloody their own hands. Recent wars have chaplains who endeavor to train and live amongst combatants more closely. In Vietnam, the chaplain David Knight fully believed that soldiers were there to kill or capture the enemy. However, he felt he should go into the war zone with the men so he could, in some way, witness to the love of the Lord.

But when do chaplains speak out about senseless slaughter and atrocities? Serving men and women who have spoken out have been demoted, transferred, and even vilified in some cases, for example the helicopter pilots at My Lai. It has to be always remembered that the chaplain serves the army and Christ—the huge problem of ambiguity. Only the

---

1. Davie, "The Military Chaplain," 43.

mature, experienced, and revered man is able to take this path and it is probable that, with today's more sophisticated training, chaplains will be able to successfully serve Christ in this continuous battlefield of ambiguity. Only a chaplain can know when it is time to act.

Chaplains in the past have made precarious decisions, which they later regretted. A significant person was Father George Zabelka, the Roman Catholic chaplain who blessed the atomic bombs that decimated 140,000 people in Hiroshima and 73,000 people in Nagasaki. Zabelka eventually became overcome with guilt and shame at the blessings he had given on those fateful days, especially when he had the opportunity to speak with survivors. He was in complete shock when he visited the silent, dying children in the hospitals. He decided to stay on in Japan working still as a chaplain. When he returned to America, he tried to talk to people about his experiences but nobody wanted to listen. It has always been the belief that the dropping of the atomic bomb was the only way to bring to cessation the war with Japan. Like Vera Brittain after World War I, Father Zabelka become a strident advocate for pacifism.

Some of the chaplain's roles are more acceptable to the serving person than others. "For example, the pastoral care of the individual soldier and his family is, for many observers, easier to affirm than the contribution that a chaplain makes to the morale of a unit caught up in military engagement. But is it possible to have one without the other?"[2] Often the "primitive" religion of the ordinary soldier is manifested as a moral code rather than as an adherence to Christianity. Many do not actively practice Christianity yet claim to believe and have an affiliation with a specific denomination. In the history of twentieth-century war it was found that the soldier often begins to feel religious when he or she takes the battlefield, but such a sense is often very basic and sometimes prone to diversification. So, it is comforting to find that the results of surveys in the United Kingdom in recent years have discovered that overall figures of Christian believers are noticeably higher in the military than in the population as a whole. This is the case when society today is becoming increasingly secular. In addition, actual experiences in the field, for example in Iraq and Afghanistan, found that soldiers from the United States often professed a strong faith in the God of Christianity.

A further quandary to this religious/moral friction is expressed when a senior commander states: "My own observation and experiences

---

2. Davie, "The Military Chaplain," 42.

. . . lead me to conclude that the role of the Padre is hugely important: a moral component force multiplier. In times of extreme stress, anxiety and grief, having a Padre allows soldiers and officers the opportunity to deal with these emotions . . . Bottom line I would not want to deploy on combat Operations without a Padre."[3] Is this commander keen to have a padre on board to keep "troops calm under fire," or does he want a spiritual counselor to prepare his soldiers for the coming battle and its consequences—note the reaction of Karl Marlantes when the padre brought him Southern Comfort when he needed spiritual comfort. Some chaplains had the incredible gift of knowing what his men needed. In the Japanese POW camps in World War II: "padres were not universally popular but sometimes they inspired respect among their fellow POWs—not just believers. Noel Duckworth, the chaplain to the Cambridgeshire Regiment, won over cynics like Russell Braddon because of the bravery with which he stood up to the Japanese and because, unlike some padres, he took an an active part in both the official and underground life of the camp . . . He delighted his fellow POWs by abusing the Japanese—who could not understand him—by delivering insults in tones so gentle and wheedling that they were mistaken for flattery."[4] He is credited with saving men from execution (for which he was often beaten), he co-operated in schemes to hoodwink the guards, he was involved in "black market" trading to obtain food for the prisoners, and he continually boosted morale. He also built a chapel and encouraged both believers and atheists to visit to be with God or to remember loved ones at home.

An important contribution to the training of military chaplains would be to do as much as possible to attain a biblical knowledge of war from God's perspective. No man can know all the answers to the types of questions a fighting soldier in his distress will ask. But a strong grounding in how war is related in the Old Testament and how Jesus teaches his gospel of peace and reconciliation can never go amiss. Unfortunately, a common thought today is that the God of the Old Testament is a God of anger and the God of the New Testament is a God of love; the Old Testament identifies with war while the New Testament identifies with pacifism. Like most assertions about the Bible, this premise is inaccurate and displays a complete lack of understanding of the vital importance of both Testaments. An in-depth study and deep reflection on God's Word

---

3. Davie, "The Military Chaplain," 42.
4. Gilles, *The Barbed-wire University*, 227–28.

beginning with Genesis and ending with the Revelation of John, reveals the complete saga of God and Man. The New Testament could not exist in any sort of intelligent form without the Old Testament as its foundation. It is the same God throughout and he is unchangeable.

There are differences of course. The Old Testament was written, redacted, and compiled over a period of more than a thousand years, when Israel was God's chosen people living amongst alien war-like nations whilst struggling to establish itself in the Promised Land. Again and again the Israelites lost their faith and dependence on the one and only loving God. God was always faithful through all their failures, "I have loved you." (Mal 1:2 NRSV) Furthermore, the Book of Psalms is a testament to the everlasting love and protection of God for his people even as they sinned against him. The New Testament documents were written over a period of approximately 100 years and covered a time when Israel was relatively secure, and though under the rule of the Romans, there was no threat of invasion from another nation. The whole history of the Jewish nation is related in the Old Testament; the new community of faith is just being established in the New Testament. From the Old to the New we see the redemptive plan of God coming to fruition, bringing mankind out of its bondage to sin. Only through the vicarious sacrifice of his son Jesus can God's righteousness be appeased.

War is a constant presence in the Old Testament and without it Israel would not have existed as a nation. The other constant is that God was the leader, the royal King, in these wars: "The LORD goes forth like a soldier, like a warrior he stirs up his fury; he cries out, he shouts aloud, he shows himself mighty against his foes." (Isa 42:13 NRSV) It should be noted that in its battles the Israelites were less brutal than their enemies, for example, Assyrian archeological inscriptions illustrate a lust for blood in conflict and a practice of rape and pillage afterwards. In the books of Chronicles and Kings we read that Israelite kings were merciful kings. The Israelite wars could be classed as holy wars because they were commanded by God: wars that were fought without God's blessing were punished by him. They were holy wars and the victory was God's victory.

The whole of the Old Testament illustrates God's covenant love for his people Israel. He leads them to victory over other nations to fulfill his promises to them. Nevertheless, God does not hesitate to use other nations, such as the Assyrians and the Babylonians, to defeat Israel and, in so doing, brings upon his people judgment for their disobedience to his commandments, and for turning away to worship other gods. Yet, even then, he is always there; he never fails his people. In this way war is redemptive:

> How beautiful upon the mountains are the feet of the messenger who announces peace, who brings good news, who announces salvation, who says to Zion, 'Your God reigns.' Listen! Your sentinels lift up their voices, together they sing for joy; for in plain sight they see the return of the LORD to Zion. Break forth together into singing, you ruins of Jerusalem; for the LORD has comforted his people, he has redeemed Jerusalem. The LORD has bared his holy arm before the eyes of all the nations; and all the ends of the earth shall see the salvation of our God. (Isa 52:7–12 NRSV)

In the New Testament we have Jesus, the Son of God, coming to bring the Kingdom of Heaven to earth, the preliminary blessing for all believers whilst dwelling in the world. He comes as a babe, then preaching and teaching as an ordinary man, trained as a carpenter. The Jews were waiting for a Messiah to save them from their enemies but, as is predicted in Isaiah 53, Jesus was the Messiah who came to save them from their sins. They looked for a mighty warrior on a great warhorse; but he came dressed in ordinary clothes on a donkey. His name is the Greek version of Joshua, the great Hebrew warrior, but his ministry preaches peace and love—a true pacifism. He comes for sinners and outcasts, for widows and orphans, for the ill and the dying. But it is the same compassion and love of the Old Testament. It the same abhorrence of sin and evil—compare, for example the first chapter of Malachi when God condemns the inferior sacrifices of the people and the corruption of the priesthood, to the words of Jesus when he denounces the scribes and the Pharisees in the 23rd chapter of Matthew. Jesus, in his anger, overturns the tables of the traders in the temple, his Father's House; he warns of the dire consequences of blaspheming the Holy Spirit—there will be much gnashing of teeth in hell!

We cannot ignore the violent warnings in the Book of Revelation. There the final battle will be fought with the devil and his followers. The wars of the Old Testament will pale in comparison with the end times. Thus, the whole Bible is the history of God's love and faithfulness to his chosen people culminating in the sending of his beloved Son to pay the sacrifice and instigate the final redemption.

In the days to come
the mountain of the LORD'S house
shall be established as the highest of the mountains,
and shall be raised above the hills;
all the nations shall stream to it.
Many peoples shall come and say,
'Come, let us go up to the mountain of the LORD,
to the house of the God of Jacob;
that he may teach us his ways
and that we may walk in his paths.'
For out of Zion shall go forth instruction,
and the word of the LORD from Jerusalem.
He shall judge between the nations,
and shall arbitrate for many peoples;
they shall beat their swords into plowshares,
and their spears into pruning hooks;
nation shall not lift up sword against nation,
neither shall they learn war any more. (Is 2:2–4 NRSV)

19

The Place of Days of Remembrance and Memorials

THERE ARE MANY TODAY who claim that Anzac Day is merely a glorification of war, but how can it possibly be claimed that Anzac Day is a celebration of war? There is no glory there—only desperation, sorrow, and loss. Anzac Day is a day devoted to remembrance—remembrance of mates gone, of cruelty and terror experienced and overcome, of survival and homecoming to loved ones—no matter how alien and frightening that homecoming may be. "No one returns from the war. Ever. Mothers get back a sad semblance of their sons—embittered, aggressive beasts, hardened against the whole world and believing in nothing except death. Yesterday's soldiers no longer belong to their parents. They belong to war, and only their body returns from war. Their soul stays there."[1]

Initially, the returning soldier needs to be welcomed and accepted into his family and his community. The ones whom he loves the most and who love him, need to validate his war history in an unspoken acceptance. Following, there are many crucial sources of public recognition, which help to affirm the status of the returning soldier. The two main ones are the initial and continuous annual marches, and the establishment of monuments to those who died. Annual marches, such as those on Anzac Day in Australia and New Zealand, can be positively compared with remembrances and ceremonies that are a vital part of all families—baptisms, birthdays, confirmations, bar mitzvahs, graduations, weddings, and award ceremonies.

1. Babcenko, *One Soldier's War*, 388.

The cruel war was over—oh the triumph was so sweet!
We watched the troops returning, through our tears;
There was triumph, triumph, triumph down the scarlet glittering street,
And you scarce could hear the music for the cheers.
And you scarce could see the house-tops for the flags that flew between;
The bells were pealing madly to the sky;
And everyone was shouting for the Soldiers of the Queen,
And the glory of an age was passing by.

And then there came a shadow, swift and sudden, dark and drear;
The bells were silent, not an echo stirred.
The flags were drooping sullenly, the men forgot to cheer;
We waited, and we never spoke a word.
The sky grew darker, darker, till from out the gloomy rack
There came a voice that checked the heart with dread;
'Tear down, tear down your bunting now, and hang up sable black;
They are coming—it's the Army of the Dead.' [2]

Memorial plaques and monuments, whether in local suburbs and villages or on overseas battlefields, can afford the solace and consolation that a funeral or a gravestone normally would provide. "No two of these memorials are ever quite alike, as communities struggled to come to terms with the enormity of their loss, the ways they chose to honour their dead were many and complex . . . War memorials were built at the busy intersections of private and collective memory: historians quarrel interminably over their meaning and use. However, there is one theme that all these monuments have in common. The Australian (and imperial) policy not to repatriate the war dead made each such monument a surrogate grave, an empty tomb for 'boys' who would never march home, a sight memory, a shrine of remembrance."[3] Even a tiny shrine brings comfort—a memorial plaque for a pilot, aged twenty-three, lost over the Bay of Biscay in August 1942, attached to a piano in the church where he spent his growing years.

Fighting men and women need to be gratefully acknowledged by the public for the sacrifices they made to serve the country they love. Both these traditions were deliberately neglected for the Vietnam veterans to the point where returnees were abused, physically and mentally, and even spat upon. Two officers were actually gunned down in the streets of Washington, DC by a passing motorist. Every aspect of confirmation

---

2. Service, "The March of the Dead," lines 1–16.
3. Scates, *A Place to Remember*, 1.

and support was taken away—men and women crept home in fear of their own countrymen and women and refused to wear their uniforms. Obviously, their recovery from a brutal and lonely war was stunted or even completely unattainable. The veterans were not welcomed; the dead were not mourned.

In 2014, the Governor of Tasmania, Peter Underwood, used the Dawn Service of Anzac Day to express his disgust in the so-called celebration of Anzac Day. To men, women, and children who had come together to mourn their loved ones, he told them that their tears were for murderers—for the men and women who had suffered the ultimate fate when their country had directed them to fight and kill. But this day of remembrance reverently brings together a nation, involving both the old and the young in recognizing the moral significance of all people, and with an unspoken prayer that all leaders will take every step to avoid such devastation and sorrow in the future. Significantly, it helps those who have participated in the unimaginable horror of war to have the strength to find the purpose of it all even where that seems impossible.

Thus, such days of remembrance and man-made memorials are for those who have suffered most, best described in John Masefield's epic poem, *A Consecration*:

> Not of the princes and prelates with periwigged charioteers
> Riding triumphantly laureled to lap the fat of the years,
> Rather the scorned—the rejected—the men hemmed in with spears;
>
> The men in tattered battalion which fights till it dies,
> Dazed with the dust of the battle, the din and the cries,
> The men with the broken heads and the blood running into their eyes.
>
> Not the be-medalled Commander, beloved of the throne,
> Riding cock-horse to parade when the bugles are blown,
> But the lads who carried the hill and cannot be known.
>
> Others may sing of the wine and the wealth and the mirth,
> The portly presence of potentates goodly in girth; -
> Mine be the dirt and the dross, the dust and scum of the earth!
>
> Theirs be the music, the colour, the glory, the gold;
> Mine be a handful of ashes, a mouthful of mould.
> Of the maimed, of the halt and the blind in the rain and the cold -
>
> Of these shall my songs be fashioned, my tale be told. Amen.

The Place of Days of Remembrance and Memorials

Remembrance of the Fallen—Lest We Forget

Days of remembrance and erection of memorials are the visible ways of demonstrating what war really means. In the United States, for nearly twenty years, the government refused to publicly recognize those who had returned from Vietnam. There had been no monuments erected and no memorial marches held. People wanted to forget. Therefore, there was nothing tangible to prompt their memory. In gripping prose, Philip Caputo maintains a fellow warrior's sacrifice was more than worthy and validates that those who choose to turn their backs should be filled with shame:

> You were a part of us, and a part of us died with you, the small part that was still young . . . whatever the rights or wrongs of the war, nothing can diminish the rightness of what you tried to do. Yours was the greater love. You died for the man you tried to save, and you died *pro patria* . . . You were faithful. Your country is not . . . It wishes to forget and it has forgotten. But there are a few of us who do remember because of the small things that made us love you—your gestures, the words you spoke, and the way you looked. We loved you for what you were and what you stood for.[4]

"There is an atavistic sense of propitiation: remembrance as a gift to the restless dead. It is an idea powerfully invoked by the First World War doctor and poet, John McCrae (who was to die in Flanders in 1918). His line 'If ye break faith with us who die/We shall not sleep' was intended to rally the boys to the flag, but to me it makes a different, equally powerful appeal."[5]

The sacrifice has to be worthwhile. Those who return alive must honor those who are brought home in body bags or, as in former wars, those left behind in some foreign grave. There must be a sense of propitiation otherwise the deaths were in vain. Those who fell kept the faith; those who live must keep the faith with them by commemorating the fallen in their hearts.

The violent and continual anti-war movement throughout the years of conflict in Vietnam; the refusal of the continuing governments to acknowledge and rectify their mistaken decisions and in so doing spare thousands of young lives; and the obstinate attitude of politicians and the

---

4. Caputo, *A Rumor of War*, 223–24.
5. Stephenson, *The Last Full Measure*, xi–xii.

military to face the fact that the United States had lost its first war in its entire history, were the reasons that no memorials were erected. At last, at the beginning of 1982, the construction of the Vietnam Veterans's Wall in Washington, DC, eventually began. However, the memorial, initially without the staple accompaniments, could easily be interpreted as a long stark block of infamy. The military, the government, and the whole of society need to recognize the returning warrior's needs. Veterans need acceptance and a reassurance that the deeds they carried out were necessary and were solely for the love of their country. Affirmation and acceptance are essential for healing.

In Australia the Commemorative Walk in Seymour, Victoria, is a moving tribute designed to bring solace to all those who will always experience pain and grief. The reddish path is planted with native trees and grasses that resemble the rubber trees and the rice paddies of Vietnam. In a clearing, a replica of the pavilion and stage has been constructed. This is where Col Joy and Little Pattie were entertaining the troops when the fighting at Long Tan began. Proceeding from here can be seen the focus of the site. A similar type of commemorative wall to that in America has been constructed, and lists all the servicemen and servicewomen who took part in this sad, lonely, and tenebrous war far from the sunburnt country. The exquisite design of this wall, with its background of photographs of combatants, helps to create a cathedral-like atmosphere in the Australian bush. It was not until 2013 that this memorial was erected.

Another form of memorial is the creation of bodies of people who can support and encourage each other in their ongoing sorrow and pain. Visaka Dharmadasa is from Sri Lanka. Her son was a soldier in the Sri Lankan military and went missing after an attack by the Tamil Tigers on a military base in 1998. Unable to mourn for him, she founded the Association of War Affected Women and Parents of Servicemen Missing in Action, an organization she still chairs today. She and many other women worldwide also support the Women Peace and Security Agenda and the Preventing Sexual Violence in Conflict Initiative.

For every one of those who has lived through the horrors of war and killing, embrace the words of this Clare Benediction by John Rutter:

> May the Lord show his mercy upon you;
>   may the light of his presence be your guide:
> May he guard you and uphold you;
>   may his Spirit be ever by your side.

> When you sleep, may his angels watch over you;
> when you wake, may he fill you with his grace:
> may you love him and serve him all your days,
> then in heaven may you see his face.

"War is brutish, inglorious, and a terrible waste. Combat leaves an indelible mark on those who are forced to endure it. The only redeeming factors were my comrades' incredible bravery and their devotion to each other. Marine Corps training taught us to kill efficiently and to try to survive. But it also taught us loyalty to each other—and love. That esprit de corps sustained us."[6] In all these memorials and days of remembrance the emphasis is on the glorious dead and the sacrifice this entailed. But it should also be a time of acknowledgment that thousands and thousands of men and women suffer with physical disfigurement and mental anguish as a result of their time of service for their countries. Time should be allocated to remembering and honoring them also. Both the agonies of the dead and continuing traumatic stress of the survivors must not become merely a heroic record on a memorial. "Loyalty and love" and thankfulness to all those who survived.

---

6. Sledge, *With the Old Breed*, 315.

20

Can War Ever Be Justified?

THERE ARE ESSENTIALLY FOUR Christian attitudes to war and one belief is in that of a just war. But even "the most just of wars brings with it a train of evils—if indeed any war can really be called just."[1]

Many people today make the sweeping claim that religion has been the cause of most of the wars throughout the world with the resultant oppression and suffering that war brings. It needs to be acknowledged that, "until the modern period, religion permeated all aspects of life, including politics and warfare, not because ambitious churchmen had 'mixed up' two essentially distinct activities, but because people wanted to endow everything they did with significance . . . Every successful empire has claimed that it has a divine mission: that its enemies are evil, misguided or tyrannical and maintained by force, religion has been implicated in the violence . . . Until the American and French revolutions, there were no 'secular' societies."[2] Because the church and the state were as one in these earlier times, it is difficult to see the true ambitions of the instigators of many hostilities. Were the combatants really Christians embarking on a holy war for their God? "The Crusades were certainly inspired by religious passion but were also deeply political."[3] The crusades really began "in the seventh century, when Islamic armies swept over the larger portions of what was then Christian territory, the Middle East, Egypt and all of North Africa, and then Spain and southern Italy as well as many major Mediterranean islands including

---

1. Erasmus, "The Education of the Christian Prince," 103.
2. Armstrong, *Fields of Blood*, 359–60.
3. Armstrong, *Fields of Blood*, 360.

Sicily, Corsica, Cyprus, Rhodes, Crete, Malta and Sardinia."[4] Islam, like Christendom of the time, saw no division between religion and state. (It still doesn't.) The appeal by Pope Urban II instigated the actual crusades of medieval times, between 1095 and 1291. Urban saw the opportunity to extend the power and influence of the papacy, both in Christian Europe and eastward into the traditionally Muslim countries. Knights flocked to the East finding a reason for exercising their strength and expertise in knightly abilities—in a real cause instead of in periodic jousts. Some indulged in carousing and looting. Conversely, there were a great many crusaders who embarked on the crusades because "they sincerely believed that they served God's battalions."[5]

The marriage between Christianity and the secular originated with the great success of the Emperor Constantine. "When Constantine overthrew his rival Maxentius at the Milvian Bridge in 312 and thus became master of the western empire, the change which portended in the fortunes of the church was such that it came to be looked upon as practically a Christian victory."[6] Previously Constantine had been a pagan—a worshipper of the "Sun," not the "Son"—but now he was convinced that the Christian God had intervened to give him victory. Constantine then proceeded to set up a Christian empire by subjection. He, and following emperors "enforced the Pax Christiana as belligerently as their pagan predecessors had imposed the Pax Romana."[7] Thus, "an originally peaceful tradition became too closely associated with the government"[8] and all as a result of a victory in a bloodied battle. The Constantinian empire saw Christianity become fashionable, "which was not really a good thing. It meant a considerable ingress of Christianized pagans into the church—pagans who had learned the rudiments of Christian doctrine and had been baptized, but who remained largely pagan in their thoughts and ways."[9] This was the beginning of being a Christian for ill purposes and so there developed throughout history events and movements that were initiated by false Christians for political purposes. Throughout the letters of the Apostles, Paul and John, we come across warnings against

---

4. Stark, *God's Battalions*, 9.
5. Stark, *God's Battalions*, 248.
6. Bruce, *The Spreading Flame*, 294.
7. Armstrong, *Fields of Blood*, 360.
8. Armstrong, *Fields of Blood*, 360.
9. Bruce, *The Spreading Flame*, 295.

these deceivers. In the gospels we read: "Beware of false prophets, who come to you in sheep's clothing but inwardly are ravenous wolves." (Mat 7:15 NRSV) Thus all these early ominous cautions grew to fruition in the coming together of Christianity and the secular world. Instead of Christianity being in the world but not of the world, it was now of the world. It is quite fascinating that in most early church history examination papers there occurs the question: Was Constantine a real Christian?

Christian viewpoints on any subject have to be based on the Bible and the Bible needs to be regarded as inerrant. This does not mean that teaching from the Bible becomes rigid and literal as the Bible uses many literary devices to express its message. Nevertheless, it is the word of God and, as such, the given truth of God. The reader needs to allow for the different literary styles—instruction, history, narrative, poetry, parables, hyperbole, epistles, prophecy, original language, hymns, proverbs, love songs, dreams, and revelation. There is historical criticism, textual criticism, source criticism, literary criticism, and narrative theology—none of these should have more influence than the other but be used to complement, not confuse. In addition, the reader must be conscious of the genre, investigating the customs of the times, not rejecting the teaching therein but seeing it in its original context. If the reader accepts some teaching and rejects others, he or she is on shifting sands. Pamela Tamarkin Reis, in her wonderful book on the (essential) close reading of the Scriptures, emphasizes the basis of the inerrancy of the Torah and this inerrancy can be applied to the whole of the Christian Bible: "Nevertheless, despite my ignorance of what my father was talking about when he told me there were no mistakes in the Torah, I was not shy to sass and did not hesitate to rebut, 'Oh, there probably are mistakes.' 'No,' my father said patiently, 'If you think there's a mistake, it's because you're too dumb to figure it out.'"[10]

Unfortunately, when people are trying to push a viewpoint, they use the Bible to prove their theory, choosing only parts of Scripture to do so. Sometimes their citations are taken out of context but even if they are not, we must use Scripture to interpret Scripture. As the Bible is inerrant there cannot be any conflict—everything agrees. It takes much thought and investigation to illustrate this, for example, we have four gospels that each tell the life and teachings of Jesus related by four different witnesses. All of these gospels can be melded together—they are just four different people telling their version of events. Where there seems to be a conflict

---

10. Reis, *Reading the Lines*, 4.

on a particular happening it is no doubt a similar healing or teaching or prophecy that was written down on a different day at a different place. As John says: "But there are also many other things that Jesus did; if every one of them were written down, I suppose that the world itself could not contain the books that would be written." (John 21:25 NRSV) Pamela Tamarkin Reis, in attempting to understand this phenomenon of differing accounts, suggests a viewing of the Japanese film, *Rashomon*, which has an unusual narrative structure that reflects the difficulty (but not impossibility) of obtaining the truth about an event when there are conflicting witness accounts. Reis also states that when listening to exegetes of specific passages of Scripture, "it was condescending and presumptive to chop, change, and reorder the Bible to make it suit their theories."[11]

In the four distinctive views of Christian teaching on war we can list, and find cases, in the Scriptures for Nonresistance, Christian Pacifism, Just War, and Preventative War. The early church took a pacifist view towards violence, becoming martyrs in the name of Christ; the medieval church was guilty of indulging in the cruel and merciless Crusades in the name of God; the modern church fluctuates from one view to the other depending on the denomination. The Church of the Brethren, Anabaptists, Quakers, and Mennonites are pacifists and generally become conscientious objectors; members of the Salvation Army refuse to bear arms but take the field as ambulance bearers, medical personnel, and padres; most major Christian denominations today such as Roman Catholics, Lutherans, Anglicans, Presbyterians, Baptists, Methodists, and other Reformed branches, follow the teaching of Augustine of Hippo and preach that certain wars are justified. All can provide scriptural references to support their stance. Nevertheless, even in the case of Just War, there is no single perspective that would combine the beliefs of each denomination.

Augustine of Hippo was not the first Christian theologian to promote the principle of a Just War. Although his ideas on this subject are scattered amongst his writings and sometimes change over the years of his life: "War, according to Augustine, must be justified before the court of morality. The primary and incontrovertible criterion is that a wrongful action must have been committed prior to the start of hostile violent action. A just war is always a reaction to wrongdoing . . . Augustine has no illusions about the essential morality or nobility of war. War inspires violence, greed, and lust and stands in sharp contrast to that peaceful

---

11. Reis, *Reading the Lines*, 14.

atmosphere which fosters piety and decency. Therefore, war should be avoided whenever possible and should be concluded as soon as morally feasible."[12] A Just War must have just cause and just intention and must be the last resort. The government makes the formal declaration and maintains its stated and limited objectives—"If the purpose is peace, then unconditional surrender or the destruction of a nation's economic or political institutions is an unwarranted objective."[13] Only the required amount of weaponry and force should be used to achieve a just peace.

One of the major problems in war is the burden of harm imposed on non-combatants (which includes prisoners of war). Governments, either governments of the country itself, or governments of the invading armies, look after their fighting men and women with weapons, shelter, food, etc., but non-combatants are exposed and vulnerable with no guarantee of protection for themselves, their families, or their homes. Protection of the population is a moral requisite of just war. In modern societies sometimes the line between civilians and the military is a fine one but this cannot be used as a moral justification for indiscriminate actions. The bombing of civilian populations in contrast to the bombing of military facilities and armament factories is an obvious deviation from just war. The use of the atomic bomb on civilians, the genocides of specific races and cultures, the killing of a country's "non-desirables" by its own government, all move into the demise of total war. "Fundamentally, the limits set on the conduct of war by morality and the law of war aim at ensuring that warfare does not destroy everything that is worth living for in peacetime, or make it hard or impossible to return to peace after the end of armed conflict."[14] Augustine believed that war was to bring peace not death for children, the elderly, the ill and disabled, the innocent non-combatants; not destruction and a "scorched earth" policy.

Considering the differing views on Just War by Christians, the Roman Catholic Church acknowledges that the entire human family is unable to build a more humane world unless all peoples are renewed in mind and dedicated to the achievement of a lasting peace. In the Second Vatican Council: The Pastoral Constitution on the Church in the Modern World, Gaudium et Spes (1965) we read in Section 1:78:

---

12. Syse, "Augustine and Just War," 39.
13. Holmes, "Just War," 121.
14. Johnson, "Maintaining the Protection of Noncombatants," 188.

> Peace is not the mere absence of war. It cannot be reduced to mere balance of power. It does not come of tyrannical domination. It is rightly and properly called 'the work of justice'. Isaiah 32:7 It exists as the fruit of the order built into human society by its divine Founder, an order to be given practical expression by men ever thirsting for more perfect justice . . . There can be no peace on earth unless personal welfare is safeguarded and men spontaneously and confidently exchange the riches of their minds and genius. The construction of peace absolutely demands a firm resolve to respect other men and peoples, and the practical determination to be brothers. Thus, peace is also the fruit of love, which advances beyond what justice can supply . . . [15]

Acknowledging that this is the ideal but not always achievable, in Section 1:79 it states: "War has decidedly not been eradicated from human affairs. So long as the danger of it persists and we have no competent international authority equipped with adequate force, it will not be possible to deny governments the right of legitimate self-defence, given that they have exhausted every peaceful means of settlement . . . Those who are serving their country in the armed forces should regard themselves as servants of the people's security and liberty. While they are fulfilling this duty they are genuinely contributing to the establishment of peace."[16]

The Protestant perspective on Just War is as united as much as it is not. Each denomination has, over the years, published their views on Just War. The State and Church are separate and God has delegated to government the authority to "execute wrath on the wrongdoer" (Rom 13:4 b NRSV) "Let every person be subject to the government authorities: for there is no authority except from God. Therefore, whoever resists authority resists what God has appointed, and those who resist will incur judgment. For rulers are not a terror to good conduct, but to bad. Do you wish to have no fear of the authority? Then do what is good, and you will receive its approval; for it is God's servant for your good." (Rom 13:1–4a NRSV) But, we know in this world all governments are not good: "Pay to all what is due to them—taxes to whom taxes are due, revenue to whom revenue is due, respect to whom respect is due, honour to whom honour is due." (Rom 13:7 NRSV) Submission to every law of the land is right provided it does not violate the laws of God. The church is responsible in the spiritual and moral realms, cf. the state in civil and political realms.

---

15. Araujo, "Catholic Christianity Part II," 153.
16. Araujo, "Catholic Christianity Part II," 153.

The state must not interfere with the church's spiritual responsibility, something that is daily being challenged in the present world.

The National Association of Evangelicals [USA] in its publication, *For the Health of the Nation: an Evangelical Call to Civic Responsibility* (2004) states: "The peaceful settling of disputes is a gift of common grace. We urge governments to pursue thoroughly nonviolent paths to peace before resorting to military force. We believe that if governments are going to use military force, they must use it in the service of peace and not merely in their national interest. Military force must be guided by the classical just-war principles, which are designed to restrain violence by establishing the right conditions for and the right conduct in fighting a war. In an age of nuclear and biological terrorism, such principles are more important than ever."[17]

It is undeniably vital for humankind to build a future of peace and security. For the church, being the light of Christ in the world, it is one of its major functions to mold and build character, and to bring people to spiritual maturity. This is a huge and crucial task "in a world enamored by and addicted to violence and warfare."[18]

It is now known that the Second Gulf War was embarked upon as a Just War but with reasons that have since proven false. Interestingly, the purpose given for this war has now been amended to condone the death and destruction of innocent people and to validate the sacrifice of so many young soldiers. When the government deceives its people, and does not do what is good, the people are justified in not honoring it and protesting against its actions. Hubris has given a country the right to act deceitfully. Just War must be just in all its parameters otherwise it becomes a crusade with a hidden agenda. Is it just for the United States of America to invade Iraq without the legal sanction of the United Nations? Are its resultant actions against the civilian population just?

Is it just for Israel to annex the West Bank and the Gaza Strip illegally? Is it just for the world to accept what Israel has done and continue to do so since 1967? Is it just that the members of the United Nations do nothing to grant the Palestinians their right to these lands? Is it just that the Palestinians are treated so ruthlessly in their own land—two-thirds of them homeless, stateless, one-third under occupation? Is it just that the Israelis have a standing army but the Palestinians are not granted

---

17. Morkevicius, "Protestant Christianity," 290.
18. Wood, *Perspectives on War in the Bible*, 178.

the same right? Then again—is it just that the Jewish people have experienced such unwarranted persecution for thousands of years? Israel *is* their promised land—the outposts in Palestinian territory are their security. It is interesting to note that when the Israelites dwelt in these lands amongst militant nations thousands of years ago, they did not become a similar military nation; they did not hero-worship their leaders when these leaders led successful campaigns against their enemies; they did not instigate compulsory military training; they did not maintain a standing army; they did not have sentries and guards on their borders.

In Israel there are some, who though often thwarted by the government, are working towards a reconciliation with the Palestinians:

> Breaking the Silence is made up of Israeli soldiers who served in the occupied territories. We are the combatants who carried out Israeli government policies in the occupied territories over the past fifty years. We implemented aggressive military mechanisms of control. We strong-armed millions of human beings into submission. We stripped people of their basic rights, their freedom, their ability to determine their own fates. Our act of speaking out—of "breaking the silence"—is an inevitable reaction to the violence and immorality we witnessed and carried out. It is a personal moral outcry, and a civic outcry. Breaking the silence, for us, entails taking responsibility for our actions, and demanding that the situation be changed. It is an expression of love for our homeland, and of our deep fear for its future.[19]

How many of our so-called Just Wars become more than that—some becoming total wars? The present-day objective is to contain the use of nuclear weapons—a never-ending and frightening challenge for all peoples on earth. The wars of tomorrow will be fought in ways beyond our imagination. We must pray that those who are in control are capable of making righteous decisions and of proceeding justly. The example of Breaking the Silence amongst the daily turmoil of the Middle East, shows that the Jews, the Christian Church, and like-minded people committed to peace, should be seeking to mold and nurture the character of individuals in their small corners of the universe, so that all peoples will see that such a goal is both urgent and worthwhile in a world that is constantly being broken by violence and warfare.

The remaining and outstanding problem is: how do future warriors function in a world without a mainstay? A true faith has enabled many

---

19. Waldman and Chabon eds., *Kingdom of Olives and Ash*, 419.

to persevere and come to terms with the results of their service. Now the world exists in a period which is called "postmodernism"—what is this and what does it mean for the warrior on the battlefield or the military pushing buttons at home?

Past generations lived in the days when, even if families did not attend church regularly, parents sent their children to Sunday schools to learn about God and the Bible. Now, family weekends revolve entirely about relaxing and enjoying worldly pleasures with the exclusion of any acknowledgment of a day of rest dedicated to honoring God and growing as Christians. It could be said that the majority of people today do not really know who Jesus is; in fact, to many "Jesus Christ" is used as a curse word. Thus, there has developed a complete ignorance of a Christian worldview. In this postmodern world men and women chase unachievable dreams—dreams that often prove to be empty and unrewarding. There is a hunger for meaning but humankind has turned away from the source of all meaning.

A book by Arthur Herman, entitled *The Scottish Enlightenment: The Scots Invention of the Modern World*, celebrates the fact that with the advent of great philosophers such as Adam Smith and David Hume, the Scots had been able to revel in a new world of humanistic meaning, breaking away from the somewhat repressive faith of John Knox and the Scottish Kirk. From the great Reformation, when Martin Luther preached "Christ Alone" as the savior of all, men, such as John Calvin in Geneva and John Knox in Scotland, preached the faithful word of God as recorded in the Bible. However, the religious revolutions in Scotland had brought violence, bloodshed, anarchy, invasions by the French, and a type of religious oppression. John Knox aimed to destroy the bastions of Roman Catholicism in much the same way that Henry VIII had destroyed the monasteries in England. Knox also imposed strict new rules for the Sabbath, which became the norm for Presbyterians well into the twentieth century. Oliver Cromwell once said: "Presbyterians, who with their rigid practices and methods laboured to hedge in the wind and bind up the sweet influence of the Spirit."[20]

The Enlightenment, to the Scots, in some ways was a breath of fresh air. Gradually, but surely, from the Enlightenment onwards and with the influence of liberal theology in the late nineteenth century, men and women have either been rejecting the Savior altogether or redesigning

---

20. Fraser, *Cromwell*, xxix.

their concept of salvation in an attempt to make humankind's own foundations for living in a modernized world. In their failures they find only meaningless in life. In the early days of the Enlightenment, Hume said: "self-interest is all there is. The overriding guiding force in all our actions is not our reason, or our sense of obligation to others, or any other innate moral sense—all these are simply formed out of habit and experience—but the most human passion of all, the desire for self-gratification. It is the one thing human beings have in common. It is also the necessary starting point of any system of morality, and of any system of government."[21]

Blaise Pascal noted that, without a sure foundation, when we look for the truth, we find uncertainty: when we look for happiness, we find wretchedness. The following are the major problems of postmodernism. Truth is decided by each individual; guilt is a destructive emotion and should be done away with; and, each person establishes his or her meaning gleaned from life experiences. There are no absolutes. If people do read the Bible, for example, they bring their own interpretation to the texts, determined by their own mindsets and on their own authority. This becomes a frightening situation to say the least.

> Postmoderns are remarkably nonchalant about the meaningless which they experience in life. Reading the works of an earlier generation of writers, existentialists authors like Jean-Paul Satre and Albert Camus, one almost developed a sense of vertigo, the kind of apprehension that one gets when standing too near the edge of a terrifying precipice, so bleak, so empty, and life-threatening was their vision. That sense, however, has now completely gone. Postmoderns live on the surface, not in the depths, and theirs is the despair to be tossed off lightly and which might even be alleviated by nothing more serious than a sitcom.[22]

David Wells calls postmodernism the culture of nothingness. The pace of the world is rapid and full of distracting events and activities. The serious advent of technology has enabled people to do away with potential hours of solitude once so coveted. Then we could meditate, refresh the mind, and rejuvenate the soul. Filling every moment means there is no time to feel guilty, to find meaning, to seek atonement, to experience forgiveness, to feed the spirit.

---

21. Herman, *The Scottish Enlightenment*, 177.
22. Wells, *Above all Earthly Pow'rs*, 177.

The present feeling of meaningless has either dissipated or is constantly being ignored. True, in times of war or other devastations, emotions of terrifying fear have pushed some back to Christ but, at the same time, we still see many who nevertheless reject their faith, and others who fail to embrace an offered saving faith that they never before experienced. Thus, how do the military go into battle in this present age? What do they use for spiritual armor? Are they all alone; each an individual, trying to fathom the depths to find how to strengthen their souls as well as their bodies when preparing for the battle ahead? The church and its chaplains face a gargantuan but not impossible task. Coming to believe the Word of God will bring the love, the purpose, and the security. The sentences of Scripture that encompass God's power over all life and expunge the fear of death are found in the eighth chapter of Paul's Letter to the Romans: "For I am convinced that neither death, nor life, nor angels, nor rulers, nor things present, nor things to come, nor powers, nor height, nor depth, nor anything else in all creation, will be able to separate us from the love of God in Christ Jesus our Lord." (Rom 8:38–39 NRSV)

Is the edge of the world the fall into depravity and insanity, or is it the door into Aslan's own country free from guilt at the feet of the Savior?

Bibliography

Addis, Ferdie, ed. *I Have a Dream: The Speeches That Changed History*. London: Michael O'Mara, 2011.
Ambrose, Stephen E. *D-Day: June 6, 1944: The Climactic Battle of World War II*. London: Simon & Schuster, 2014.
Applebaum, Anne. *Iron Curtain: The Crushing of Eastern Europe, 1944–56*. London: Penguin, 2013.
Appy, Christian G. *Patriots: The Vietnam War Remembered from All Sides*. New York: Viking, 2003.
Araujo, Robert John. "Catholic Christianity. Part II. Contemporary Sources." In *Religion, War and Ethics: A Sourcebook of Textual Traditions*, edited by Gregory M. Reichberg and Henrik Syse, 103–63. Cambridge: Cambridge University Press, 2014.
Archer, Stuart M. "The Racket and the Fear." *History Today* 66 (2016) 11–18.
Armstrong, Karen. *Fields of Blood: Religion and the History of Violence*. London: Bodley Head, 2014.
Aronson, Shlomo. *Crowns in Conflict: The Triumph and the Tragedy of European Monarchy, 1910–918*. Manchester, NH: Salem House, 1986.
———. *Hitler, the Allies and the Jews*. Cambridge: Cambridge University Press, 2006.
Arthur, Max. *Lest We Forget: Forgotten Voices from 1914–1945*. London: Ebury, 2007.
———. *We Will Remember Them: Voices from the Aftermath of the Great War*. London: Weidenfeld & Nicolson, 2009.
Atkinson, Rick. *The Long Gray Line: The American Journey of West Point's Class of 1966*. New York: Henry Holt, 2013.
Australia. Department of Veterans' Affairs. *The Australian Light Horse*. Canberra, ACT: AGPS, 2007.
Avnery, Uri. *1948: A Soldier's Tale: The Bloody Road to Jerusalem*. Translated by Christopher Costello. Oxford: Oneworld, 2008.
Babchenko, Arkady. *One Soldier's War*. Translated by Nick Allen. New York: Grove, 2007.
Baker, A. B. "The Story of a W.A.A.C." In *On the Front Line: True World War I Stories*, edited by C. B. Purdom, 395–401. Rev. ed. London: Constable, 2009.
Bao Ninh. *The Sorrow of War: A Novel*. English version by Frank Palmos, from the original translation by Phan Thanh Hao. London: Vintage, 1998.
Barrett, Michele. *Casualty Figures: How Five Men Survived the First World War*. London: Verso, 2007.

Bean, C. E. W. "Trommelfeuer: The Battle of Today: Its First and Last Weapon." *Auckland Star* XLVIII 244 (1916) 7.
Beer, Edith Hahn, and Susan Dworkin. *The Nazi Officer's Wife: How One Jewish Woman Survived the Holocaust*. London: Abacus, 2001.
Berkhof, Louis. *Systematic Theology*. Grand Rapids, MI: Eerdmans, 1941.
Bessel, Richard. *Violence: A Modern Obsession*. London: Simon & Schuster, 2015.
Bible: *New Revised Standard Version: Containing the Old and New Testaments and the Deuterocanonical books*. Peabody, MA: Hendrikson, 2005.
Biggs, Jason. *Skies of WWII: Courage, Battle and Victory in the Air*. New York: Chartwell, 2014.
Bilton, David. *The Germans in Flanders, 1914: Rare Photographs from Wartime Archives*. Images of War. Barnsley, South Yorkshire: Pen & Sword Military, 2012.
Bonhoeffer, Dietrich, and Maria von Wedemeyer. *Love Letters from Cell 92*. Edited by Ruth-Alice von Bismarck, and Ulrich Kabitz. Translated by John Brownjohn. London: HarperCollins, 1994.
Bourke, Joanna. *An Intimate History of Killing: Face-to-face Killing in Twentieth-Century Warfare*. London: Granta, 1999.
Bown, Stephen R. *The Last Viking: The Life of Roald Amundsen*. Boston, MA: Da Capo, 2012.
Brandt, Anthony, ed. *The North Pole: A Narrative History*. Washington, DC: National Geographic Society, 2005.
Bridgland, Tony. *Waves of Hate: Naval Atrocities of the Second World War*. Barnsley, South Yorkshire: Leo Cooper, 2002.
Brigham, Robert K. *Is Iraq Another Vietnam?* New York: Public Affairs, 2006.
Brittain, Vera. *Chronicle of Youth: War Diary, 1913–1917*. Edited by Alan Bishop. London: Fontana, 1982.
———. *Testament of Youth: An Autobiographical Study of the Years 1900–1925*. London: Virago, 1976.
Brown, Malcolm. *The Imperial War Museum Book of the First World War*. London: Pan Books, 2002.
Brown, Malcolm, and Patricia Meehan. *Scapa Flow*. London: Pan Books, 2002.
Bruce, F. F. *The Spreading Flame: The Rise and Progress of Christianity from the First Beginning to the Conversion of the English*. Grand Rapids, MI: Eerdmans, 1958.
Buchan, John. "Mr Standfast." In *The Complete Richard Hannay Stories*, 307–559. Ware, Hertfordshire: Wordsworth Editions, 2010.
Burns, Ken, and Lynn Novick, dirs. *The Vietnam War: A Film*. Written by Geoffrey C. Ward. Walpole, NH: Florentine Films, 2017.
Burroughs, Bryan et al. "The Path to War: Gathering the Troops." *Vanity Fair* 30 Oct 2010. http://www.vanityfair.com/politics/features/2004/05/pathtowar
Byrnes, Paul. *The Lost Boys: The Untold Stories of the Under-age Soldiers who Fought in the First World War*. South Melbourne, VIC: Affirm, 2019.
Cadbury, Deborah. *Princes at War: The British Royal Family's Private Battle in the Second World War*. London: Bloomsbury, 2016.
Caputo, Philip. *A Rumor of War*. London: Arrow Books, 1978.
Carlyon, Les. *Gallipoli*. Sydney, NSW: Pan Macmillan Australia, 2001.
———. *The Great War*. Sydney, NSW: Pan Macmillan, 2006.

Caulfield, Michael. *The Unknown Anzac: The Real Stories of Our National Legend Told through the Rediscovered Diaries and Letters of the Anzacs Who Were There*. Sydney, NSW: Hachette Australia, 2013.

Cawthorne, Nigel. *Vietnam: A War Lost and Won*. Enderby, Leicester: Arcturus, 2003.

Chalker, Jack Bridger. *Burma Railway Artist: The War Drawings of Jack Chalker*. Ringwood, VIC: Viking, 1994.

Clark, C. M. H. *A History of Australia. Volume 6. 'The Old Dead Tree and the Young Tree Green,' 1916–1935*. Melbourne, VIC: Melbourne University Press, 1987.

Clay, Catrine. *King, Kaiser, Tsar: Three Royal Cousins Who Led the World to War*. London: John Murray, 2007.

Clouse, Robert G., ed. *War: 4 Christian Views*. Downers Grove, IL: InterVarsity Press, 1981.

Cobb, Matthew. *Eleven Days in August: The Liberation of Paris in 1944*. London: Simon & Schuster, 2013.

Colburn, Larry. "They Were Butchering People." In *Patriots: The Vietnam War Remembered from all Sides*, by Christian G. Appy. 346–49. New York: Viking, 2003.

Cornwell, Bernard. *Waterloo: The History of Four Days, Three Armies and Three Battles*. London: William Collins, 2014.

Cornwell, John. *Hitler's Pope: The Secret History of Pius XII*. London: Penguin, 2000.

Craig, Gordon A. *Theodor Fontane: Literature and History in the Bismarck Reich*. New York: Oxford University Press, 1999.

Damousi, Joy. *Living with the Aftermath: Trauma, Nostalgia and Grief in Post-war Australia*. Cambridge: Cambridge University Press, 2001.

Dante Alighieri. *The Divine Comedy. Inferno*. Translated and edited by Robin Kirkpatrick. London: Penguin, 2006.

Dapin, Mark. *The Nashos' War: Australia's National Servicemen and Vietnam*. Camberwell, VIC: Viking, 2014.

Dapin, Mark. ed. *The Penguin Book of Australian War Writing*. Camberwell, VIC: Viking, 2011.

Davidson, Andrew. *A Doctor in the Great War*. New York: Marble Arch, 2013.

Davie, Grace. "The Military Chaplain: A Study in Ambiguity." *International Journal for the Study of the Christian Church* 15 (2015) 39–53.

de Man, Henry. "The Remaking of a Mind: A Soldier's Thoughts on War and Reconstruction." London, 1920. Cited in *An Intimate History of Killing: Face-to-face Killing in Twentieth-century Warfare*, by Joanna Bourke, 31.

Dennis, David B. *Inhumanities: Nazi Interpretations of Western Culture*. Cambridge: Cambridge University Press, 2012.

Dimbleby, Jonathan. *Russia: A Journey with Jonathan Dimbleby*. London: BBC, 2008. Film.

Dos, Margarete, and Kerstin Lieff. *Letters from Berlin: A Story of War, Survival and the Redeeming Power of Love and Friendship*. North Sydney, NSW: Vintage Australia, 2012.

Downing, Taylor. *Breakdown: The Crisis of Shell Shock on the Somme, 1916*. London: Little, Brown, 2016.

Dunbar, Raden. *The Secrets of the Anzacs: The Untold Story of Venereal Disease in the Australian Army, 1914–1919*. Melbourne, VIC: Scribe, 2014.

Dunlop, E. E. *The War Diaries of Weary Dunlop: Java and the Burma-Thailand Railway, 1942–1945*. Melbourne, VIC: Nelson, 1986.

Dyer, Gwynne. *War*. London: Guild Publishers, 1985.

Ebury, Sue. *Weary: The Life of Sir Edward Dunlop*. Ringwood, VIC: Viking Australia, 1994.

Eman, Diet, and James Schaap. *Things We Couldn't Say*. Grand Rapids, MI: Eerdmans, 1994.

Engelke, Gerrit. "To Death." Translated by Merryn Williams. *The Interpreter* 9 (1998), 65.

Erasmus, Desiderius. *The Education of the Christian Prince*. Edited by Lisa Jardine. Cambridge Texts in the History of Political Thought. Cambridge: Cambridge University Press, 1977.

Fadiman, Anne. *Ex Libris: Confessions of a Common Reader*. London: Penguin, 2000.

Farrar-Hockley, Anthony. *The Edge of the Sword*. London: Companion Book Club, 1954.

Faust, Drew Gilpin. *This Republic of Suffering: Death and the American Civil War*. New York: Vintage Civil War Library, 2009.

Fenby, Jonathan. *The Sinking of the Lancastria: Britain's Greatest Maritime Disaster and Churchill's Cover-up*. London: Simon & Schuster, 2005.

Fewster, Kevin et al. *A Turkish View of Gallipoli: Canakkale*. Richmond, VIC: Hodja Educational Resources, 1985.

Feigel, Lara. *The Love-charm of Bombs*. London: Bloomsbury, 2014.

Figes, Orlando. *The Whisperers: Private Life in Stalin's Russia*. Camberwell, VIC: Penguin, 2008.

Frankl, Viktor E. *Man's Search for Meaning: An Introduction to Logotherapy*. Translated by Ilse Lasch. New York: Simon & Schuster, 1962. [Rev. ed. *From Death-camp to Existentialism*]

Fraser, Antonia. *Cromwell: Our Chief of Men*. London: Phoenix, 2002.

Fredriksen, Paula. *Augustine and the Jews: A Christian Defense of Jews and Judaism*. New Haven, CT: Yale University Press, 2010.

Funder, Anna. *Stasiland: Stories from Behind the Berlin Wall*. New York: Harper Perennial, 2003.

Garrett, Stephen A. *Ethics and Air Power in World War II: The British Bombing of German Cities*. London: Palgrave Macmillan, 1993.

Geddes, Giorgio. *Nichivo: Life, Love and Death on the Russian Front*. London: Cassell, 2001.

Gilbert, Adrian. *Challenge of Battle: The Real Story of the British Army in 1914*. Oxford: Osprey, 2013.

Gilbert, Martin. *A History of the Twentieth Century. Volume One. 1900–1933*. London: HarperCollins, 1997.

———. *A History of the Twentieth Century. Volume Two. 1933–1951*. New York: William Morrow, 1998.

———. *The Holocaust: The Jewish Tragedy*. London: Fontana, 1987.

———. *The Righteous: The Unsung Heroes of the Holocaust*. New York: Henry Holt, 2003.

Gillies, Midge. *The Barbed-wire University: The Real Lives of Allied Prisoners of War in the Second World War*. London: Aurum, 2011.

Grandin, Robert. *The Battle of Long Tan: As Told by the Commanders*. Crows Nest, NSW: Allen & Unwin, 2004.
Graves, Robert. *Goodbye to All That*. Camberwell, VIC: Penguin, 2009.
Griffin, A. Harry. *Heritage of Lakeland: A Centenary Collection*. Edited by Peter Hardy. London: Frances Lincoln, 2011.
Grossmann, Atina. *Jews, Germans, and Allies: Close Encounters in Occupied Germany*. Princeton, NJ: Princeton University Press, 2007.
Grossman, Dave. *On Killing: The Psychological Cost of Learning to Kill in War and Society*. New York: Back Bay Books, 1995.
Gullett, H. S., and Chas Barrett eds. *Australia in Palestine*. Sydney, NSW; Angus & Robertson, 1919.
Gullett, H. S. *The Australian Imperial Force in Sinai and Palestine, 1914–1918*. 7th ed. Volume VII of *The Official History of Australia in the War of 1914–1918*. 7. Sydney, NSW: Angus and Robertson, 1939.
Ham, Paul. *Hiroshima Nagasaki*. Sydney, NSW: HarperCollins, 2011.
———. *1914: The Year the World Ended*. North Sydney, NSW: William Heinemann Australia, 2013.
———. *Vietnam: The Australian War*. Pymble, NSW: HarperCollins, 2010.
Hambrook, Michael. *On the Front Line: Real Life Stories of Spying, Escaping and Surviving War*. London: New Holland, 2012.
Hamilton, R. *The History of World War I in Photographs: Photographs by the Daily Mail*. Bath, Somerset: Parragon, 2014.
Harding, Thomas. *Hanns and Rudolf: The German Jew and the Hunt for the Kommandant of Auschwitz*. London: William Heinemann, 2013.
Harris, Mark Jonathan, and Deborah Oppenheimer. *Into the Arms of Strangers: Stories of the Kindertransport*. London: Bloomsbury, 2000.
Haste, Cate. *Nazi Women: Hitler's Seduction of a Nation*. London: Channel 4, 2003.
Hastings, Max. *Nemesis: The Battle for Japan 1944–45*. London: William Collins, 2014.
Helm, Sarah. *If This Is a Woman: Inside Ravensbrück: Hitler's Concentration Camp for Women*. London: Little Brown, 2015.
———. *A Life in Secrets: The Story of Vera Atkins and the Lost Agents of SOE*. London: Abacus, 2006.
Henderson, Kenneth T. *Khaki and Cassock*. Melbourne, VIC: Melville & Mullen, 1919.
Herma, Hans. "Goebbels' Conception of Propaganda." *Social Research* 10 (1943) 200–218.
Herman, Arthur. *The Scottish Enlightenment: The Scots Invention of the Modern World*. London: Fourth Estate, 2003.
Herr, Michael. *Dispatches*. London: Picador, 1978.
Hersey, John. *Hiroshima*. London: Penguin, 1986.
Hillenbrand, Laura. *Unbroken: An Extraordinary True Story of Courage and Survival*. London: Fourth Estate, 2010.
Hilton, Christopher. *The Wall: The People's Story*. Stroud, Gloucestershire: Sutton, 2001.
Holmes, Arthur. "The Just War." In *War: 4 Christian Views*, edited by Robert G. Clouse. 118–35. Downers Grove, IL: InterVarsity, 1981.
Holmes, Stephen. *The Matador's Cape: America's Reckless Response to Terror*. New York: Cambridge University Press, 2007.
Horne, Alistair. *Hubris: The Tragedy of War in the Twentieth Century*. New York: HarperCollins, 2015.

Hudson, Edward ed. *Poetry of the First World War: 'The Hell Where Youth and Laughter Go.'* Hove, East Sussex: Wayland, 1988.

Huie, Shirley Fenton. *The Forgotten Ones: Women and Children under Nippon.* Pymble, NSW: Angus & Robertson, 1992.

Hunter, Douglas J. *My Corps Cavalry: A History of the 13th Light Horse Regiment (AIF).* McCrae, VIC: Slouch Hat, 1999.

James, Harold. *Europe Reborn: A History, 1914-2000.* Abingdon, Oxon: Routledge, 2003.

Johnson, James Turner. "Maintaining the Protection of Noncombatants." In *Ethics, Nationalism and Just War: Medieval and Contemporary Perspectives,* edited by Henrik Syse and Gregory Reichberg, 151–89. Washington, DC: Catholic University of America Press, 2012.

Jones, Gregg. *Honor in the Dust: Theodore Roosevelt, War in the Pacific, and the Rise and Fall of America's Imperial Dream.* New York: New American Library, 2012.

Jones, Ian. *The Australian Light Horse.* Australians at War. North Sydney, NSW: Time-Life Books Australia, 1987.

Josephs, Jeremy. *Swastika over Paris: The Fate of the French Jews.* London: Bloomsbury, 1989.

Keith, Agnes Newton. *Three Came Home.* New York: MacFadden-Bartell, 1965.

Kelly, Terence. *By Hellship to Hiroshima.* Barnsley, South Yorkshire: Pen & Sword Military, 2006. [Originally entitled *Living with Japanese.* 1997.]

Kempowski, Walter. *Swansong 1945: A Collective Diary of the Last Days of the Third Reich.* Translated by Shaun Whiteside. New York: W. W. Norton, 2015.

Kenez, Peter. *The Coming of the Holocaust: From Antisemitism to Genocide.* New York: Cambridge University Press, 2013.

Kershaw, Alex. *Escape from the Deep: The Epic Story of a Legendary Submarine and Her Courageous Crew.* Philadelphia, PA: Da Capo, 2008.

———. *The Liberator: One World War II Soldier's 500-day Odyssey from the Beaches of Sicily to the Gates of Dachau.* New York: Crown, 2012.

Kershaw, Ian. *The End: The Defiance and Destruction of Hitler's Germany, 1944–45.* New York: Penguin, 2011.

Kertzer, David I. *The Pope and Mussolini: The Secret History of Pius XI and the Rise of Fascism in Europe.* New York: Random House, 2014.

Knop, W. G. ed. *Beware of the English!: German Propaganda Exposes England.* London: Hamish Hamilton, 1939.

Knopp, Guido, and Peter Hartl. *Joseph Goebbels: The Propagandist Firebrand.* Hitler's Henchmen. Mainz: ZDF with ARTE and SBSTV, 1996. Film.

Koonz, Claudia. *The Nazi Conscience.* Cambridge, MA: Belknap, 2003.

Kramer, Rita. *Flames in the Field: The Story of Four SOE Agents in Occupied France.* London: Penguin, 1996.

Kuhn, Rita J. *Broken Glass, Broken Lives: A Jewish Girl's Survival Story in Berlin, 1933–1945.* Piedmont, CA: Barany, 2012.

Kwan, Michael David. *Things That Must Not be Forgotten: A Childhood in Wartime China.* Sydney, NSW: Flamingo HarperCollins, 2002.

Kyle, Chris et al. *American Sniper: The Autobiography of the Most Lethal Sniper in U.S. Military.* New York: William Morrow, 2014.

Ladd, George Eldon. *A Theology of the New Testament.* Grand Rapids, MI: Eerdmans, 1974.

Laffin, John. *Damn the Dardanelles!: The Agony of Gallipoli*. Gloucester, Gloucestershire: Sutton, 1989.

Lagnado, Lucette Matalon, and Sheila Cohn Dekel. *Children of the Flames: Dr Josef Mengele and the Untold Story of the Twins of Auschwitz*. London: Pan Books, 1992.

Lamont-Brown, Raymond. *Kamikaze: Japan's Suicide Samurai*. London: Cassell, 1999.

Langewiesche, William. "The Distant Executioner: Sharpshooters." *Vanity Fair* 30 Oct 2010. http://www.vanityfair.com/politics/features/2010/12/sniper

Langner, Rainer K. *Scott and Amundsen: Duel in the Ice*. Translated by Timothy Beech. London: Haus, 2007.

Leckie, Robert. *Helmet for my Pillow*. London: Ebury, 2010.

Levine, Joshua. *Forgotten Voices of the Somme: The Most Devastating Battle of the Great War in the Words of Those who Survived*. London: Ebury, 2009.

Lewis, C. S. *The Chronicles of Narnia*. London: HarperCollins, 2001.

Lewis, Jonathan, and Ben Steele. *Hell in the Pacific: From Pearl Harbor to Hiroshima and Beyond*. London: Channel 4, 2001.

Lewis-Stempel, John. *Six Weeks: The Short and Gallant Life of the British Officer in the First World War*. London: Weidenfeld & Nicolson, 2010.

Linder, Robert D. *The Long Tragedy: Australian Evangelical Christians and the Great War, 1914–1918*. Adelaide, SA: Openbook, 2000.

Long, Gavin. *Greece, Crete and Syria*. Rev. reprint. Australia in the War of 1939–1945. Series 1 Army II. Sydney, NSW: Collins, 1986.

Longden, Sean. *Blitz Kids*. London: Constable, 2012.

Lord, Walter. *The Miracle of Dunkirk*. London: Allen Lane, 1983.

Lower, Wendy. *Hitler's Furies: German Women in the Nazi Killing Fields*. London: Vintage, 2014.

Lunn, Hugh. *Vietnam: A Reporter's War*. St Lucia, QLD: University of Queensland Press, 1986.

Lynch, E. P. F. *Somme Mud: The War Experiences of an Infantryman in France, 1916–1919*. Edited by Will Davies. North Sydney, NSW: Random House Australia, 2008.

Macdonald, Lyn. *1914*. London: Penguin, 1989.

———. *The Roses of No Man's Land*. London: PAPERMAC, 1984.

———. *Somme*. London: PAPERMAC, 1984.

Macintyre, Ben. *Agent Zigzag: The True Wartime Story of Eddie Chapman: The Most Notorious Double Agent of World War II*. London: Bloomsbury, 2010.

———. *Operation Mincemeat: The True Spy Story that Changed the Course of World War II*. London: Bloomsbury, 2010.

MacKenzie, S. P. *The Colditz Myth: British and Commonwealth Prisoners of War in Nazi Germany*. Oxford: Oxford University Press, 2004.

MacKinnon, Marianne. *The Naked Years: Growing up in Nazi Germany*. London: Chatto & Windus, 1987.

Main, J. M. ed. *Conscription: The Australian Debate, 1901–1970*. Stanmore, NSW: Cassell, 1970.

Marlantes, Karl. *What It Is Like to Go to War*. New York: Atlantic Monthly, 2011.

Marlow, Joyce ed. *The Virago Book of Women and the Great War, 1914–1918*. London: Virago, 1999.

Martin, David. *Reflections on Sociology and Theology*. Oxford: Clarendon, 1997.

Maspero, Francois. *Out of the Shadows: A Life of Gerda Taro*. Translated by Geoffrey Strachan. London: Souvenir Press, 2008.

Matthews, Rupert. *Hitler: Military Commander*. Enderby, Leicester: Arcturus, 2003.

Maynard, Roger. *Ambon: The Truth about One of the Most Brutal POW camps in World War II and the Triumph of the Aussie Spirit*. Sydney, NSW: Hachette Australia, 2014.

McKernan, Michael. *Australian Churches at War: Attitudes and Activities of the Major Churches, 1914–1918*. Studies in the Christian Movement 6. Sydney, NSW: Catholic Theological Faculty, 1980.

———. *Padre: Australian Chaplains in Gallipoli and France*. Sydney, NSW: Allen & Unwin, 1986.

———. *This War Never Ends: The Pain of Separation and Return*. St Lucia, QLD: University of Queensland Press, 2001.

McNaughton, John T. "Proposed Course of Action re: Vietnam: Draft Memorandum to Robert McNamara, 24 March 1965." *The Pentagon Papers: Gravel ed.* v.3, 694–702. http://www.mtholyoke.edu/acad/intrel/pentagon3/doc253.htm

Metaxas, Eric. *Bonhoeffer: Pastor, Martyr, Prophet, Spy: A Righteous Gentile vs. the Third Reich*. Nashville, TN: Thomas Nelson, 2010.

Mitchell, Elyne. *Light Horse: The Story of Australia's Mounted Troops*. South Melbourne, VIC: Macmillan Australia, 1978.

Moore, Harold G., and Joseph L. Galloway. *We Were Soldiers Once . . . and Young: Ia Drang: The Battle that Changed the War in Vietnam*. London: Corgi, 2002.

Moorehead, Caroline. *A Train in Winter: An Extraordinary Story of Women, Friendship and Resistance in Occupied France*. New York: Harper LUXE, 2012.

Moreman, John. *Victory in the Pacific, 1945: Australians in the Pacific War*. Canberra, ACT: Australia. Department of Veterans' Affairs, 2005.

Morkevicius, Valerie Ona. "Protestant Christianity." In *Religion, War and Ethics: A Sourcebook of Textual Traditions*, edited by Gregory M. Reichberg and Henrik Syse, 235–99. Cambridge: Cambridge University Press, 2014.

Morris, Ian. *War! What Is it Good For?: Conflict and the Progress of Civilization from Primates to Robots*. New York: Farrar, Straus and Giroux, 2014.

Mortimer, Barbara. *Sisters: Memories from the Courageous Nurses of World War Two*. London: Hutchinson, 2012.

Murdoch, Keith. *The Gallipoli Letter*. Crows Nest, NSW: Allen & Unwin, 2010.

Murray, Nicholas. *The Red Sweet Wine of Youth: The Brave and Brief Lives of the War Poets*. London: Little, Brown, 2010.

Newbolt, Henry. "Vitaï Lampada." http://www.firstworldwar.com/poetsandprose/newbolt.htm

Newby, Wanda. *Peace and War: Growing Up in Fascist Italy*. London: Picador, 1992.

Nguyen, Kien. *The Unwanted: A Memoir of Childhood*. Boston, MA: Back Bay Books, 2002.

Nicolson, Juliet. *The Perfect Summer: England 1911, Just Before the Storm*. New York: Grove, 2006.

Nicholson, Mavis. *What Did You Do in the War, Mummy?: Women in World War II*. London: Chatto & Windus, 1995.

Ohler, Norman. *Blitzed: Drugs in Nazi Germany*. Translated by Shaun Whiteside. London: Penguin, 2017.

Olsen, Jack. *Silence on Monte Sole*. New York: Simon & Schuster, 2002.

Ousby, Ian. *The Road to Verdun: World War I's Most Momentous Battle and the Folly of Nationalism*. New York: Doubleday, 2002.

Owen, James. *Danger UXB: The Heroic Story of the WWII Bomb Disposal Teams.* London: Little Brown, 2010.
Pakenham, Thomas. *The Scramble for Africa, 1876–1945.* London: Abacus History, 1992.
Pakula, Hannah. *An Uncommon Woman: The Empress Frederick: Daughter of Queen Victoria, Wife of the Crown Prince of Prussia, Mother of Kaiser Wilhelm.* London: Phoenix, 1997.
Palmer, Michael A. *The German Wars: A Concise History, 1859–1945.* Minneapolis, MN: Zenith Press, 2010.
Parry, Naomi, and Brad Manera. *New South Wales and the Great War.* Haberfield, NSW: Longueville Media, 2015.
Parsons, Martin. *War Child: Children Caught in Conflict.* Stroud, Gloucestershire: Tempus, 2008.
Passingham, Ian. *All the Kaiser's Men: The Life and Death of the German Soldier on the Western Front.* Port Stroud, GL: History Press, 2011.
Poole, Robert M. *Section 60 Arlington National Cemetery: Where War Comes Home.* New York: Bloomsbury, 2014.
Posner, Gerald. *Hitler's Children: Inside the Families of the Third Reich.* London: Heinemann, 1991.
Price, Sian. *If You're Reading This . . . Last Letters from the Front Line.* London: Frontline, 2011.
Price-Jones, David. *Unity Mitford: A Quest.* London: W. H. Allen, 1978.
Purdom, C. B. ed. *On the Front Line: True World War I Stories.* Rev. ed. London: Constable, 2009.
Ramsay, Roy. *Hell, Hope and Heroes: Life in the Field Ambulance in World War I: The Memoirs of Private Roy Ramsay, AIF.* Dural, NSW: Rosenberg, 2005.
Rappaport, Helen. *Caught in the Revolution: Petrograd, Russia, 1917: A World on the Edge.* New York: St Martin's, 2017.
Rees, Peter. *The Other ANZACS: Nurses at War, 1914–18.* Crows Nest, NSW: Allen & Unwin, 2008.
Reichberg, Gregory M., and Henrik Syse eds. *Religion, War, and Ethics: A Sourcebook of Textual Traditions.* New York: Cambridge University Press, 2014.
Reid, Anna. *Leningrad: The Epic Siege of World War II, 1941–1944.* New York: Walker, 2011.
Reilly, Robin. *The Sixth Floor: The Danish Resistance Movement and the RAF Raid on Gestapo Headquarters, March 1945.* London: Cassell Military, 2002.
Reis, Pamela Tamarkin. *Reading the Lines: A Fresh Look at the Hebrew Bible.* Peabody, MA: Hendrickson, 2002.
Rex, Christina. *Doodlebugs, Gas Masks & Gum: Children's Voices from the Second World War.* Stroud, Gloucestershire: Amberley, 2008.
Reymond, Robert L. *A New Systematic Theology of the Christian Faith.* Nashville, TN: Thomas Nelson, 1998.
Richie, Alexandra. *Warsaw 1944: The Fateful Uprising.* London: William Collins, 2013.
Roberts, Craig, and Charles W. Sasser. *The Walking Dead: A Marine's Story of Vietnam.* London: Grafton, 1990.
Robertson, Stuart. *A Pocket Guide to the D-Day Beaches.* Caen, Normandy: the Author, 2015.

Rolfe, Mel. *Looking into Hell: Experiences of the Bomber Command War*. London: Rigel, 2004.

Rose, Gideon. *How Wars End: Why We Always Fight the Last Battle: A History of American Intervention from World War I to Afghanistan*. New York: Simon & Schuster, 2011.

Russell of Liverpool, Edward Frederick Langley, 2nd Baron. *The Knights of Bushido: A History of Japanese War Crimes during World War II*. New York: E. P. Dutton, 1958.

Salmon, Andrew. *Scorched Earth, Black Snow: Britain and Australia in the Korean War*. London: Aurum, 2011.

Sarkar, Dilip. *Last of the Few: 18 Battle of Britain Fighter Pilots tell their Extraordinary Stories*. Stroud, Gloucestershire: Amberley, 2011.

Scates, Bruce. *A Place to Remember: A History of the Shrine of Remembrance*. Melbourne: Cambridge University Press, 2009.

Schanberg, Sydney. *Beyond the Killing Fields: War Writings*. Edited by Robert Miraldi. Washington, DC: Potomac Books, 2010.

Schwarz, Fred C. *You Can Trust the Communists (to Do Exactly as They Say)*. New York: Prentice-Hall, 1961.

Sereny, Gitta. *Albert Speer: His Battle with Truth*. London: Macmillan, 1995.

———. *The German Trauma: Experiences and Reflections, 1938–2001*. London: Penguin, 2001.

———. *Into That Darkness: From Mercy Killing to Mass Murder*. London: Pimlico, 1995.

Service, Robert William. "The March of the Dead." http://www.public-domain-poetry.com/robert-william-service

Shelley, Percy Bysshe. *Selected Poems of Percy Bysshe Shelley*. London: Oxford University Press, 1919.

Simon, Marie Jalowicz. *Underground in Berlin: A Young Woman's Extraordinary Tale of Survival in the Heart of Nazi Germany*. Translated by Anthea Bell. New York: Little, Brown, 2015.

Sledge, Eugene B. *With the Old Breed: At Peleliu and Okinawa*. New York: Ballantine, 2007.

Smith, Lyn. *Forgotten Voices of the Holocaust*. London: Ebury, 2005.

———. *Voices Against War: A Century of Protest*. Edinburgh: Mainstream, 2009.

———. *Young Voices: British Children Remember the Second World War*. London: Viking, 2007.

Smith, Mark S. *Treblinka Survivor: The Life and Death of Hershl Sperling*. Stroud, Gloucestershire: Spellmount, 2011.

Smith, Michael. *The Debs of Bletchley Park: And Other Stories*. London: Aurum, 2015.

Southard, Susan. *Nagasaki: Life after Nuclear War*. New York: Viking, 2015.

Spilsbury, Julian. *The Thin Red Line: An Eyewitness History of the Crimean War*. London: Weidenfeld & Nicolson, 2005.

Stark, Rodney. *God's Battalions: The Case for the Crusades*. New York: HarperOne, 2009.

Steinhoff, Johannes, Peter Pechel, and Dennis Showalter. *Voices from the Third Reich: An Oral History*. London: Grafton, 1991.

Stephenson, Michael. *The Last Full Measure: How Soldiers Die in Battle*. London: Duckworth Overlook, 2013.

Summers, Julie. *The Colonel of Tamarkan: Philip Toosey and the Bridge on the River Kwai*. London: Downtown, 2006.

———. *Stranger in the House: Women's Stories of Men Returning from the Second World War.* London: Simon & Schuster, 2008.
Syse, Henrik. "Augustine and Just War: Between Virtue and Duties." In *Ethics, Nationalism and Just War: Medieval and Contemporary Perspectives*, edited by Henrik Syse and Gregory M. Reichberg, 36–50. Washington, DC: Catholic University of America Press, 2007.
Syse, Henrik, and Gregory M. Reichberg, eds. *Ethics, Nationalism and Just War: Medieval and Contemporary Perspectives.* Washington, DC: Catholic University of America Press, 2007.
Taylor, Rosemary, and Wende Grant. *Orphans of War: Work with the Abandoned Children of Vietnam, 1967–1975.* London: Collins, 1988.
Tec, Nechama. *When Light Pierced the Darkness: Christian Rescue of Jews in Nazi-occupied Poland.* New York: Oxford University Press, 1987.
Teilhard de Chardin, Pierre. *The Making of a Mind: Letters from a Soldier-Priest, 1914–1919.* London: Collins, 1965.
ten Boom, Corrie et al. *The Hiding Place.* London: Hodder and Stoughton, 1976.
Thompson, Peter Alexander, and Robert Macklin. *Keep Off the Skyline: The Story of Ron Cashman and the Diggers in Korea.* Milton, QLD: John Wiley Australia, 2004.
Toosey, Philip. "Tamarkan Base Hospital." In *The Colonel of Tamarkan: Philip Toosey and the Bridge on the River Kwai*, by Julie Summers. London: Downtown, 2006.
Ungerer, Tomi. *Tomi: A Childhood Under the Nazis.* Boulder, CO: Roberts Rinehart, 1998.
van Emden, Richard. *The Soldier's War: The Great War through Veterans' Eyes.* London: Bloomsbury, 2008.
von Hassell, Fey. *A Mother's War.* Edited by David Forbes-Watt. London: Corgi, 1991.
Waldman, Ayelet, and Michael Chabon eds. *Kingdom of Olives and Ash: Writers Confront the Occupation.* London: 4th Estate, 2017.
Wallis, Sarah, and Svetlana Palmer. *We Were Young and at War: The First-hand Story of Young Lives Lived and Lost in World War II.* London: Collins, 2009.
Walters, Guy. *Berlin Games: How Hitler Stole the Olympic Dream.* London: John Murray, 2007.
———. *Hunting Evil: The Nazi War Criminals Who Escaped and the Quest to Bring Them to Justice.* New York: Broadway, 2009.
Weale, Adrian. *Army of Evil: A History of the SS.* New York: NAL Caliber, 2012.
Wells, David F. *Above All Earthly Pow'rs: Christ in a Postmodern World.* Grand Rapids, MI: Eerdmans, 2005.
West, Arthur Graeme. *Diary of a Dead Officer: Being the Posthumous Papers of Arthur Graeme West.* London: Greenhill, 2007.
Westminster Abbey. *A Service of Commemoration and Thanksgiving to Mark ANZAC Day, Thursday 25th April 2019 Noon.* London: The Abbey, 2019.
White, David Fairbank. *Bitter Ocean: The Battle of the Atlantic, 1939–1945.* New York: Simon & Schuster, 2006.
Wilcockson, Michael. *Issues of Life and Death.* 2nd ed. Access to Religion and Philosophy. London: Hodder Education, 2009.
Willingham, Matthew. *Perilous Commitments: The Battle for Greece and Crete, 1940–941.* Staplehurst, Kent: Spellmount, 2005.
Witkop, Philipp ed. *German Students' War Letters.* Translated and arranged from the original edition by A. F. Wedd. London: Methuen, 1929.

Wood, John A. *Perspectives on War in the Bible*. Macon, GA: Mercer University Press, 1998.
Wright, Pattie. *The Men of the Line: Stories of the Thai-Burma Railway Survivors*. Carlton, VIC: Miegunyah, 2008.
Ziino, Bart. *A Distant Grief: Australians, War Graves and the Great War*. Crawley, WA: University of Western Australia Press, 2007.
Zimmerman, Dwight Jon, and John D. Gresham. *Uncommon Valor: The Medal of Honor and the Six Warriors who Earned it in Afghanistan and Iraq*. New York: St Martin's, 2010.

Index

American Civil War, 219–20
Amundsen, Roald, 10–11
Antisemitism, origins, 129–30
   in Germany, 120–21
   in the Church of Rome, 140–42
   See also Jews and Judaism
ANZAC Day. *See* Days of Remembrance
Arlington National Cemetery, 201
Armenian Massacre WW1, 90–91
Ataturk. *See* Mustafa Kemel

Balkan countries, post WW1, 105
Barth, Karl, 119–21
Bismarck, Otto von, 4–5
Boer War, 91
Bombing, Britain's campaign, 150
   Hamburg, 151
Bonhoeffer, Dietrich, on Germany's
      guilt WW1, 112
   and the German Church, 146–47
   imprisonment and execution, 148
Breaking the Silence, 259
Brittain, Vera, 87–88, 95–96
Brooke, Rupert, 68, 70–71

Chaplains, in WW1, 72–80
   in Vietnam, 236–37
   training, 238–42
China, conflict with Japan, 106
Christian attitudes to war, *pax*
      Christiana, 253
   modern day, 252–60
Christian faith, British and Allies, 65–67
   German, 62–64

Christian soldiers, Morality of killing,
      74, 77–78, 92–93
Church in Germany. *See* German
   Church
Church in Rome, 139–44
Churches in Australia, attitudes in
   WWI, 82–86
Churches in Great Britain, attitudes in
   WWI. 80–81
Communism, in China, 106–7
   in Germany, 102

Dante Alighieri, the Inferno, 60–61
Days of Remembrance, 246–49
Death, 218–20
   See also in specific Wars
Dirlewanger, Oskar, 131–32

Egypt, 13th Light Horse, 17–47
Enemy as subhuman, 227
Engelke, Gerrit, 71

Fascism, in Italy, 105
Franklin, John, 12
Franz Ferdinand, Archduke,
      assassination of, 6
   Austro-Hungarian response, 7

George V, King-Emperor, 7, 100
German Army WWII, attitude to SS,
      131
   massacres, 133–34
   use of drugs, 135–37

German Church WWI, Lutheran
    doctrine, 64
  WWII, 120–22, 146–48
  theologians, 118–21
German Concentration Camps,
    treatment of Jews, 125–28
  medical experiments, 125–26
Germany, Treaty of Versailles, 102–3
  continuing battles after WWI, 102
  threat of a German Soviet Republic,
    102
  economic crisis post WWI, 111–12
  re-armament, 103–4
  See also Hitler, Nazism
Gestapo, See Nazism
God and war, 79–80, 242–45
Goebbels, Josef, 116–17, 122–23
Great Britain, early attitude of the
    military, 8–9, 12–13
  failures in exploration, 10–12
Grief, 95–101, 249–51

Halsall, George Samuel, journal Egypt,
    16–47
  Western Front, 48–54
Hamburg, 151
Hell on earth, 60–61
Himmler, Heinrich, 123
Hiroshima, 175
Hitler, beginnings of National Socialism,
    112
  organizational ability, 112
  Nazi Party, 112
  indoctrination of the people, 114–20
  as Chancellor, 116–17
  and Mussolini, 137
  and Pope Pius XII, 143–45
  and Warsaw (Pabst Plan), 132
  drug addiction, 135, 137
  See also Nazism
Hitler Youth, 149–50
Hodgson, W. N., 68
Holocaust. See Jews and Judaism

Ireland, Home Rule, 107

Japan, invasion of China, 158–60
  invasion of Manchuria, 107, 158
  attack on Singapore, 161–62

Japanese brutality, conditioned, 158–59,
    162–63
  death marches, 165, 169
  POW camps, 165–74
  hell-ships, 170–71
  civilian prisoners, 174
Japanese culture, race superiority, 161–62
  isolation from other cultures, 167
Jews and Judaism, New Testament,
    129–30, 140–41
  persecution under Nazism, 120–28
Just War, 252–60

Killing, experiences, 220–23
  adapting to kill, 233–24, 227
  avoidance, 226
  atrocities, 228
  effects, immediate, 223–24, 231–32
  effects, long-term, 232–37
  guilt, 224–25
  from a distance, 229–30
  snipers, 225
  training to kill, 227
  See also in specific wars
Korean War, Chinese soldiers with
    North Koreans, 187–88
  interrogation methods of Koreans,
    186
  Peace Negotiations, 189

League of Nations, 107
Lenin, Vladimir, 104–5
Leningrad, Siege, 152–54
Liberal Theology, in Germany, 119–20

Magee, John Jr., 138
Manchuria, Japanese invasion, 107, 158
Mao Tse-tung, 106–7
Masefield, John, 248
Medical personnel WWI, 87–90
Medical advances WWI, 89
Memorials, 247, 250–51
Mongolia, 106
Mussolini, Benito, glorifies war, 105
  and Pope Pius XI, 142–43
  and Hitler, 137
Mustafo Kemal, message to mothers,
    98–99
Mustard gas WWI, 202–3

Nagasaki, 175
Napalm, 188, 203
National Socialism. *See* Nazism
Nazi propaganda, 115–17, 122–23
Nazism, beginnings, 112
   study of genetics, 124
   practice of euthanasia, 124–25
   Gestapo (Secret State Police), 123
   SS (Schutzstaffeln), 123, 131
   SS use of criminals, 131–32
   persecution of the Jews, 120–28
   unrestricted submarine warfare, 163–64
Newbolt, Henry, 55–56
Nurses WWI, 87–89

Padres. *See* Chaplains
Palestine, British mandate, 106
Pax Christiana, 253
Pershing, General John J. 93, 94–95
Poetry WWI, 67–71
Poison gas. *See* Mustard gas
Pope Pius XI, 142–43
Pope Pius XII, 143–46
Postmodernism, 261–62
Post-traumatic stress disorder, 233–36
Prisoners of war, in Germany, 154
   in Japan, 165–74

Racism in war, Americans in the Philippines, 178–79
   Americans in Vietnam, 181, 200
   African-Americans WWII, 180–81
   Australian aborigines, 181–82
Russia, co-operating in German rearmament post WWI, 104
Russia *See also* Stalin

Sassoon, Siegfried, 68–69, 71
Scorched earth policy WWI, 91
Scoresby, William Jr., 11
Scott, Robert Falcon, 10–11
Serbia and Serbians, 6–7
Service, Robert William, 247
Shelley, Percy Bysshe, 157
Shell-shock WWI, 52–54

Spiritual armor, 78–79, 262
SS (Schutzstaffeln). *See* Nazism
Stalin, Josef, as leader of the Soviet States, 104–5, 151–53
   ethnic cleansing, 155
   treatment of returning soldiers, 152
   treatment of prisoners of war, 154–56

Treaty of Versailles, 102–3, 107
Turkey, 14, 90, 93

United States of America, Iraq war, 214

Verdun, war memorial, 3
Vietnam War. Australia, use of National Servicemen, 191–94
   Battle of Long Tan, 195–99
   Prime Minister apologizes, 194
Vietnam War. United States of America, involvement, 199–201
   training of troops, 202
   trauma of battles, 205–6, 211
   massacre at My Lai, 206–7, 228–29
   use of chemical defoliants, 202–3
   use of napalm, 203
Vietnam War, release of American prisoners of war, 212–13
Vietnam War, war correspondents, 209–11

War cemeteries WWI, 98–101
Warsaw Uprising, 132–33
West, Arthur Graeme, 69–70
Western Front WWI, 13th Light Horse, 48–51
   experiences of soldiers, 50–54, 59–62
   British treatment of Germans, 58–59, 91
   problems with morality, 77–78, 92–93
   Shell-shock, 52–54
Wilhelm II, German Emperor, upbringing, 4–5
   beginning of WWI, 1, 6–8, 13.

www.ingramcontent.com/pod-product-compliance
Lightning Source LLC
Chambersburg PA
CBHW050841230426
43667CB00012B/2095